The Library of

Crosby Hall

The National Trust and
The National Trust for Scotland

REVISED EDITION

The National Trust and The National Trust for Scotland

COMPLETE IN TEXT AND PICTURES

REVISED EDITION

by

PETER
RYAN

J. M. DENT & SONS LTD
LONDON

Made in Great Britain
at the
Aldine Press · Letchworth · Herts
for
J. M. DENT & SONS LTD
Aldine House · Albemarle Street · London
First published 1969
Revised edition 1974

ISBN: 0 460 04223 8

Contents

———⊂◯⊃———

ENGLAND

5

6

11

13

15

17

18

19

20

23

27

National Trust Properties of Special Interest

Illustrations

BLACK‑AND‑WHITE ILLUSTRATIONS

By county, in alphabetical order

COLOUR PLATES

MAPS

Author's Note

———— ⊸ ⊸ ————

Fully revised, the second edition of this book aims to be both a useful work of reference and an agreeable volume for browsing, being a record of all the properties acquired by the Trusts to the end of 1973.

It may help to say something of how it was compiled.

I made first a list of properties which would, between them, illustrate the great diversity of buildings and landscape that the Trusts have undertaken to preserve. I collected photographs of those properties and wrote notes on them, intending to outline what, in my opinion, are the most notable features of a property and its history, and to give a brief factual account of what the visitor may expect to see there, drawing attention to any aspects of its past that may enhance its interest. Properties not illustrated are covered by briefer notes or a simple listing.

I apologise to architects, botanists, art historians, archaeologists, ornithologists and the many other specialists whose studies can be enjoyably pursued on Trust property if I have failed to emphasise particularly what are to each the most significant points. Please treat my notes as a menu, something which even in the best of restaurants can provide no more than an indication of what is available. To be proven and enjoyed, the pudding must be eaten.

The counties are listed in alphabetical order for England, Wales, Northern Ireland and Scotland, and the properties in turn are grouped alphabetically under the counties to which they now belong, except in some instances where it has appeared helpful to depart from this. Thus, for example, the five properties within ten miles of Worthing are grouped under Worthing, and some of the coastal properties in South Wales are made the subject of a little perambulation from Carmarthen Bay round St David's Head to Cardigan. Should you find this confusing, names of properties and place names are included in the index.

I am indebted to Mr Philip Sked, Publicity Officer of the National Trust for Scotland. He placed at my disposal his knowledge of the Scottish properties, and his own enthusiasm and love for them encouraged and helped me in a most agreeable task. Although he has generously volunteered to accept blame for any deficiencies or errors in the Scottish part of the book, they should in fairness be charged to my Sassenach pen.

Publisher's Note

The author and publisher are grateful to the National Trusts, theacknow-
ledged publishers and photographers for their indispensable aid in the
preparation of this book.

Approximate locations are given for all properties. It is assumed that the
intending visitor will be equipped with a large-scale map or will be using the
Trusts' publications *Properties of the National Trust* and *The National Trust for
Scotland Year Book*, which give more precise locations.

Unless otherwise indicated with the description of the property, or unless it
is obviously closed (e.g. where it is leased to a private body), the property is
open to the public at certain seasons, days and times. Intending visitors
should always check opening times in the annual *Properties Open* booklet
since they frequently change. This is why opening times are not given in this
book.

Introduction

THE NATIONAL TRUST which operates in England, Wales and Northern Ireland has been in existence since 1895, and the National Trust for Scotland since 1931.

Both work on the same lines, and their object is to preserve places of historic interest or natural beauty. They are independent charities; that is to say, they are not under government control and have the legal status of charities. They are run by their own members, subject to the requirement, contained in the National Trust Acts, that half the members of their councils must be nominated by other bodies. The present lists of nominating bodies include museums, the Royal Institute of British Architects, scientific societies, the County Councils Association and the Youth Hostels Association.

Service on the councils and on the committees which run the Trusts' affairs is voluntary. Each Trust employs a paid staff which deals with day-to-day property management and accounting, and includes specialists in matters with which the Trusts are much concerned such as gardens.

The Trusts are dependent financially on voluntary support which they receive in the form of donations, legacies and members' annual subscriptions, membership being open to all.

The National Trust was founded at a time when, although both the Society for the Protection of Ancient Buildings and the Commons Preservation Society had been established for a number of years, public interest in preservation was far less widespread than it is now. Also, there were then no Town and County Planning Acts as we have them today. Sir Robert Hunter, Octavia Hill and Canon Hardwicke Rawnsley, who were effectively the founders of the National Trust, had been active in campaigns to prevent unsuitable development, notably on Wimbledon Common and in the Lake District. They decided that the time had come to form a society which could act as a holding body, in appropriate cases, for buildings and lands which rank for permanent preservation. In framing the constitution of the society and defining its objects they were remarkably far-sighted. The National Trust was registered under the Companies Act in 1895 as a non-profit-making company. In 1907, when it had grown in public confidence to the extent that Parliament recognized the importance of its work by passing the National Trust Act of 1907, the constitution of the 1895 Society needed no amendment. Nor has it since been altered, subsequent legislation affecting the Trust having been designed to facilitate its work, not to amend its constitution or powers. When the National Trust for Scotland was incorporated by statute (in 1935) the Confirming Act followed closely the provisions of the National Trust Act of 1907.

The history of the Trust's work in furthering the aims so clearly established by its founders is a record of growth. This growth has not followed any recognizable pattern, but it has been a continuous process. The first acquisition—by the gift of $4\frac{1}{2}$ acres of cliff-land at Dinas Oleu above Barmouth in Merioneth, overlooking Cardigan Bay—was made in 1895. By 1974 the total acreage in the Trust's ownership had grown to nearly 400,000 acres (approximately the equivalent in area of the county of Hertfordshire). The figure for the National Trust for Scotland was about 85,000 acres excluding Fair Isle and St Kilda. In the same year the list of buildings, gardens and other places which are opened to the public at stated times and on payment of an admission fee contained some three hundred entries, and that for the National Trust for Scotland, forty-three.

Some properties have been acquired after public appeal for funds for their purchase. Gifts of property have been made not only by private individuals and some commercial and industrial firms, but also by local authorities, many of whom in addition help the Trusts by making grants towards the upkeep of Trust properties. Since 1946 there has been a further important factor in this growth. In that year the Treasury was empowered, when accepting buildings or lands in payment of death duty, to transfer them, with the Trust's agreement, to the ownership of one of the Trusts. Among the well-known places acquired by the Trusts in this way are Hardwick Hall, Brodick Castle and Brownsea Island.

Membership of the Trust, which in 1974 was 450,000 (that for the National Trust for Scotland being 65,000), has grown mainly in the years since 1945. Before the 1914–18 war and during the 1920s and 1930s, although numbers increased each year, the rate of increase was very small and total membership of the National Trust in 1939 was under 10,000.

As property owners the Trusts have one unique privilege—they are empowered by the National Trust Act of 1907 and later legislation to declare land inalienable. Such a declaration having been made, the property is protected against compulsory purchase by local authority or by a ministry; it can only be taken from either Trust by special will of Parliament.

From their beginnings the Trusts have regarded themselves as trustees for the nation, and for that reason adopted the name 'National Trust'. For that same reason the public have access to Trust properties; it is not restricted to

Trust members. At many properties a charge is made for admission and the proceeds put towards upkeep. Access to open spaces is usually free but is always subject to the needs of farming, forestry and the protection of nature.

In deciding what should interest them, i.e. what constitutes 'historic interest or natural beauty', the Trusts take a very broad view. As this volume shows, the properties which they have accepted for protection include industrial monuments, nature reserves and prehistoric sites as well as historic buildings of interest and beautiful countryside.

PROTECTIVE COVENANTS AND RESTRICTIVE AGREEMENTS

In addition to being a property owner, the National Trust has been given or has bought protective covenants over some properties which are not in its ownership. These covenants are legal agreements which provide, for example, that alterations to the exterior of a building may not be made without the Trust's consent. The covenant continues despite changes in ownership. Thus it affords a useful measure of protection for the appearance of the property under covenant.

There is, however, an important difference between the legal position of land owned by the Trust and that of land under covenant. Under the National Trust Act of 1907 the Trust has, as explained above, the power to declare its land inalienable. Land under covenant is not eligible for this unique protection.

There is also an important difference in regard to public access. Subject to the needs of farming, forestry and nature protection, there is access to all properties *owned* by the Trust. But covenants do not include any provision for access, and visitors are not usually admitted to covenanted land. The total acreage over which the Trust held covenants in 1973 was 61,000 acres.

In Scotland the term 'protective covenant' is not used, but the term 'restrictive agreement' covers very similar arrangements. The National Trust for Scotland is party to a number of such agreements which, between them, protect a total of nearly 15,000 acres. In recent years there has been an increasing interest in affording this form of protection to the coast line and some eighteen miles of the Scottish coast is now so protected.

—◦—

AVON

Trust properties now in the new county of Avon were formerly in Gloucestershire and Somerset.

Bath

ASSEMBLY ROOMS The eighteenth-century Assembly rooms, designed by John Wood about 1770, were gutted by fire in an air raid in 1942, but have been restored. They are let to the Corporation.

RAINBOW WOOD FARM *a mile south-east of Bath* A farm with adjoining fields (*300 acres*). A half-mile north is a further sixty acres of farmland between Claverton Manor and the golf course.

LITTLE SOLSBURY HILL *north of Bath, between Batheaston and Swainswick* Land of twenty acres on a flat six-hundred-foot hill top with an Iron Age hill fort.

—◦—

Bristol

BLAISE HAMLET *4 miles north of central Bristol, just north of B 4057* These cottages (page 46), grouped round a green, were built in 1809 by John Harford to house pensioners of the Blaise estate.

There are ten cottages, all different, designed by John Nash. Given to the Trust in 1943. (Not open.)

The Trust owns the following smaller properties near Bristol:

FAILAND *4 miles to the west* Farm and woodland (*360 acres*).

FRENCHAY MOOR *5 miles to the north-east* Land under the management of Winterbourne Parish Council (*8 acres*).

LEIGH WOODS *left bank of the Avon by Clifton Suspension Bridge* This woodland is now a Nature Reserve (*160 acres*).

Blaise Hamlet, Avon

SHIREHAMPTON PARK *4 miles to the north-west* Overlooking the Avon; part is now a golf-course (*99 acres*).

WESTBURY COLLEGE *3 miles to the north, in Westbury* Belonging to the Trust is the fifteenth-century gatehouse of the College of Priests, of which John Wycliffe was a prebend.

CADBURY CAMP *2½ miles east of Clevedon* The site of an Iron Age hill fort (*40 acres*).

Clevedon Court, Avon

Clevedon Court

1½ miles east of Clevedon, on Bristol road, B3130

Although alterations have been made at times, Clevedon Court (above) remains substantially a medieval manor-house. It was built about 1320, incorporating the tower of an earlier building. The plan of the building was in accordance with the fashion of the day, except that it included a chapel. This is on the first floor of the house and has a graceful south window. In Tudor times some comfort was added by providing the Great Hall with a fireplace and new windows. In the eighteenth century the Great Hall was given a new ceiling.

Clevedon was built by Sir John de Clevedon and has had several owners. It passed by marriage in Henry VI's reign to a Northamptonshire family called Wake. They sold it in 1630 to John Digby, first Earl of Bristol. After the death of the third and last earl it was bought in 1709 by Abraham Elton, Merchant Venturer, Mayor of Bristol, and MP for the city. It remained in the possession of the Elton family until 1961, when it was accepted by the Treasury in payment of death duty and transferred to the Trust.

The house contains a number of Elton family portraits and a collection of Elton ware. Sir Edmund Elton, who succeeded to the estate in 1884, established a pottery at Clevedon which enjoyed widespread popularity, urns, jars and vases receiving awards at exhibitions all over the world.

The garden has an eighteenth-century garden house and many rare plants growing on the ancient terraces.

Dyrham Park

7 miles north of Bath and 12 miles east of Bristol, approached from A46

Dyrham (below) was built at the end of the seventeenth century, part of it being designed by a well-known architect, William Talman, and part by an otherwise unknown French architect called S. Hauduroy. It is a fine building and has been described as looking, for all its parkland setting, as though it might be a town house. Inside the house the rooms are panelled, and there are tapestries and leather wall-hangings. The contents include Delftware tulip holders, Dutch paintings and Dutch furniture contemporary with the house.

Dyrham Park, Avon: the east front

Sir William Blathwayt, who built the house, made a very highly successful career as a civil servant and spent much time in Holland, being as a young man a secretary at the embassy at The Hague and later, while Secretary at War, accompanying King William to Flanders on a number of campaigns. He came to Dyrham when he married Mary Wynter, whose family had owned the estate since Tudor times.

The house that he had built has been very little altered. The formal gardens that he had made were transformed into parkland late in the eighteenth century and some fine trees have survived.

Blathwayts remained in possession of Dyrham until 1856, when house, contents and eleven acres of garden were sold to the Ministry of Works, who transferred them to the Trust in 1961.

Dyrham is one of the properties where concerts are held and its great Hall provides most gracious surroundings for this purpose. Among concerts held here have been those arranged by the National Trust Concerts Society and the Bath Festival.

HORTON COURT *3 miles north-east of Chipping Sodbury* A Cotswold manor house, altered in the last century but retaining its twelfth-century hall.

REDCLIFFE BAY A two-acre coastal belt, across which runs the mariners' footpath from Clevedon to Portishead.

Weston-super-Mare

BREAN DOWN *2 miles south-west of Weston-super-Mare* The south arm of Weston Bay; 159 acres of three hundred feet high headland, with a small Iron Age promontory fort. (Actually in Somerset.)

MIDDLE HOPE (WOODSPRING PRIORY) *5 miles north of Weston-super-Mare* A two-mile coastal stretch covering 158 acres, with views across the Bristol Channel. There is access to Middle Hope from Sand Bay.

MONK'S STEPS A viewpoint on the north edge of Weston-super-Mare.

SAND POINT (KEWSTOKE) The thirty-two acres of headland here adjoin the Middle Hope property.

BEDFORDSHIRE

DUNSTABLE DOWNS *At Whipsnade, 2 miles south of Dunstable* Part of the Chilterns, this 285-acre stretch of land includes the Tree Cathedral close to Whipsnade village green, and twenty acres, known as Dell Fields, acquired with contributions from members of the Camping Club of Great Britain, local Girl Guides and Bedfordshire County Council.

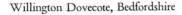

SHARPENHOE: THE CLAPPERS *1½ miles south-west of Barton-in-the-Clay* This Chiltern site has a fine woodland viewpoint (140 acres).

Willington Dovecote, Bedfordshire

Willington Dovecote

4 miles east of Bedford

The birds that lived in dovecotes were actually pigeons, and were not fed but foraged abroad for their own food. This foraging naturally led them to any cultivated fields there might be in the neighbourhood: so the keeping of pigeons in the Middle Ages was a privilege reserved for the lord of the manor, in some cases a layman, in others a churchman. Willington Dovecote (page 50) was built by Sir John Gostwick, Cardinal Wolsey's Master of the Horse. It has fifteen hundred nesting boxes. Close by it are stables and a barn, also Trust property, built at the same time as the dovehouse. These buildings were given to the Trust by different donors in 1914 and 1947 respectively.

BERKSHIRE

Under the new county boundary reorganisation several Trust properties formerly in Berkshire are now in Oxfordshire (see page 265).

Manor of Cookham and Maidenhead

In 1934 local residents bought and gave to the Trust a variegated parcel of property which includes land on the right bank of the Thames between Cookham and Winter Hill, land on Winter Hill, part of Cookham Dean Common including the village green, land on Widbrook Common, also two miles west of Maidenhead, Maidenhead Thicket where there is a Belgic farm enclosure, and Pinkney's Green which is a continuation of Maidenhead Thicket to the north.

Crowthorne

AMBARROW HILL *just south of the station*   A pine-clad hill top.

FINCHAMPSTEAD RIDGES *¾ mile west of the station*   Woodland and a heather ridge with extensive views. To the north-east of the Ridges is Heath Pool with its surrounding woodlands, and Simons Wood which contains a variety of species. (*107 acres.*)

Newbury

BUCKLEBURY *8 miles east of Newbury* Farmland adjoining Bucklebury Common.

FALKLAND MEMORIAL *a mile south-west of the town* A nineteenth-century memorial to the Viscount Falkland who fell in the first of the Civil War battles of Newbury. Given in 1897 by a local Society.

PANGBOURNE MEADOW *just below Pangbourne Bridge* Seven acres on the right bank of the Thames, just below the bridge.

STREATLEY *north of the town* Downland on Lardon Chase and on Lough Down, which forms part of the same hill top and has views over the Chilterns and the Thames. (On Oxfordshire–Berkshire border.)

WINDSOR: THE GOSWELLS *off Thames Street* Bought in 1910 to preserve the view of the Castle, and now a Corporation recreation ground (*3 acres*).

The Hall, Ascott, Buckinghamshire

BUCKINGHAMSHIRE

Ascott House

2 miles south-west of Leighton Buzzard

The nineteenth-century house contains a fine collection of pictures, including works by Rubens, Hogarth, Gainsborough, Hobbema, Stubbs, Cuyp and other masters, collections of French and Chippendale furniture and oriental porcelain with examples of the Ming and K'ang Hsi periods and Chun ware of the Sung dynasty (page 52). Given by Mr and Mrs Anthony de Rothschild in 1950 with 261 acres of grounds, and gardens with views of the Chilterns which contain many rare trees under which are naturalised various bulbs. Rich collection of variegated evergreen shrubs and trees and a topiary clock. Victorian sunken flower garden.

AYLESBURY: THE KING'S HEAD Partly fifteenth-century and still let as an inn.

BOARSTALL TOWER *between Bicester and Thame* A fourteenth-century gatehouse, with sixteenth- and seventeenth-century alterations. The rest of the house was pulled down. (Not open.)

BRADENHAM *4 miles north-west of High Wycombe* A thousand-acre estate of farms, woodland and most of the village. The manor house, which is not open, was for a time the home of Disraeli's father.

BUCKINGHAM: CHANTRY CHAPEL *on Market Hill* The chapel has a fine Norman doorway, but was otherwise rebuilt in 1475. Once a Royal Latin School, it is now used for meetings.

Claydon House, Buckinghamshire

Claydon House

13 miles north-west of Aylesbury at Middle Claydon

Claydon House (above and next) contains what the Trust's guide-book describes as 'the most astounding rococo suite of rooms in Great Britain'— and, for good measure, a quite exceptionally fine staircase.

It is part of what was intended to be a very much larger house. It is complete in itself, a delightful two-storey building of 1768 agreeably sited in its own parkland and having a great wealth of interest inside.

The builder was the second Lord Verney. He came of a family which had owned land in Claydon since the fifteenth century. One of his ancestors was Edmund Verney, the Royalist standard-bearer killed in the battle of Edge-

Claydon House, Buckinghamshire: the north wall of the north hall

hill. Another—his grandfather—made a fortune after the Restoration trading with eastern countries. It was this grandfather's fortune which enabled Lord Verney to embark on, among other things, some ambitious building projects.

He built a brick stable block to the east of the present house and altered the old manor-house (which was further altered in 1860) to the south of it. Then he got down to his major plan for a 250-ft west wing that included a ballroom and a hall with an observatory over it. He ran out of money before he could finish. Some of what he built was pulled down by his niece when she inherited his unfinished mansion. What remains is one block: the delightful house one sees today.

He employed as architect for the whole plan Thomas Robinson of Rokeby Hall, in Yorkshire. But from correspondence in the Claydon papers it seems that the surviving part of the building may have been designed by a carpenter-contractor called Lightfoot, who certainly contributed much of the interior decoration. The correspondence reveals Lightfoot as extremely eccentric. Nothing else at all is known about him; but the wood carving at Claydon is of amazing delicacy and richness of detail. In addition to the carving there is beautiful plasterwork in the saloon, library and stairwell, most if not all of it by the famous stuccoist Joseph Rose. The staircase has an ironwork balustrade with a continuous garland of ears of corn so delicately wrought that they rustle when somebody walks upstairs. The stairs themselves are in mahogany with holly, ebony and ivory parquetry.

The house remained in the Verney family until they gave it to the Trust in 1956.

Florence Nightingale frequently stayed at Claydon after her sister married Sir Henry Verney in 1858, and many objects associated with her have been preserved in the house.

Cliveden

3 miles upstream from Maidenhead bounded north and east by B476

Cliveden was built in 1850 by Sir Charles Barry for the Duke of Sutherland on the wide terraces which had been constructed for an earlier house. This earlier house was built in about 1670 by William Winde for the Duke of Buckingham, the Zimori of Dryden's *Absalom and Achitophel*. It was very seriously damaged by fire in 1795 and remained derelict for thirty years; it was then rebuilt, but in 1849 was again burned down.

In preparing his design for the impressive building in the classic style which stands there today, Barry fitted it most skilfully to the terraces of the earlier building. Mr Gladstone thought highly of Barry's design and recorded his approval in a sentence in Latin which the Duke of Sutherland had inscribed on the house. Rendered into English this reads: 'Built with the skill and devotion of Charles Barry.' The Clock Tower and Stable Block were built a little later, to designs of Henry Clutton. The interior is not as Barry intended it, having been altered in the 1870s and again in the 1890s when J. L. Pearson redesigned the hall and staircase.

The gardens, like the house, command sweeping views of the Thames below, and they are flanked by magnificent woodlands. Apart from the magnificent nineteenth-century parterre, there are herbaceous borders, a rose garden and a water garden. The main drive is an ancient lime avenue. Various owners have introduced buildings and statuary of beauty and interest. These include an octagonal temple (now a chapel) designed here for Lord Orkney in 1735 by Giacomo Leoni; and a balustrade brought from gardens in Rome by Lord Astor.

The then Cliveden House was let from 1739 to 1751 to Frederick, Prince of Wales, father of George III, and during his tenancy Cliveden heard the

Cliveden, Buckinghamshire

first performance of *Rule, Britannia!* This was part of the music composed by Dr Arne for a *Masque of Alfred* which was given its first performance in the Rustic Theatre in the woods below the gardens.

The Cliveden estate was bought in 1893 by William Waldorf Astor—the first Viscount Astor. After the 1914–18 war his son, the second Viscount Astor, entertained British and foreign politicians, journalists and men of affairs at Cliveden—hence references in memoirs and histories of the 1930s to 'the Cliveden Set'. In 1942 he gave the property to the Trust with the expressed wish that, should it cease to be used as a private residence, it should be used 'as my wife and I have tried to use it, to bring about a better under-standing between the English-speaking world and between various groups or sections of people of this and other countries'.

The house is now let to Stanford University, California.

DORNEYWOOD *south-west of Burnham Beeches* The house and more than two hundred acres were given to the Trust during the 1939–45 war, with the condition that it be used as an official residence for a Minister of the Crown.

HOGBACK WOOD *a mile west of Beaconsfield Station* Twenty acres of woodland.

Hughenden Manor

1½ *miles north of High Wycombe*

Hughenden was the house of Disraeli's choice and in large measure of his making. When he bought it in 1847 it was a very plain late-Georgian house outside as well as in. He and Mrs Disraeli added the ornamental parapet and other decorative detail which gave the house, as he wrote, 'a new form and character'. It has not been altered since his time, except for the addition of the west wing. The interior is decorated and furnished in the style that they adopted and many of the rooms, including his study, contain the furniture which belonged to them.

Disraeli got great pleasure from Hughenden, which he used, from 1848 until his death in 1881, whenever parliamentary duties did not tie him to

Hughenden Manor, Buckinghamshire: Disraeli's study

London. He enjoyed the surroundings as well as the house itself. Describing how he spent his time there he wrote: 'When I come down to Hughenden I pass the first week in sauntering about my park and examining all the trees, and then I saunter in the library and survey the books.'

There are many portraits of Disraeli's family, political colleagues and others with whom he was associated. There is a bronze of Queen Victoria which she presented to him and an inscribed copy of her *Leaves from the Journal of Our Life in the Highlands*, the publication which allowed him to say to her: 'We authors, ma'am.' The Queen also planted a tree in the grounds, but this has not survived. In the drawing-room, which has a delightful view of the small garden and was in Disraeli's time the library, there is a charming miniature of his wife, Mary Anne Disraeli. A great many items connected with his career, which have been gathered there in recent years, are also on view in the house.

After Disraeli's death Hughenden was lived in first by a nephew and then by a niece, until the latter sold it in 1937 to Mr W. H. Abbey, who vested it in a special trust. It was given to the National Trust in 1947, the Disraelian Society contributing funds for decorating and adapting the house.

———

IVINGHOE: PITSTONE WINDMILL *half a mile south of Ivinghoe* Dating from the seventeenth century, one of the oldest post mills in England and a landmark from Ivinghoe Beacon.

———

LONG CRENDON COURTHOUSE *2 miles north of Thame* A fourteenth-century building, partly half-timbered. The upper floor is open.

———

MEDMENHAM: LODGE FARM *north of the church* 75 acres of farmland and a seventeenth-century flint farmhouse (not open).

Princes Risborough

COOMBE HILL $3\frac{1}{2}$ *miles north of Princes Risborough* Downland rising to 850 ft, the highest viewpoint in the Chilterns. A nature walk has been provided here.

MANOR HOUSE *opposite the church* A seventeenth-century red brick house with a Jacobean oak staircase.

WHITELEAF FIELDS *three-quarters of a mile north-east of Princes Risborough* Land near the Nags Head at Monks Risborough. Given, after a local appeal, to preserve the view over the Vale of Aylesbury.

———

STOKE POGES: GRAY'S MONUMENT *east of the churchyard* This was designed by James Wyatt and erected in 1799.

———

Waddesdon Manor, Buckinghamshire: the south front

Waddesdon Manor

6 miles north-west of Aylesbury, gates in Waddesdon Village on A41

The superb contents of Waddesdon come from three collections. Baron Ferdinand de Rothschild, who built the manor to house his collections, had a great knowledge of French eighteenth-century art. His sister Miss Alice de Rothschild lived there after him and added to the collections, particularly much of the Sèvres china. She left Waddesdon to her great-nephew, Mr James de Rothschild, who brought over from France the pictures, furniture and china which he inherited from his father, Baron Edmond de Rothschild of Paris. When he died in 1957 he left Waddesdon and these three remarkable collections to the Trust.

Waddesdon Manor, Buckinghamshire: the red drawing-room

They include paintings of the French eighteenth-century school, Dutch seventeenth-century paintings, and portraits by Reynolds and Gainsborough; Sèvres and Dresden china; Savonnerie carpets and some of the magnificent eighteenth-century French furniture made for the French royal palaces.

Baron Ferdinand had the house built between 1874 and 1889, employing a French architect to design a building in French Renaissance style. He also had the grounds laid out, planting the bare hillside with full-grown trees. He was active in local affairs, as J.P. and as Member of Parliament for the local constituency, and received many notable visitors at his new house, Queen Victoria, Lord Rosebery and de Maupassant among them.

West Wycombe Park

at the west end of West Wycombe

Wycombe sets one wondering—how many cooks is *too* many? No less than six people had a hand in the designing of the house and park: three architects, two landscape architects—and Sir Francis Dashwood, who owned the property. Yet so far from spoiling the broth they produced an unusual, handsome mansion set in one of the best of eighteenth-century landscaped parks, with numerous temples, one of which is on an island in the lake.

It took them from around 1740 till about 1800 to transform an earlier house. Sir Francis Dashwood (later Lord le Despencer) was, among other things, a founder of the Dilettante Society, and from his travels and study well versed in architectural styles. At different times he commissioned Robert Adam and Nicolas Revett to produce designs, and the garden buildings and various parts of the house are attributable to them. He also employed John Donowell, who designed the south front (page 64), and Thomas Cook, who laid out the grounds about 1760. Twenty years after Francis Dashwood's death his successors employed Humphry Repton to make improvements in the gardens.

The exterior of the house is on neo-classical lines with a double colonnade along the south front and porticoes at both the east and west sides of the house. The interior is handsomely decorated and has some splendid ceiling paintings. These are copies of pictures by Raphael and others which were executed by an artist brought by Sir Francis from Italy, Giuseppe Borgnis. There are beautiful marble fireplaces and a staircase of mahogany, satinwood and walnut. The contents of the house, which belong to the present Sir

West Wycombe Park, Buckinghamshire: the south front

West Wycombe Park, Buckinghamshire: the dining-room

Francis Dashwood, include some fine eighteenth-century English furniture and portraits of his ancestor who built the house.

The house and grounds were given to the Trust in 1943 by the late Sir John Dashwood, who also (in 1935) gave Church Hill, which looks on to the grounds from the other side of West Wycombe village. It was on this hill that Francis Dashwood had built a mausoleum for members of the Hell Fire Club, of which he was a founder. The mausoleum remains. It is not Trust property. Most of West Wycombe village belongs to the Trust.

West Wycombe village, Buckinghamshire

West Wycombe Village

west of High Wycombe on A40

At West Wycombe, as at Lacock (in Wiltshire), the Trust owns virtually the whole village (above). The buildings are let as private dwellings or shops and are not open to visitors. The Trust as landlord is concerned to preserve the attractive appearance of the village, which has an agreeable mixture of architectural styles from the fifteenth century onwards.

Most of the cottages were bought and modernised by the Royal Society of Arts and sold to the Trust in 1934. Church Hill was given by Sir John Dashwood.

CAMBRIDGESHIRE

Of the five properties in the new county, three were formerly in the old county and two, Houghton Mill and Ramsey Abbey Gatehouse, were previously in Huntingdon.

Anglesey Abbey

6 miles north-east of Cambridge, in the village of Lode

There have been three phases in the long life of Anglesey Abbey. First, it was a foundation of the Augustinian Order; the Canons' Parlour, built in 1236, remains the dining-room of the present-day house. Secondly, after the dissolution of the monasteries, when part of the building was pulled down, it was rebuilt as an Elizabethan manor-house; substantially the house which is there today (below). Thirdly, in 1926 the late Lord Fairhaven and his brother bought it, made some alterations to the interior, and during the following forty years transformed the grounds and created there a garden (over) of outstanding interest. Earlier owners had planted trees, including cedars, which are now mature. Lord Fairhaven extended these plantings and

Anglesey Abbey, Cambridgeshire: the north front

A view in the gardens of Anglesey Abbey

established formal areas such as the hyacinth garden, herbaceous garden, arboretum and avenues and long walks embellished with temples, sculpture and seats, an area of almost a hundred acres. To mark the eight hundredth anniversary of the founding of the abbey he erected a commemoration urn. Sections of the gardens are laid out in formal style with statuary, grass and trees.

Lord Fairhaven was also a collector of pictures. When he died in 1966 he left the abbey and gardens to the Trust, together with the exceptionally fine paintings (including works by Claude, Cuyp, William Etty and Constable) which hang there.

Houghton Mill

Houghton Mill

midway between Huntingdon and St Ives

Houghton Mill (above) is a timber water-mill on the River Ouse given to the Trust by the River Ouse Catchment Board and the borough councils of Huntingdon and Godmanchester in 1939. An external fire escape has been added to the building, which is among those let by the Trust to the Youth Hostels Association (others are Wilderhope in Shropshire, Winchester City Mill and the Palace Stables at the head of Boscastle Harbour in Cornwall).

69

Ramsey Abbey Gatehouse, Cambridgeshire

Wicken Fen, Cambridgeshire: evening light

Ramsey Abbey Gatehouse

at the south-east edge of Ramsey

The remains of the fifteenth-century gatehouse of the Benedictine abbey (page 70) were given to the Trust in 1952.

Wicken Fen

17 miles north-east of Cambridge via A10

Wicken Fen (page 71) is a famous nature reserve where for many years naturalists have studied the plants, insects and birds of the fenlands. It has been described as 'an open-air laboratory for biological study in its widest sense'. It is much visited not only by specialists but also by school parties and by the general public. There is a resident warden and visitors are required to keep strictly to the rules for access to different areas.

In 1967 the committee which administers the fen for the Trust launched an appeal for funds to improve facilities for study, and to create a new marsh-land reserve. This reserve, to quote the committee, 'will produce a new range of aquatic and marsh communities, providing a valuable breeding habitat and migration refuge for many species of birds'.

The first gift to the Trust of a part of the fen was made in 1899 and further gifts have been made since. The property now extends to about 730 acres.

Wisbech: Peckover House

on the north brink of the River Nene

Peckover House is one of the Georgian merchant houses in Wisbech over-looking the River Nene. The stables are to the side, and there is a garden at the back. The house was built in 1722 in brick for a local family called Southwell. The exterior, except for some detail of the garden front which may have been added later in the century, remains unaltered. Inside the house a great deal of remarkably fine decoration was added to the rooms

Peckover House, Wisbech, Cambridgeshire: the chimney-piece in the drawing-room

between 1730 and 1750. All the rooms are panelled; the fireplaces have carved overmantels. There is a good Georgian staircase. In the pale blue, grey and white drawing-room the overmantel is described in the Trust's guide-book as 'a *tour de force* of applied carving, outstanding in its elegance and grace'.

Towards the end of the eighteenth century the house was bought by Jonathan Peckover, founder of the local bank which was merged with Barclays in 1896. During the nineteenth century the Peckovers added the two low wings on either side of the house. They also laid out the garden and planted some rare trees, including a maidenhair tree which has flourished. In the glasshouse orange trees bear good fruit. The house and garden were given to the Trust in 1943 by the Hon. Alexandrina Peckover, and the latter contains two Victorian summer houses and flower borders.

The Trust also owns the much plainer early eighteenth-century houses on either side of Peckover House, Nos. 14 and 19 North Brink. These were accepted by the Treasury in payment of death duties and transferred to the Trust in 1949.

CHESHIRE

Alderley Edge

4½ miles north-west of Macclesfield

A wooded sandstone escarpment with fine views across the Cheshire plain, the Edge was the site of a Neolithic Settlement and of copper mining from pre-Roman times to the last century. 1½ miles to the south, at Nether Alderley, the Trust owns Alderley Old Mill and holds covenants over the house that was formerly the Eagle and Child Inn. The fifteenth-century mill was in use up until 1939 and has recently been repaired (*200 acres*).

BURTON WOOD (see THE WIRRAL, MERSEYSIDE).

Alderley Edge, Cheshire: a view of the Cheshire plain

Congleton

THE CLOUD and MOW COP *respectively 3 miles to the east and 5 miles to the south of Congleton* Both sites are just over a thousand feet high and give views over the Cheshire plain. The first camp meeting of the Primitive Methodists was held on Mow Cop in 1807. Mow Cop Castle is an eight-eenth-century imitation ruin.

⟶ ⟵

HELSBY HILL *half a mile south of Helsby* From the top of this hill are views of the Mersey and the Welsh mountains. The Trust owns forty acres of the summit on which is an Iron Age promontory fort.

⟶ ⟵

Little Moreton Hall

4 miles south-west of Congleton on east side of A34

A most apt description of Moreton is given by James Lees-Milne in the Trust's guide-book to the house: 'Moreton appears like some great doll's house about to collapse into the waters of the moat, in which its chequered surface is quietly reflected.'

It was not planned like that, indeed it was never planned as one whole

Little Moreton Hall, Cheshire: seen from within the courtyard

but grew at intervals during the sixteenth century as successive Moretons contributed the accommodation they thought desirable. It seems that the hall itself and the lower parts of the gatehouse were built about 1520; a porch and a parlour were added around 1560. Then twenty years later, feeling the urge to follow fashion and have a long gallery, the owners decided that the only place for it was above the gatehouse range. So there it sits, the whole structure looking a bit top heavy but with the aid of brick buttresses still secure. Since that date virtually no changes or additions have been made, although the garden is being redesigned.

The presence of the moat makes it clear that the Tudor Moretons were building where their medieval ancestors had established a secure lodging. Inside, the hall and gallery and other rooms are decorated with carving and plasterwork and contain some interesting pieces of furniture.

For a time during the nineteenth century the hall was used as a farmhouse. But its last two Moreton owners, Miss Elizabeth Moreton, who died in 1912, and her cousin Bishop Abraham, who with his son gave the hall to the Trust in 1938, ensured its preservation.

Lyme Park

6½ miles south-east of Stockport on the south side of A6

The house was built originally in about 1560 and the Long Gallery and the Drawing Room with its exceptionally fine Elizabethan woodwork are still there to proclaim the fact. But without ever being pulled down it has been completely—and very grandly—transformed inside and out. Alterations have been made at various times, but principally about 1720. Then it was that Sir Peter Legh brought the distinguished Venetian architect Giacomo Leoni to Lyme: he remodelled the south front (page 78) into what James Lees-Milne describes in the Lyme guide-book as 'one of the boldest achieve-ments of English Palladian architecture to survive'. The box-like structure behind the portico was not in Leoni's design. It was added in 1816. Leoni also refashioned the inner courtyard (page 79) and much of the interior of the house.

Inside, as well as the fine woodwork in the Elizabethan rooms, there is some remarkable pear-wood carving in the saloon. It consists of six eight-foot panels of fruit, flowers, musical instruments and cherubs. This beautiful work is strongly reminiscent of Grinling Gibbons and it is possible, though by no means certain, that it is by him.

Lyme Park, Cheshire: the south front

Lyme Park, Cheshire: the inner courtyard

The extensive garden is noted for spring and summer bedding and herbaceous borders. There is an orangery, formal terraces and a sunken rose garden.

The park at Lyme runs to thirteen hundred acres and rises to 850 ft on a Cheshire spur of the Pennines. It still has a herd of deer, and has been a deer-park since medieval times. It used also to be famous for Lyme mastiffs, exceptionally large beasts, some of them the size of a small pony. The Sir Piers Legh who fought at the battle of Agincourt is said to have taken one to the campaign, and in the shield of arms of his descendant, Lord Newton, two mastiffs act as supporters. The park also has a nature trail.

The Leghs first came into possession of Lyme through the marriage of Sir Piers Legh to the daughter of the then owner in 1388. This Sir Piers is believed to have served with his father-in-law at Crécy. The family remained continuously in occupation for nearly six hundred years. In 1946 Richard Legh—the third Lord Newton—gave the property to the Trust and left there on loan the principal tapestries and furniture. The house has been leased to Stockport Corporation. A part of the property has now been made a country park.

Macclesfield

EDDISBURY PARK FIELD   16 acres of meadowland a mile east of
Macclesfield along the Buxton road.

⟨ornament⟩

MAGGOTY'S WOOD *south-west of Macclesfield near Gawsworth* A little
wood in which Maggoty Johnson, an eighteenth-century dramatist, dancing
master and eccentric, was buried.

⟨ornament⟩

MOBBERLEY *3 miles north-east of Knutsford House* (not open)   given with
twenty acres to protect the approach to the church.

⟨ornament⟩

Styal

about 10 miles south of Manchester, 1½ miles north-west of Wilmslow

Quarry Bank Cotton Mill was built in 1784. Millworkers' cottages were
added shortly afterwards, to form a planned and self-contained industrial
community. No longer a textile mill, part of it now is let. It is situated on
a beautiful wooded stretch of the River Bollin and was given with the
cottages and 250 acres of the valley in 1939 by Mr A. C. Greg. Part of Styal
Woods, illustrated on page 82, has now been made a country park.

⟨ornament⟩

Tatton Park

3½ miles north of Knutsford

Tatton offers an unusually varied choice of interest. The imposing stone-
built mansion (page 83) is surrounded by fifty-four acres of variegated
gardens and set in a two-thousand-acre park with a large lake. The principal
rooms contain the collections of paintings, furniture and silver made by the
Egerton family over the last 450 years. In the huge room which he had built

Styal, Cheshire: Quarry Bank Mill

to house them are displayed the curiosities and big game hunting trophies which the last Lord Egerton brought back from his travels—and with them a motor car that he bought in 1900 (a Benz) which bears Cheshire's first registration number, M.1.

The house is beautifully sited, looking over the terraced garden to the park and meres, and is described in the guide book as 'of a severely classical design with little external ornamentation'. It was started by one architect and completed by another (Samuel Wyatt and his nephew Lewis Wyatt) between the years 1780 and 1810. Inside, the principal rooms are of a size and proportions to match the imposing exterior. The books in the library (page 83) were collected mainly in the eighteenth century or earlier. But the furniture is early nineteenth century, some of it made for the room. The two Canalettos in the drawing room were commissioned from the artist by Samuel Egerton while he was living in Venice about 1729.

81

Styal, Cheshire: Styal Woods

Tatton Park, Cheshire: from the south-west

The gardens, too, are the work of successive generations of the family. The orangery, which was designed about 1810 by one of the architects of the house, contains orange trees in tubs and various exotic plants. The tall glasshouse containing New Zealand tree-ferns dates from the middle of last century. The Japanese garden, laid out round a Shinto temple, was

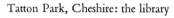

Tatton Park, Cheshire: the library

started in 1910. There are also a rose garden, an arboretum, extensive rhododendron plantings, and a nature trail in the park.

The Trust was given the house by the last Lord Egerton in his will and acquired the park from the Treasury, which had accepted it in part payment of death duties. Both are leased to the Cheshire County Council.

—∞⊃ ⊂∞—

CLEVELAND

ORMESBY HALL *3 miles south-east of Middlesbrough* A mid-eighteenth-century house with contemporary plasterwork (below). Bequeathed by Colonel J. B. W. Pennyman in 1962 with 273 acres.

Ormesby Hall, Cleveland: the saloon

CORNWALL

Antony House

5 miles west of Plymouth via the Torpoint car ferry

Antony was built between 1711 and 1721, the centre block in Pentewan stone and the two wings, joined to it by colonnades, in brick. Except for the addition of a nineteenth-century porch it has not been altered since. The architect is unknown, but it is agreed that he achieved a most successful design.

Many rooms are panelled, and some of them contain furniture which is contemporary with the house and has always been there. They also contain some fine china and an unusually interesting collection of family portraits.

The Carew family came to Antony in 1492, and in the present house are portraits and treasures both of generations who lived at Antony before this house was built and of those who have lived there since. In the entrance hall (page 86) is a portrait of Richard Carew, the Elizabethan author of the *Survey of Cornwall*, with a chest and other furniture which probably came

Antony House, Cornwall: the east front

Antony House, Cornwall: the entrance hall

from the house of his time. His book gives a vivid picture of Cornwall at the period of the Armada.

In the garden, where there is a fine maidenhair tree, are a collection of stone carvings from the North West Frontier of India and a temple bell from Burma. These were brought to Antony by General Sir Reginald Pole-Carew, who campaigned in India and Burma.

Antony was given to the Trust in 1961 by Sir John Carew Pole, who also gave the Bath Pond House in 1971. This late eighteenth-century building has a plunge bath with a panelled changing-room, and is situated to the north of Antony House by the estuary of the River Lynter.

⸺⊙⊙⸺

BODIGGA CLIFF *1 mile east of Looe*   Thirty acres of cliff-land with views over Looe Bay. Also 13 acres of foreshore.

⸺⊙⊙⸺

BODRUGAN'S LEAP *1½ miles south of Mevagissey*   Three acres of the head-land from which, it is said, Sir Henry Trenowth of Bodrugan, being pursued by Sir Richard Edgcumbe of Cotehele, jumped into the sea and escaped (during Henry VII's reign).

Boscastle Harbour

3½ miles north-east of Tintagel on the Bude road (B3263)

There are fine high views from the cliffs surroundings Boscastle Harbour and many wild flowers. Part of the harbour works were built by Sir Richard Grenville in 1584. Other parts had to be rebuilt in 1962 by the Trust. These had been originally made about 1820 but were blown up in 1941 by a drifting mine. The harbour belongs to the Trust, as do about 270 acres of adjoining cliffs including the 317-ft Willapark Headland. The harbour was given to the Trust in 1955 by Mr T. P. Fulford, and the following year additional land was given by another donor. The Palace Stables at the head of the harbour have been let to the Youth Hostels Association.

There are two other Trust properties close to Boscastle Harbour. At Forrabury Common (adjoining it) sixty-seven acres were bought in 1955-7

Boscastle Harbour, Cornwall

with monies given for purchases in the west of England. Here there persists a survival of Celtic agricultural planning—a 'Stitchmeal' system of land holding. The Trust owns thirty-four of the forty-two 'stitches' into which the area is divided.

In the Valency Valley (two miles north-west) over a hundred acres were given in 1958 by the Treasury, who had accepted them in payment of death duty. Further land was acquired in 1968 and in 1971, including twenty-five acres on the north side of the valley given in memory of Thomas Hardy and his first wife.

CADSONBURY *2 miles south-west of Callington* A hill fort, as yet unexcavated, but probably early Iron Age.

CAMEL ESTUARY Six acres of cliff fields near Trebetherick Point.

CHAPEL PORTH *1½ miles south-west of St Agnes* Cliff and moorland around the valley leading into Chapel Porth cove. Ruined engine houses of disused mines stand on the site (*360 acres*).

East Pool and Agar mine, Cornwall:
rotative winding engine

Cornish Engines

on both sides of Camborne–Redruth road, A30

Rotative winding engines of this kind (page 88) were among the first applications of steam power to industry. The Trust acquired five nineteenth-century examples in 1967 with the help of the Cornish Engines Preservation Society, which had been looking after them for some time, and with further help from the local and county councils and a public appeal. They are situated at Levant Mine, St Just; South Crofty Mine, Camborne; Holman's Museum, Camborne; and at East Pool and Agar Mine, Camborne.

These are the most recent additions to the list of Industrial Monuments preserved by the Trust. Other properties in this category are the Stratford-upon-Avon Canal, the eighteenth-century limekilns at Beadnell near Seahouses in Northumberland, and the eighteenth-century cotton mill and cottages at Styal, south of Manchester.

The engine illustrated is the type of winding engine in general use in Cornish mines during the last century and was built in 1887 by Holman Bros to the design of F. W. Michell and used for hoisting men and ores. It is a double-acting rotative engine of 30-inch cylinder bore by nine-foot stroke, designed to work at from twenty-seven to thirty revolutions per minute and at a rope speed of a thousand feet per minute.

—⌒ ⌒—

Cotehele

8 miles south-west of Tavistock on the west bank of the Tamar

When Sir Richard Edgcumbe and his son, who succeeded him, rebuilt their home between 1490 and 1520 they continued the plan of the medieval manor that they were improving and enlarging. Alterations and additions made since then have not touched their principal work, so Cotehele provides basically a most authentic example of a medieval house (page 90). The interior is embellished by the tapestries, needlework, furniture, pewter and brass collected during the seventeenth century. The tapestries which decorate the walls include Brussels and Flemish work as well as products of Soho and Mortlake. The furniture includes some unusually interesting English pieces. There is also a collection of arms and armour in the hall. The chapel clock is a great rarity. It was installed in about 1489 when the chapel was com-

Cotehele House, Cornwall: the courtyard

pleted. It is a pre-pendulum clock, powered by two ninety-pound weights, which has never been converted to pendulum working.

The gardens are on many different levels as they descend to the valley below the house. There are ponds and rills, old yew hedges, terraced flower borders, a tulip tree, golden ash and other fine trees, a medieval dovecote, and shrubs which provide colour through the season. A nature trail follows a circular path of $1\frac{1}{2}$ miles through the woods surrounding the house.

Cotehele continued in possession of the Edgcumbe family until 1947, when it was offered to the Treasury in payment of death duty, accepted and given to the Trust—the first property to be acquired by the Trust in this way. The contents of the house are on loan from Lord Mount Edgcumbe's trustees. Morden Mill, the manorial water-mill on the estate, has recently been restored.

Crackington Haven

halfway between Boscastle and Bude

Here the Trust owns a three-mile stretch of this wild and unspoiled part of the north coast of Cornwall. It covers Tremoutha Haven, Crackington

Crackington Haven, Cornwall: looking from Pencannow Point towards Cambeak

Haven (above), Cambeak, High Cliff—the highest in Cornwall (731 ft) —and Pencannow or Pentenna Point (400 ft). High Cliff was the setting for part of Hardy's novel *A Pair of Blue Eyes*.

The property is made up of farmland, cliff and foreshore, and access is by footpath only. The high points command superb views along the coast.

The major part of the property was given, in 1959, in memory of Flight-Lieutenant Denis Parnall and air crews who gave their lives in the Battle of Britain, by his brother Wing-Commander A. G. Parnall. Additional land was bought in 1959, 1966 and 1968.

Cubert

4 miles west of Newquay

The Cubert properties embrace 559 acres of cliff, farm and common land with sand dunes.

CUBERT COMMON An enclosed common, one of the few remaining in England, and grazed by the commoners.

THE KELSEYS   Three hundred acres covering the Kelsey Head, the south side of Porth Joke, Holywell Beach and an island called The Chick.

WEST PENTIRE FARM   Includes the north side of Porth Joke and West Pentire Head.

———

THE DIZZARD *2 miles north-east of Crackington Haven*   A wild headland overlooking Chipman Strand, with wide views (*56 acres*).

———

The Dodman

about 10 miles south of St Austell

In this area Trust property amounts to 465 acres. Dodman Point itself is the Dead Man's Rock of Q's novel and the Trust has been acquiring parts of it at intervals since 1919.

HEMMICK BEACH *west of the Dodman*   An unspoilt cove; the surrounding land belongs to the Trust.

LAMBSOWDEN COVE *1½ miles west of The Dodman Point*   The Trust has farmland between the coast road and the cliffs.

LAMLEDRA FARM   A sixty-acre farm west of Gorran Haven above Vault Beach.

———

Duckpool to Sandymouth

5 miles north of Bude

Steep cliffs rise behind a sandy beach, and Trust property here of nine hundred acres includes two and a half miles of coast. The coastal footpath runs the whole length of the property.

COOMBE   Farmland and cliff with wide views from Steeple Point (300 ft).

HOUNDAPIT CLIFFS   Open farmland extending to the cliff edge.

STOWE BARTON   A seven-hundred-acre farm, the site of Sir Richard Grenville's family home—the 'Chapel' in Kingsley's *Westward Ho!*

ERTH BARTON and ERTH ISLAND *4 miles west of Saltash*   Saltings and foreshore at the junction of the Tiddy and the Lynher (*200 acres*).

FAL ESTUARY: ARDEVORA   Foreshore on the reach known as Ruan River, on the south bank of the Fal, and on the east bank at Trelonk.

Fowey

There are a number of small properties in the immediate neighbourhood of Fowey.

HALL WALK, LANTEGLOS *opposite Fowey*   Forty acres of walks and cliff.

HAY POINT, ST VEEP *on east bank of estuary*   Steep land immediately above Penpol Creek.

PONT PILL, LANTEGLOS *on south bank of Pont Creek*   Land of fifty-six acres, including the farm at the head of the creek. The Trust has rebuilt the quays and footbridge to reopen the circular walk from Fowey.

READYMONEY COPSE *on north side of Readymoney Cove*   A small copse. Also eight acres of hanging woodland forming the south side of the cove.

ST CATHERINE'S POINT   Land on the summit and the south slopes behind the castle (which belongs to the D.O.E.).

ST SAVIOUR'S POINT *on east side of Fowey Harbour*   Four acres at Polruan.

STATION WOOD *on right bank of the estuary*   Woodland and meadow above the town (*30 acres*).

GODREVY to PORTREATH *on the north coast, about 15 miles south-west of Newquay* This property of cliff and farmland includes most of the Godrevy peninsula and extends six miles to Western Hill overlooking Portreath harbour. A footpath runs the length of the property. There are several small beaches and coves used by Atlantic seals. The property has been built up since 1939 by a series of gifts and purchases (*750 acres*).

THE GRIBBIN and POLRIDMOUTH *2 miles west of Fowey* Since 1966, through purchases from Enterprise Neptune funds of land and protective covenants and through a gift, the Trust has secured protection of about five miles of unspoilt coast including most of the east side of St Austell Bay. Access by coastal footpath only. The property includes the east side of Polridmouth Cove and Gribbin Head.

GUNWALLOE TOWANS *a mile north-west of Mullion village* Land between Poldhu Cove and Church Cove including a golf course and marsh (*130 acres*). Also 126 acres of Winnianton Farm, which includes the northern half of Church Cove, given in 1974.

Helford River, Cornwall, near Mawnan on the north side of the river mouth

Helford River

between Falmouth and the Lizard

The Trust has property in many parts of this beautiful estuary. On the north side is land near Mawnan Church (page 94) and to the south and east of Mawnan Smith village. Also Glendurgan Garden, a gift of members of the Fox family. One of the most beautiful and sensitively planted Cornish gardens, there are tender shrubs, a formal walled garden and a water garden, remarkable trees, magnolias and rhododendrons. On the south side, land surrounding Penarvon Cove, at Trewarnevas and Coneysburrow Cove and at Frenchman's Creek, which inspired Daphne Du Maurier's novel. There are also cottages at Carne Vean and Penarvon Cove (not open).

On Rosemullion Head, north of the river mouth, there is land with views over Falmouth Bay.

Helston

THE LOE POOL *2 miles south of Helston* Acquired in 1974 by gift of Commander J. P. Rogers, whose family have been owners of the property since 1771. The Loe Pool is a mile and a half long freshwater lake separated from the sea by the shingle beach of Loe Bar. Included with the gift were fifteen hundred acres of the surrounding countryside and the beautiful woods around the lake. Access to the lakeside walks is on foot only, as the Trust is continuing the long-established rule of 'no vehicles'.

HOR POINT and HELLESVEOR CLIFF $1\frac{1}{2}$ *miles west of St Ives* Rocky coast with good views bought and given to the Trust—in the face of a threat to use Hor Point as a refuse tip—as a family memorial (*24 acres*).

Land's End

There are several properties in the neighbourhood of Land's End. The 'first and last' hill in England is three miles to the north-east, CHAPEL CARN BREA, which rises to 657 feet. Still on the north side, there is cliff-land between Sennen Cove and Land's End.

To the south, between Land's End and Porthcurno, there is more land on the St Levan Cliffs and four miles to the south-east at Penberth Cove and Treen Cliff, nearly two hundred acres, including an Iron Age fort and the well-known Logan Rock.

Lanhydrock House

2½ miles south of Bodmin on B3268

Lanhydrock House overlooks the beautiful valley of the River Fowey. It stands in a park of about 250 acres, largely wooded. The park trees were planted during the eighteenth and nineteenth centuries. The delightful gardens, near the house, were given their present layout in 1857.

The house itself was built between 1630 and 1651. The north wing and the gatehouse (page 97) remain from this original building, but the rest, which had been altered in 1780, was badly damaged by fire in 1881. It was rebuilt on a larger scale.

The great gallery (page 97), in the north wing, retains its charming plasterwork. On the ceiling and over the two fireplaces the plasterers illustrated many of the well-known Old Testament stories, and did so most vividly. The craftsmen have not been identified, but it is believed that they did other work in the neighbourhood.

The contents of the house include Mortlake and Brussels tapestries, and a number of portraits, some of them by Kneller and Romney.

In the garden are some bronze garden urns by Louis XIV's goldsmith, Louis Ballin. These were brought to this country from the Château de Bagatelle in Paris during the last century, and to Lanhydrock when the gardens were laid out in 1857. The general plan of this nineteenth-century garden has been retained, but it has been largely replanted and now has a unique Victorian formal parterre and an extensive herbaceous garden. The grounds contain many very fine magnolias, azaleas, camellias, hydrangeas and other trees and shrubs. Mr Gladstone and Lord Rosebery each planted a copper beech by the tennis courts.

In the Middle Ages Lanhydrock had belonged to the priory at Bodmin. The tithe barn, in the garden, remains as evidence of this ownership. It changed hands several times after the dissolution of the monasteries. It was bought in 1620 by Sir Richard Robartes, who came of a family which had prospered as merchants and bankers connected particularly with the Cornish tin trade. He began the seventeenth-century house. This was completed by his son, who had a long and active public life, attaining high rank in the

Lanhydrock House, Cornwall: the gatehouse and house seen from the park
Lanhydrock House, Cornwall: the great gallery

Parliamentary forces during the Civil War and holding a number of important offices after the Restoration, including that of Lord President of the Council. The house and park remained in the ownership of the family until given to the Trust in 1953 by the seventh Viscount Clifden. In 1970 his brother added about a hundred acres of woodland to the south and east of the park. There is a circular nature walk of two miles through the park and woods.

Lantivet Bay

east of Fowey between Polruan and Polperro

Trust properties in this area cover nearly a thousand acres of cliff, farmland and beach. They include Pencarrow Head, from which there are wide ranging views, the coves of Lantivet Bay and the farmland surrounding Lansallos church (below). There is access by footpaths. These properties were acquired between 1936 and 1971 by gift and public subscription, and included the purchase of land at Lansallos Barton Farm in 1965 from funds subscribed to Enterprise Neptune, the Trust's appeal for preservation of the coast.

Lantivet Bay, Cornwall, looking eastwards across the bay with Lansallos church in background

LAUNCESTON: LAWRENCE HOUSE *in Castle Street* Let to the Borough Council as a museum.

—

LERRYN CREEK *on the east bank of the Fowey estuary* Ethy House (not open) and its 377-acre wooded park were given by Lord St Levan as part of the endowment for St Michael's Mount.

—

LESCEAVE CLIFF *5 miles west of Helston* Cliff-land at the end of Prah Sands, with access by coastal footpaths (*13 acres*).

—

Lizard Peninsula

South Coast

Trust properties on the Lizard Peninsula provide a variety of interest as well as scenic beauty and amount to more than a thousand acres. A mile west of Mullion village, on the cliff from which Marconi's transmitter sent the first wireless message across the Atlantic in 1901, there is a memorial erected by the Marconi Company.

At Lowland Point on the east side of the peninsula, the cliff and farmland overlooks the Manacles Rocks, scene of many shipwrecks. The land on Lizard Downs and at Kynance Cove includes some fantastic rock formations. The farmland at Inglewidden, south of Cadgwith, surrounds the Devil's Frying Pan. There is a view point on Bass Point, the southernmost tip of Cornwall. On the west side of the peninsula, two miles south of Mullion, at Predannack, is farm and coastal land, including some of special botanical interest, which is let to the Cornwall Naturalists' Trust. The National Trust also owns Mullion Cove and part of Polurrian Cove.

—

MORWENSTOW *6 miles north of Bude on Devon border* Robert Stephen Hawker, the parson poet, was vicar here for nearly forty years during the last century. Hawker's Hut on the 450 ft Vicarage Cliff, where he wrote, is owned by the Trust, together with about ninety acres of cliff and farmland.

—

NARE HEAD and VERYAN BAY *4½ miles south of Tregony* Nare Head is about ten miles east of Falmouth Bay and Veryan Bay about four miles farther east. The Trust owns 375 acres of farmland and cliffs forming the south-west side of Veryan Bay, including Nare Head. There are good coastal views. Also some land near the village of Portloe.

―∽ ∾―

NEWQUAY The Trust owns a number of small areas of sandhills and farmland, about eighty acres in all, mainly on the south bank of the Gannel estuary forming part of the view from Newquay. Also a little orchard called the Round Garden in Crantock village.

―∽ ∾―

PARK HEAD, ST EVAL *6 miles south-west of Padstow* The Trust's two-hundred-acre property here includes Pentire Farm and some small coves. Park Head is a backdrop to the view from the remarkable granite cliff formation called Bedruthan Steps (not Trust property) south-west of the headland. A good view overlooking the steps is from a Trust-owned view-point on Pendarves Point (*west of B3276*).

―∽ ∾―

PENDOWER BEACH *south coast, 6 miles south-west of Tregony, a mile south-west of Veryan* Includes Gwendra Farm, overlooking the large sandy beach, the east side of the valley opening on to it at Pendower, and Carne Beacon (*247 acres*).

―∽ ∾―

PENTIRE HEAD and PORTQUIN BAY *north coast, 6 miles north-west of Wadebridge* The Trust's property (680 acres) of cliff and farmland here, with footpaths along the cliffs, is made up of Pentire Farm, which includes Pentire Point and an Iron Age cliff castle (excavated in 1963-5); Pentire-glaze Farm, the approach to Pentire; land at Carnweather Point; land at Lundy Bay; and land on the south side of Portquin harbour, including Doyden Point. Doyden Castle, on the point, is a nineteenth-century folly. Also four acres of mine burrows, the site of the disused Pentireglaze silver-lead mine.

―∽ ∾―

Penzance

LANYON QUOIT *4 miles north-west of Penzance* A huge granite capstone, the remains of a megalithic burial place.

TRENCROM HILL *4½ miles north-east of Penzance* A gorse-covered hill-side with an Iron Age B hill fort, given as a memorial to Cornish men and women of the two wars. Also Bowl Rock on the north side of the hill (*64 acres*).

TRENGWAINTON *2 miles west of Penzance, between the St Just and Morvah roads* Planted mainly in the last forty-five years, the ancient walled gardens contain an unrivalled collection of rare and tender shrubs and trees, including magnolias, rhododendrons, primulas and hydrangeas.

POLPERRO *about 5 miles east of Fowey* A fishing village on the south coast. The Trust owns about ninety acres on both sides of the harbour, including farmland and terraced walks on the west side.

PORT GAVERNE *north coast, 7 miles north of Wadebridge* The Trust owns part of the beach and foreshore and some cottages, given to preserve the character of the hamlet. Also fish cellars on the west side of the stream.

PORTHCOTHAN *north coast, 5 miles south-west of Padstow* Land forming the north side of the inlet (*17 acres*).

PORTHMINSTER POINT *north coast, near St Ives* Cliff-land and small fields on the south edge of St Ives, with views of the town and its harbour.

RINSEY CLIFF *south coast between Helston and Marazion* Heather-covered cliff-land dominated by the ruin of the Wheal Prosper Mine's engine house, which was abandoned over a hundred years ago (*35 acres*).

ROSEMERGY and TREVEAN CLIFFS *north of the Land's End–St Ives road (B3306), north-east of Morvah church* This cliff-land property of fifty-five acres includes four rocky viewpoints. Given as a memorial to Mr D. W. Thomas, the first chairman of the Trust's Cornwall Advisory Committee.

Rough Tor

3 miles south-east of Camelford

As a memorial to men of the 43rd (Wessex) Division who fell in the 1939–1945 war, a 170-acre stretch of Bodmin Moor was given to the Trust in 1957.

Rough Tor, Bodmin Moor, Cornwall: the view to the south-west

Rough Tor (1,300 ft) is the second highest point in Cornwall (above). On its westerly slopes there are remnants of human settlements which are thought to be of an Early–Middle Bronze Age date.

Access to Rough Tor is by vehicle to the edge of the Moor (from Camelford by the Jubilee Drive) and thence on foot.

—◦◦—

ST AGNES BEACON *north coast, a half-mile west of the Truro–St Agnes road (B3277)* Sixty acres of heath land rising to 629 ft, with wide-ranging views both up and down the coast and inland. Also three stone cottages (not open).

—◦◦—

ST ANTHONY-IN-ROSELAND *south coast, 2½ miles east of Falmouth (by steamer)* The Trust's farmland and foreshore here (*470 acres*) surround the hamlet of Bohortla and make up about half the St Anthony peninsula. Included is part of St Anthony Head, the eastern entrance to Falmouth

Harbour. The Trust bought the land on the headland both to provide public access and to remove the coastal artillery buildings left there from the 1939–45 war, which were an eyesore. Wide views across Falmouth Bay.

St Michael's Mount

3 miles east of Penzance, south of Marazion

When Sir John St Aubyn bought St Michael's Mount in 1660 he came into possession of a group of buildings standing in an enclosure against the central pinnacle of the rock. Some were monastic, some secular, the Mount having been in the previous five hundred years both monastery and fortress or at times a combination of the two (below).

Edward the Confessor founded a chapel here in 1044 in a grant to the Benedictine Abbey of Mont Saint Michel in Brittany. By 1154 there was a church and quarters for thirteen brothers.

Later in the century, while Richard I was on Crusade, some of John's partisans seized the Mount to hold as a fortress. It reverted to monastic use but was again treated as a stronghold during the Wars of the Roses, during the Cornish rebellion against Edward VI and during the Civil War.

Since Sir John's purchase in 1660 it has led a peaceful existence.

The monastic church is of the late fifteenth century but probably incorporates masonry of a much earlier church. The other buildings have been remodelled and added to at different times since 1660, most recently in 1878.

The Mount, which is an island at high tide, is itself a romantic sight and from its terraces affords splendid views towards Land's End and the Lizard.

St Michael's Mount,
Cornwall

The Mount continued in the ownership of the St Aubyn family until 1954 when the third Lord St Levan gave it to the Trust.

Tintagel

In addition to land overlooking TREBARWITH STRAND, 1½ miles south of Tintagel (below), the Trust has several other properties near by—a view-point on Barras Nose to the north of King Arthur's Castle; land between Tintagel Church and the sea, from which are fine views; a view-point on Penhallick Point given to mark the Coronation in 1953; and, 3 miles south of Tintagel, at TREGARDOCK BEACH are sixty acres of cliffs to which there is access only on foot. In Tintagel is the small fourteenth-century house known as the Post Office, which was used from 1844 to 1892 as the GPO's letter-receiving office for the district. The building is now open to the public. These properties were acquired between 1897 and 1968 by public subscriptions and the gifts of a number of donors.

Trebarwith Strand, near Tintagel, Cornwall

Trelissick, Cornwall: looking from the park to the estuary of the River Fal

TREGASSICK and TREWINCE *on east bank of the St Mawes estuary, 2 miles east of Falmouth* The 140-acre Tregassick Farm includes a mile and a half of the shore of the estuary.

Trelissick

4 miles south of Truro astride B3289

370 acres of park, farm and woodland, including woods on the west bank of the Fal above and below King Harry Passage, and Round Wood on the east bank (above). The park, from which there are beautiful views of the estuary, is open to visitors at advertised times. It is rich in rhododendrons, azaleas and hydrangeas. There are fine trees, a circular nature walk, and a formal terraced garden has been recently replanted. Trelissick House is not open.

Trerice, Cornwall: the hall

Trerice

3 miles south-east of Newquay via A392 and B3058

Trerice is an Elizabethan stone manor-house, built about 1570 on the site of an earlier house, and has been very little altered. The hall (above) and solar (now the drawing-room) have fine ceilings and fireplaces. There is no record of who executed the excellent plasterwork in these rooms, but it is thought, from the evidence of similar work done at that time in other houses in Cornwall and parts of Devon, that it was a local craftsman. There is a formal terraced garden.

The builder of the house, Sir John Arundell, had inherited Trerice from his father and with it the means to rebuild. His father, another Sir John, had a remarkable career in the service of the Crown and profited by it. He was knighted at the battle of the Spurs, was Esquire of the Body to Henry VIII, and also served both Edward VI and Mary. The Arundells supported the Crown during the Civil War with much gallantry and loss, but recovered something of their position after the Restoration. Trerice passed during the eighteenth century to a nephew of the fourth Lord Arundell, and from him to the Acland family of Killerton in Devon. The property was sold in 1915 and the house changed hands several times. The Trust bought it in 1954 with money bequeathed by Mrs Annie Woodward, and restored it with the help of Mr J. F. Elton and a grant from the Historic Buildings Council.

Whitesand Bay

south coast, 3 miles north-west of Rame Head, about 8 miles east of Looe

SHARROW POINT and HIGHER TREGANTLE CLIFFS Farm and cliff-land overlooking Whitesand Bay with good coastal views (*280 acres*).

TRETHILL CLIFFS *1 mile west of Whitesand Bay* Again, farm and cliff-land—seventy acres between the road and the sea with access to a small cove.

Visitors are warned not to stray to the south, where there is a Ministry of Defence firing range.

ZENNOR *north coast, 5 miles north-west of St Ives* Eighty-four acres of cliff at Zennor Head and Tregerthen Cliff where there are views and good cliff flora. Access is by footpath.

CUMBRIA

ACORN BANK: TEMPLE SOWERBY MANOR *6 miles east of Penrith, just north of Temple Sowerby* A part sixteenth, but mainly eighteenth-century red sandstone house. Public access to gardens which contain an extensive collection of medicinal and culinary herbs. Also 186 acres of land by the Crowdundle Beck.

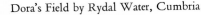

Ambleside

BEE HOLME *west side of Windermere* A one and a half acre peninsula between Wray Castle and Pull Wyke.

BORRANS FIELD *a half-mile south of Ambleside, on the left bank of the Brathay, where it flows into Windermere* In the field are remains of Galara, a Roman fort, objects from which can now be seen in the National Park Centre at Brockhole (*21 acres*).

BRIDGE HOUSE *on a bridge over the Stock Ghyll, in Ambleside* A curious small building, possibly an eighteenth-century garden house, now used as a Trust Information Centre.

Dora's Field by Rydal Water, Cumbria

DORA'S FIELD $1\frac{1}{2}$ *miles north-west of Ambleside on north side of A591* Formerly known as the Rashfield, Dora's Field lies opposite Rydal Water and extends to an acre and a half (page 108). It belonged for a time to Wordsworth, who bought it in 1826 and planted daffodils there for his daughter. It was given to the Trust by his grandson in 1935.

FORCE HOW Seven acres of woodland running down to the Lancashire side of Skelwith Force.

GREAT BOG *beside Lake Road, Ambleside* A one and a half acre field given to preserve the view.

KELSICK SCAR and HIGH SKELGILL FARM $1\frac{1}{2}$ *miles south-east of Ambleside, south of Wansfell* Wood, fell and farmland with wide-ranging views (*200 acres*).

SCANDALE FELL *3 miles north of Ambleside* Grazing land at the top of Scandale beck (*73 acres*).

WANSFELL *a mile south of Ambleside* Wood and grassland on the east shore of Windermere, with views over the lake (*190 acres*).

WRAY CASTLE *2 miles south of Ambleside* On the west side of Windermere stands this nineteenth-century castle. Grounds are open, though not the house (*64 acres*).

—————

ARNSIDE: THE KNOTT *a mile south of Arnside* Land overlooking Morecambe Bay. 106 acres with two nature walks.

—————

Buttermere Valley

roughly half way between Whitehaven and Keswick

In this part of the Lake District the Trust owns three lakes (Buttermere, Crummock Water (page 110) and Loweswater), several areas of woodland and the waterfall at Scale Force about three-quarters of a mile up Scale Beck south-west from Crummock Water. Much of this property was bought by public subscription in the 1930s, some since the last war, and some was given by Dr G. M. Trevelyan and other donors.

Fishing and boats are to let on all three lakes.

Buttermere Valley,
Cumbria:
dry stone walling

Buttermere Valley,
Cumbria:
Buttermere and
Crummock Water
from Green Crag

These are the main properties:

BUTTERMERE *10 miles south-west of Keswick* The 230-acre lake (page 110) with 94 acres of woodland on the south shore and a three-acre field where the river flows out of the lake. Also five acres of oak woodland beside Sail Beck.

CRUMMOCK WATER *7–10 miles south of Cockermouth* The whole lake (*623 acres*) with Lanthwaite Wood (*69 acres*) at the north end and Backhows Wood (*7 acres*) and Fletcher Fields (*9 acres*).

HONISTER PASS Land extending for two miles on either side of the road from Gatesgarth to the Hause.

KIRK CLOSE *east of Hassness* Nineteen acres of land on a steep slope.

LONG HOW and NETHER HOW *between Buttermere village and Crummock Water* Fifteen acres of woodland.

LOWESWATER The whole lake (*160 acres*) with two acres of woodland to the north, Holme Wood (*122 acres*) on the south shore and Palace How Wood (*5 acres*).

SCALE FORCE *three-quarters of a mile up Scale Beck* Two acres of land and a waterfall.

————

CARTMEL: PRIORY GATEHOUSE Built about 1330; all that remains —with the exception of the church—of an Augustinian Priory. It is now used as a gallery and local museum.

————

CAUTLEY: CROSS KEYS INN *5 miles north-east of Sedburgh* Early seventeenth-century with later alterations. By the donor's wish, an unlicensed inn.

————

COCKERMOUTH: WORDSWORTH HOUSE *in Main Street* The house where Wordsworth was born—a mid-eighteenth-century building. Its original staircase, fireplaces and panelling remain. Wordsworth in *The Prelude* referred to the garden, which leads from the back of the house to the Derwent. The property was acquired by the Trust after a public appeal in 1938.

————

Coniston Water

CONISTON HALL *a mile south of Coniston village* An estate including the seventeenth-century hall with farmlands which give access to about a mile of the west shore of Coniston Water. Bought in 1971 with help from the Countryside Commission (*542 acres*).

FIR ISLAND A half-acre island half way down the lake and towards its east side.

HIGH AND LOW ARNSIDE FARM *2½ miles north-west of the lake* Two farm houses (below) and three hundred acres crossed by footpath and giving westerly views. Today's tenants are law-abiding farmers, but in the early nineteenth century Low Arnside Farmhouse was the home of Lanty Shee. He set up an illicit still and reputedly did a useful trade until arrested and jailed in 1833.

MONK CONISTON The Trust's Monk Coniston Estate stretches from Coniston to Little Langdale and amounts to just over four thousand acres. Monk Coniston Hall is let to the Holiday Fellowship. There are a number

High and Low Arnside Farm, near Coniston, Cumbria

Tarn Hows, near Coniston, Cumbria

of farms and at Tarn Hows (above) there is a splendid view-point and a nature walk. The estate has been built up since 1930 by subscription and gifts from several donors.

NIBTHWAITE WOODS   Situated towards the southern end of the lake on the east side (*147 acres*). Also Peel Island given by the 8th Duke of Buccleuch.

PARK-A-MOOR   Four hundred acres of woodland and fell on the east side of the lake.

DALTON CASTLE: DALTON-IN-FURNESS *main street*   A four-teenth-century tower, housing a small collection of armour.

113

Derwentwater and Borrowdale

Trust properties in this most prized area of the Lake District amount to more than five thousand acres of woodland, farmland and hillsides. At Brandlehow on the west side of the lake is the Trust's first acquisition in the Lake District—some woods, parkland and foreshore bought with public subscription in 1902. At Castle Crag (900 ft) between Rosthwaite and Grange, is one of several famous viewpoints. The summit of Castle Crag was given by Sir William Hamer as a memorial to his son, who was killed in the First World War. On the east side of the Lake, Calf Close Bay and Friar's Crag were bought by public subscription in 1922 as a memorial to Canon Rawnsley, one of the founders of the Trust. There is now a nature trail at Friar's Crag. Cockshott Wood and Stable Hills were added to this stretch of farm and woodland in 1925 and 1929. Seatoller Farm, its land and woods surrounding the hamlet of Seatoller, has fell land reaching to the top of Honister Pass.

These and other properties have been acquired at intervals since 1902 from public subscriptions and a variety of donors, and in one instance from the Treasury, which had accepted Seatoller Farm in payment of death duty.

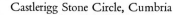

Castlerigg Stone Circle, Cumbria

Other properties in the area are:

ASHNESS FARM *3 miles south of Keswick* Farm and woodlands with good views.

BANKS INTAKE A hillside on the east side of Langstrath Beck.

BULL CRAG *4 miles south of the lake* A fine rocky bluff at the foot of Langstrath.

CASTLE HEAD Woodland half a mile south-east of Keswick rising to five hundred feet, with views of Derwentwater.

CASTLERIGG STONE CIRCLE *2 miles east of Keswick* Sometimes referred to as 'Druids' Circle' or 'The Carles' (page 114). It is a free standing megalithic circle, a hundred feet in diameter, of unhewn local boulders consisting of thirty-eight stones, five of which are fallen. There is an interior rectangular setting of smaller stones. Excavations in 1882 yielded only charcoal.

COOMBE ALLOTMENT and TROUTDALE Woodland on the east flank of Borrowdale (*180 acres*).

CROW PARK An open space on the north shore of the lake (*40 acres*).

DERWENT ISLAND A seven-acre island opposite Keswick boat-landing (*no access*).

Derwentwater: early morning

DERWENTWATER LAKE   The Trust owns the bed of the west half of the Lake.

GRANGE FELL   A three-hundred-acre property south of the Lake which includes the Bowder Stone (an estimated two thousand tons) and the 1363-ft King's How.

GREAT WOOD, KESWICK   Fine woodland south of Keswick on the east side of the Borrowdale road.

HAWSE END *north of Brandelhow*   Twenty acres on the west shore of the lake, excluding house and cottage.

HIGH RIGG FIELDS *west of Grange*   Part of Riggside Farm.

ISTHMUS *south-west of Keswick*   The Keswick bathing place and a cottage let to the County Association of Boys' Clubs.

JOHNNY'S WOOD and HIGH DOAT   Eighty acres adjoining existing Trust property in the heart of Borrowdale, with a two and a half-mile nature walk at Johnny's Wood.

LANGSTRATH INTAKE   Open hillside in Borrowdale on the west side of the Borrowdale–Langdale track.

LORD'S and ST HERBERT'S ISLANDS and RAMPSHOLME   Three small wooded islands in Derwentwater within a mile by boat from Keswick.

MANESTY PARK   107 acres at the south end of the lake. Wood, park and rough land part of which is let to the Caravan Club of Great Britain for touring caravans.

NOOK FARM *south-west of Rosthwaite*   Most of this farmland was given in memory of Captain John Diver, RAMC, in 1947.

SEATHWAITE FARM   Situated at the head of the valley, and at the foot of Styhead Pass. The property includes Taylor Gill Waterfall (*600 acres*).

STONETHWAITE and ROSTHWAITE   This property comprises Croft Farm and other land across the foot of Langstrath, cottages in the two hamlets and The How, and a hill in Rosthwaite village.

Watendlath Village, Cumbria, before the larch wood was felled

WATENDLATH *1½ miles north-east of Rosthwaite* This hamlet was bought in 1960–2 together with the Tarn, the land surrounding it and common rights which extend two thousand acres to the south (above). The purchase was made from funds bequeathed by several donors.

Duddon Valley

The Trust owns a number of farms in the Duddon Valley, covering between them nearly five thousand acres. They include high ground running up to the top of Hardknott Pass, to Grey Friar (2536 ft) and the Carrs (2550 ft). Three of these farms were gifts from the Rev. H. H. Symonds and one was given as a memorial to him. The farms are as follows:

BASKELL FARM Links Pikeside and Hazel Head Farms (see below).

BLACKHALL FARM At the head of the valley opposite Cockley Beck and reaching the top of Hardknott Pass.

BRIGHOUSE and HAZEL HEAD FARMS At Ulpha on the Cumberland side.

BROWSIDE and THRANG FARMS Up the valley above Seathwaite (*170 acres*), extending to the cascade of Thrang Force.

COCKLEY BECK and DALE HEAD FARMS Accessible only over Wrynose or Hardknott Pass, or twelve miles up the valley from Broughton. The lands rises to Grey Friar and adjoins the Trust's Monk Coniston estate at the 2550-ft Carrs.

PIKESIDE FARM and BECKSTONES A fell farm 900 ft up, at Low Ulpha.

TROUTAL FARM *2 miles north of Seathwaite* A Youth Hostel on the left bank of the Duddon with 145 acres.

WALLOWBARROW CRAG *half a mile west of Seathwaite* Rough fell on the right bank of the Duddon (*84 acres*). Also Crag End Wood.

———— ⌐ ⌐ ————

DUNTHWAITE *2 miles west of the north end of Bassenthwaite* Farmland and woodland bordering the Derwent for one and a half miles (*427 acres*).

———— ⌐ ⌐ ————

Ennerdale

To the south and east of Ennerdale Water the Trust owns nearly four thousand acres of fell on both sides of the River Liza, leased mainly from the Forestry Commission, and also the following farms on the north and north-west of the lake:

BECKFOOT FARM *on the north shore (48 acres)*.

HOW HALL FARM   Land at the north-west of Ennerdale Water and also further up Ennerdale.

HOWSIDE FARM   Fifty acres adjoining other Trust property.

~ ~

Eskdale

BOOT   Agricultural land near Eskdale church. Not open (*20 acres*).

BURNMOOR TARN   Beside the path from Eskdale to Wasdale (*57 acres*).

BUTTERILKET FARM   Land running down the left bank of the River Esk from the source at Eskhause to Wha House Bridge including the 2,960 ft summit of Bow Fell. Beyond Hardknott Pass on to Harter Fell it runs with Trust property in the Duddon Valley (Blackhall Farm).

PENNY HILL   Land on the left bank of the river, bequeathed to the Trust by Mrs W. Heelis, better known as Beatrix Potter, the authoress (*156 acres*).

TAW HOUSE FARM   Situated under the foothills of Scafell, on the right bank of the Esk.

WHA HOUSE FARM   Adjoining Taw House on the south-west. The Eskdale Youth Hostel stands on part of this land.

~ ~

Grasmere

In the village the Trust owns a cottage opposite the church called CHURCH STILE, in which there is an Information Centre; a half-acre at MOSS PARROCK; one-and-a-half acres at BROADGATE FIELD; and ALLAN BANK, the house where Wordsworth lived from 1808 to 1811. The house is not open, but there is a public footpath through its park leading to Score Crag and Kell Crag.

   In the neighbourhood are several cottages, a small house and the following properties:

ALCOCK TARN, BRACKENFELL and CHAPEL GREEN   Hillside behind Dove Cottage leading up to and including Alcock Tarn.

BRIMMER HEAD FARM, EASEDALE Two hundred acres of farmland acquired in 1973.

BUTTERLIP HOW Rising out of the Vale of Grasmere behind the village. Wordsworth recommended this as a good view-point when he wrote his *Guide to the Lakes* (6 acres).

LAKESIDE LAND Land with a lake-shore footpath on the south-west shore of Grasmere (20 acres).

EASEDALE *a mile north-west of Grasmere village* A house with several small pieces of land.

NICHOLAS WOOD *a mile south of Grasmere village* Woodland (10 acres).

STUBDALE COTTAGE At the foot of Easedale, including some land opposite.

WHITE MOSS INTAKE *a mile east of Grasmere village* Six acres of rough pasture adjoining White Moss Common through which runs Dunnery Beck. Views of Rydal Water.

THE WRAY *adjoining Allan Bank Park and St Oswalds* Meadow and rough pasture land (15 acres).

———— ⊂ ⌐ ————

Hawkshead

HAWKSHEAD COURT HOUSE *about 3 miles east of Coniston and 5 miles south of Ambleside* The Court House (page 121) dates mainly from the fifteenth century, though parts may be older. Furness Abbey held the Manor of Hawkshead during the Middle Ages, and the Court House is all that remains of the manorial buildings. It was given to the Trust by Mr H. S. Cowper, whose grandfather had bought it in 1860, and it is now let to the Lake District Museum Trust.

   The National Trust owns several cottages in the village of Hawkshead and land in the neighbourhood including, about two miles to the north-east, Blelham Bog, which is part of Low Wray Farm (385 acres) and is let to the Nature Conservancy, Blelham Tarn, and 260 acres of farmland overlooking the tarn.

Hawkshead, Cumbria: the Court House

Other properties in this area are:

DAN BECK *north-east of Hawkshead* 150 acres bequeathed by Mrs W. Heelis; nearby GREEN END 170 acres including Syke Side Farm and Latterbarrow, from which are fine views; HIGH AND LOW LOAN-THWAITE FARM *a mile north of Hawkshead* with 160 acres and Crag Wood, bequeathed by Mrs Heelis; NORTH FEN *at the north-east edge of Esthwaite Water*, seventeen acres, four acres of which are leased to the Nature Con-servancy; ROUND PARROCK WOOD *north-west of Hawkshead (1 acre)*.

—◦—◦—

HOBCARTON CRAG *4 miles west of Derwentwater* Twenty-seven acres of the face of the Crag, which reaches a height of 2,525 ft.

—◦—◦—

Langdales, Cumbria: Langdale Pikes, from Elterwater

Langdales

west-north-west of Ambleside

The section in the Trust's list of properties which is headed 'Langdales' notes the property belonging to the Trust at the head of Great Langdale, which consists of several farms and the Old Dungeon Ghyll Hotel; and other property, some adjoining the shore of Elterwater, some in Little Langdale, some at the head of Great Langdale, Four of the Great Langdale farms were given by Dr G. M. Trevelyan. Side House Farm, at the head of Great Langdale, was bought in 1963 with the help of Mrs Moorman and Trinity College, Cambridge as a memorial to him. Two of the farms in Little Langdale and some woodland were bequeathed to the Trust by Mrs W. Heelis (Beatrix Potter). The 'Langdales' section also refers the reader to another entry headed 'Lord Lonsdale's Commons'. Langdale Pikes (above) are included in Lord Lonsdale's Commons, which comprise the high land from the slopes of Helvellyn to the head of Great Langdale, and at the low level White Moss and Elterwater Commons with parts of Grasmere Lake and Rydal Water, in all nearly seventeen thousand acres. These the seventh Earl of Lonsdale leased to the Trust in 1961 for a peppercorn rent for thirty-five years or his lifetime, whichever is the longer.

Other properties in the Langdales area are:

BLEA TARN FARM *9 miles west of Ambleside* This 290-acre farm includes Blea Tarn and links existing Trust property at the head of Great and Little Langdales.

BRUNT HOW *half a mile east of Skelwith Bridge* An acre and a half by the Langdale Road.

HIGH CLOSE Stretching from the north-east shore of Elterwater to the south-west shore of Grasmere, this property includes two farms, Loughrigg Tarn with a nature walk on Loughrigg Fell, and High Close House, which is let to the Youth Hostels Association.

PYE HOW *on the north flank of the valley between Harry Place and Dungeon Ghyll* A footpath leads up from the road to nine acres of open fell.

———

NEWLANDS VALLEY *4 miles south-west of Keswick* High Snab Farm (*90 acres*).

———

Sawrey

between Esthwaite Water and Windermere

Mrs Heelis (Beatrix Potter) left about half Near Sawrey village to the Trust, including HILL TOP, the small seventeenth-century house behind the Tower Bank Arms where she wrote the Peter Rabbit books. Her furniture and some of her drawings are still in the house. She was an ardent and generous supporter of the Trust and her gifts and bequests, including that noted above, amounted to over four thousand acres together with farm and cottage buildings in different parts of the Lakes.

———

Scafell Pike, Cumbria: Glaramara and Scafell Pike viewed from Castle Crag

Great Gable and the Innominate Tarn, Cumbria

Scafell

between Borrowdale, Eskdale and Wastwater

The photograph of Scafell Pike (opposite) was taken from another Trust property, Castle Crag between Rosthwaite and Grange. Of this Scafell Group the Trust holds altogether about 2,500 acres. Forty acres on Scafell Pike itself (3,210 ft and the highest summit in England) were given in 1920 as a war memorial for the Lake District. In 1923 the Fell and Rock Climbing Club gave about twelve hundred acres above the 1500-ft mark near Styhead Pass as a war memorial to club members. Other land has been given by private donors. Great Gable (photograph opposite) is part of the group.

———

SHAP: KELD CHAPEL *a mile south-west of Shap near the River Lowther*   A small pre-Reformation building.

———

Silverdale

4 miles north-west of Carnforth (partly in Lancashire)

Properties here are:

CASTLEBARROW *overlooking Morecombe Bay (20 acres).*

EAVES AND WATERSLACK WOODS *just east of Castlebarrow Head* Woodland, a nature trail and an acre of Waterslack quarry.

THE KNOTT, ARNSIDE   See ARNSIDE KNOTT, page 109.

Sizergh Castle

3 miles south of Kendal

The name Sizergh, like other names in Cumberland and Westmorland, has its origin in the Scandinavian occupation of northern England in the ninth and tenth centuries. The first part, now reduced to Siz, had a variety of spellings such as Sirith in its early days, and was a personal name. The

Sizergh Castle, Cumbria: the pele tower

second part, erg, meant a summer pasture. The core of Sizergh Castle is the fourteenth-century pele tower (above). A pele was a tower within a stockade. Before the Union of 1603 those who lived near the Scottish border thought it sensible to take their own security measures, and many of these pele towers, and castles as well, were built. The tower at Sizergh has nine-feet-thick walls which still rise sixty feet to the battlements. Its fourteenth-century fireplaces and windows have remained unaltered during all the additions and changes which have been made through the centuries to render the castle a more convenient and handsome dwelling house. There is a variety of interest in the other parts of the building and their contents. The Great Hall, built in 1450, was altered and decorated between 1558 and 1575, and has a large Tudor fireplace. During this same period the wings, with their fine panelling and interior decoration, were added to the castle. Some further changes were made late in the eighteenth century. The castle contains English and French furniture of different periods, silver and china and, in addition to family portraits, a collection of Stuart portraits and Stuart and Jacobite relics. The

Strickland family acquired Sizergh by marriage in 1239 and it has continued to be their main residence ever since. Sir Thomas Strickland who had been Keeper of the Privy Purse to the Queen in Charles II's reign, and his second wife who was a member of the household of James II's queen, went into exile with James II and his family in 1688. Lady Strickland acted as governness to the young prince and the Stuart portraits in the Dining Room were given to her by the Queen. Sir Thomas's son was allowed to return to England and Sizergh in 1700. The grounds contain a notable sunken rock garden, and collections of dwarf conifers and hardy ferns.

—⚬——⚬—

SOLWAY COMMONS *on south shore of the Firth* Eighteen hundred acres of common land having twelve miles of coastline, mainly between Anthorn and Bowness. On a long lease from the Earl of Lonsdale at a peppercorn rent.

—⚬——⚬—

STOCKDALE MOOR *4 miles south of Ennerdale* Two and a half thousand acres, with enclosures and cairns, including the long barrow known as Sampson's Bratfull.

—⚬——⚬—

Troutbeck

3 miles south-east of Ambleside

TOWNEND A farm and farmhouse at the south end of the village, built about 1626 and occupied by the same family until 1944. It contains their furniture, books and papers. The farm runs to eight hundred acres.

TROUTBECK PARK FARM North of Troutbeck, this is a famous Lake District sheep farm of two thousand acres, mostly acquired under the will of Mrs Heelis.

—⚬——⚬—

Ullswater Valley

The Trust owns some very beautiful property around Ullswater, including parts of the lake shore, and was most actively engaged at all levels in the battles of the early 1960s that preserved the lake from being converted into a reservoir.

Ullswater, Cumbria

The photograph above is taken from Glencoyne Park, which is flanked on one side by Glencoyne Wood. These Trust properties lie to the west of the lake running up to Stybarrow Dodd (2,760 ft) and Raise (2,885 ft). On the same side of the lake, Gowbarrow Park (two and a half miles north of Glenridding, between the Penrith and Dockray roads) includes the sixty-five-feet-high waterfall of Aira Force and a mile of the lake shore. The Trust also owns 95 acres of the bed of Ullswater near Glenridding. South of Patterdale at the bottom end of the lake the Trust has farmlands in the valley including Hartsop Hall Farm and open spaces on the fells above, which run

Cumbria: Little Langdale Tarn, from the east, with Blake Rigg in the background on the left

Chartwell, Kent: the study

up to the Kirkstone Pass. This property, which includes the whole of Brotherswater, was given by the Treasury in 1947 having first been accepted in payment of death duty—the first property acquired by the Trust in this way. On the east shore of Ullswater, Side Farm runs for a mile northwards from Goldrill Beck at the south-east corner.

There are five more properties here:

CAUDALE BECK 1132 acres on both sides of the road down Kirkstone Pass towards Patterdale.

GREAT MELL FELL *2 miles south of Troutbeck* A hill of 364 acres rising to 1760 feet.

MILLSES FARM *east of the village of Dockray* Ninety-two acres adjoining Gowbarrow Park.

RIDDINGS PLANTATION Open fell flanking the north boundary of Gowbarrow Park (*146 acres*).

STYBARROW CRAG WOOD *between Glencoyne Wood and Glenridding* A strip of woodland along the western shores of Ullswater.

Wasdale

Here the Trust owns several large farms, including land at the head of the lake and fell land reaching up towards Scafell and towards Blacksail Pass; lake shore and woodland at the foot of Wastwater; and fourteen hundred acres to the west between Netherwasdale village and Santon Bridge. The individual properties are:

BOWERDALE A strip of woodland between the road and the north shore of Wastwater from Netherbeck Bridge to Overbeck Bridge.

MIDDLE ROW FARM *in the hamlet at the head of Wasdale* Land running down to the lake and up towards Scafell and Blacksail Pass (*2735 acres*).

NETHER WASDALE Comprising land between Bolton Wood, north of the Gosforth–Wasdale road, the River Irt and Kidbeck Farm near Netherwasdale village.

ROWHEAD FARM *At the head of Wasdale* Fifteen hundred acres with two nature walks, each one and a half miles long.

WASDALE HALL   Includes thirty-five acres of woodland and a half-mile stretch of lake shore at the foot of Wastwater.

WASDALE HEAD FARM *at the head of Wastwater*   Nineteen hundred acres of fell land running down towards the screes and also on High Fell, on the other side of the lake.

WETHERAL WOODS *south of Wetherall*   Twenty-one acres of land on the left bank of the Eden.

Windermere

The Trust has several properties here which are view-points, several which provide access to the lake, two islands and a nineteenth-century folly. The properties are:

ALLEN KNOTT and LATTER HEATH *2 miles north of Windermere Station*   The first is twelve acres overlooking the lake, and the second, sixty-three acres, a little to the east.

BORDRIGGS BROW   A view-point a half-mile south of Bowness.

CLAIFE WOODLAND, stretching from Wray Castle to Ferry Nab on the west shore of the lake, giving full access to the shore. There is a nature walk extending around a one and a half mile circular route.

COCKSHOTT POINT   On the lake shore on the outskirts of Bowness, with fine views (*21 acres*).

COMMON FARM   169 acres adjoining a view-point known as Orrest Head, on the south-east side of Windermere.

FELL FOOT   Eighteen acres providing access to the lake at the south end on the east shore. Now a Country Park with camping and sailing facilities and an Information Centre.

LADYHOLME   A half-acre island north of Bowness, upon which once stood a pre-Reformation chantry chapel.

POST KNOTT   Rough land east of the Kendal road, above Bowness (*7 acres*).

QUEEN ADELAIDE'S HILL *a mile by road west of Windermere Station* Twenty acres on the east shore of the lake with views and a boat landing. Also two acres to the south given in 1937 to commemorate King George VI's Coronation.

RAMPHOLME ISLAND   A wooded one-acre island south of Ferry Nab.

STORR'S TEMPLE   Built as a folly in 1804, it juts out from the east shore of the lake, south of the ferry (no access).

DERBYSHIRE

ALPORT HEIGHT *2 miles south-east of Wirksworth*   A nine-acre view-point on a thousand-foot hilltop.

ALSOP MOOR PLANTATION *8 miles north of Ashbourne*   Sixteen acres giving views of Wolfscote Dale and of Beresford and Biggin Dales.

BIGGIN DALE   Fifty-one acres on the western slopes of Wolfscote Hill.

CURBAR GAP *a half-mile east of Curbar village*   An eight-acre view-point with magnificent views of the Derwent Valley.

Dovedale

4 to 7 miles north-west of Ashbourne

On the Derbyshire-Staffordshire border, in the Dove, Manifold and Hamps valleys and the hills which divide them, Trust properties embrace a variety of areas of unspoiled country (pages 132–3). Altogether two thousand acres there belong to the Trust, and over a further three thousand acres protective covenants have been granted. In addition to the three places illustrated, the Trust has property in Dovedale which includes the remarkable rock forma-tions known as Jacob's Ladder and the Twelve Apostles. At Ilam, in Staffordshire, the park and woodland on both sides of the Manifold and the home farm are Trust property. The nineteenth-century Ilam Hall is let to the Youth Hostels Association, and there is a nature walk in the grounds.

131

Hall Dale, Derbyshire: the entrance, just above Dovedale, on the Staffordshire side
of the River Dove

Bunster Hill,
Derbyshire:
a view taken from
the Ilam–Blore road
showing Bunster
Hill, which stands
between Dovedale
and Ilam

Mill Dale,
Derbyshire:
Viator's Bridge at
the top end
of Dovedale

A little farther north on the east bank of the Dove (at High Wheeldon about five miles south-east of Buxton), some thirty acres on the hills bounding the upper reaches of the river were given in 1947 as a memorial to men of Derbyshire and Staffordshire who fell in the 1939–45 war.

In the Manifold valley (Staffordshire) the Grindon and Swainsley estates cover nearly nine hundred acres of farmland to the west of Alstonfield, reaching up to Grindon Moor and Welton Hill. On the right bank of the Hamps between Sparrowlee and Beeston Tor, the Throwley Estate includes Oldpark Hill and parts of Beeston Tor.

These properties were acquired by the Trust since the 1930s through the generosity of many donors, notable among them being the late Sir Robert McDougall.

—— ⇀ ⇀ ——

DUFFIELD CASTLE 2½ *miles south of Belper*   Foundations of a Norman keep razed in 1266.

—— ⇀ ⇀ ——

ECCLES PIKE 1½ *miles west of Chapel-en-le-Frith*   Six acres on the 1200-ft summit given to commemorate George VI's Coronation. Fine views.

—— ⇀ ⇀ ——

Edale

MAM TOR *a mile west of Castleton*   Mam Tor (page 135) commands wide-ranging views of the Peak District. Below it on its west side is the village of Castleton at the head of the Hope Valley and to the east is Edale. To the north it looks up from its 1,700-ft summit to the 2,000-ft flat top of Kinderscout. In the Edale area the Trust owns more than 1,400 acres, including several hill farms, eight hundred acres of Mam Tor, the nearby Winnats Pass, the limestone gorge which leads down to Castleton, and Hardenclough on the west side of the col of Mam Nick.

At the top of Mam Tor is an Iron Age hill fort, the largest in the county.

Other properties in the area include Edale End Farm on the western slopes of Kinderscout; four farms totalling four hundred acres at the foot of the Vale of Edale and at the head of the valley; thirty-seven acres including the summits of Lord's Seat and Ashton Bank, with fine views; Lose Hill Pike—fifty-five acres of hilltop two miles east of Edale Village.

At Fieldhead an Information Centre has been set up jointly by the Trust and the Peak District National Park.

Mam Tor, Derbyshire

EYAM: THE RILEY GRAVES *5 miles east of Tideswell* On a hillside a half-mile east of the village, where seven members of one family were buried in 1665 when the village, stricken by the plague, heroically isolated itself.

―⌒ ⌒―

FROGGATT WOOD *3 miles south of Hathersage on west side of B6054* Seventy acres of wood and pasture given mainly by the Sheffield and Peak District Branch of the Council for the Preservation of Rural England.

―⌒ ⌒―

Hardwick Hall

6½ miles north-west of Mansfield

Hardwick Hall (over) is much praised by critics as a masterpiece of Renaissance building. Its interior is embellished by a wealth of magnificent plasterwork, and it has a unique collection of tapestries and needlework.

135

Hardwick Hall, Derbyshire: the west front

In a brief account of the house Sacheverell Sitwell wrote of the Great High Chamber that in his opinion it is 'the most beautiful room not in England alone, but in the whole of Europe'.

To less learned visitors, too, Hardwick is immensely satisfying: a grand, impressive building, richly decorated, splendidly furnished and with a fine formal garden laid out in three large, walled areas with herbaceous plants and shrubs in long borders, an orchard and a herb garden. It has suffered very little change for three hundred years and more. Some of the contents listed in the present-day guide-books are also to be found in the inventory that 'Bess of Hardwick' had made when she moved into her new house in 1601. Her descendants, who became Earls and then Dukes of Devonshire, added to her furniture and tapestries during the seventeenth century. But since then little has been changed, because Chatsworth became their preferred family home. So Hardwick remains outside as Bess built it, and inside substantially as she knew it.

It is not known who was the architect, but it is likely that Bess herself (who, when she came to this task, was an experienced and indeed compulsive builder) worked with Robert Smythson. He had been working at Wollaton Hall not far away, and among his papers are plans which look like Hard-wick. It took from 1591 to 1597 to build and decorate. But Bess (born Elizabeth Hardwick and married four times, lastly to the Earl of Shrewsbury; hence the initials ES on the towers) was a lady of prodigious determination. Also, in her fourth widowhood she controlled the considerable wealth which her four husbands had bequeathed to her. Further, she seems to have done some advance planning. Thus the Brussels tapestries, in the High Great Chamber, she had bought a few years before the building was begun, and the detail of the room was evidently planned to display them.

There is a wealth of interesting portraits in the house. They include three of Bess herself, two of Mary Queen of Scots and others of Queen Elizabeth, Lord Burghley, James I and Thomas Hobbes the philosopher, who was tutor to the Earl of Devonshire and died at Hardwick in 1679.

Hardwick was accepted by the Treasury in part payment of death duties on the death of the tenth Duke of Devonshire and transferred to the Trust in 1959.

The eighteen-thousand-acre estate includes over two thousand acres of park and farmland, and the sixteen-thousand-acre Hope Woodlands Estate (below). There is a nature walk through the open parkland, which is grazed by cattle and a flock of White Faced Woodland (horned) Sheep.

HAYFIELD: SOUTH RIDGE FARM *a quarter-mile south of Hayfield* Has good views of Kinderscout and the Peak and rises above a thousand feet.

HAYWOOD: LAND AT NETHER PADLEY *north-west of B6045* Pasture, moor and woodland linking the Trust's Longshaw and Froggatt Wood properties. 171 acres acquired in 1973.

HOPE WOODLANDS *6 miles east of Glossop* The sixteen-thousand-acre Hope Woodlands estate, between Glossop and Sheffield, was given to the Trust with Hardwick Hall. Weathering has exposed a section of Roman road, just off the A57 near Doctor's Gate culvert.

137

LANTERN PIKE *1¼ miles north-west of Hayfield* This moorland hilltop with views was given as a memorial to Edwin Royce, a past President of Manchester Ramblers' Federation.

LONGSHAW *a mile south-east of Hathersage, on south side of A625* Eleven hundred acres of moor and woodland extending from Fox House Inn to below the Surprise View. Includes Padley Woods and the Padley Gorge Nature Walk.

MILLER'S DALE and RAVENSTOR *2 miles south of Tideswell* Sixty-four acres of wooded cliffs astride the River Wye.

SHINING CLIFF WOOD *4 miles north of Belper* Two hundred acres of woodland at Alderwasley on the west bank of the Derwent, leased to the Forestry Commission.

STANTON MOOR EDGE *4 miles south-east of Bakewell* A three-quarter-mile strip over nine hundred feet high with views over the Derwent valley. Also five acres of woodland on the lower slopes (no access).

Sudbury Hall

6 miles east of Uttoxeter on A50

Sudbury Hall, seen from the outside, is a most impressive red brick mansion (opposite) and inside it is rich in fine decoration. It was built by Sir George Vernon, who seems to have been his own architect. He was building in the 1660s and 1670s, and in later years added to the interior decoration. Although succeeding generations of Vernons made plans for transforming the house to suit eighteenth- and nineteenth-century fashions in architecture, these were not put into effect. Apart from a changed garden layout and alterations in the east part of the house Sudbury is substantially as Sir George left it in 1701.

For the interior he initially employed local craftsmen, and also other men from further afield, including Grinling Gibbons, who did some very fine carving in the Drawing Room. Later Sir George employed the painter

Sudbury Hall, Derbyshire: the south front

Louis Laguerre, whose contributions include the Four Seasons on the ceiling of the Saloon.

The staircase is described in the Trust's guide book as 'the finest staircase of its date *in situ* in an English country house'.

Sir George included in his interior plan a Long Gallery, which his con-temporaries considered very old fashioned. Why he did so is a matter for speculation, for although detailed accounts of his expenditure on the building have survived, no record of his ideas on the design, except for the building itself, has been found.

The house and principal contents were transferred to the Trust in 1967, having been accepted by the Treasury in part payment of estate duty. Lord Vernon gave an endowment and the Derbyshire County Council offered grants towards maintenance.

Sudbury Hall, Derbyshire: the saloon

TADDINGTON WOOD *1½ miles east of Taddington*   Fifty acres of wooded slope on the south side of the Buxton–Bakewell road.

WINSTER MARKET HOUSE *4 miles west of Matlock*   The market house at Winster (below), a town noted for its mumming dance, was built about 1700. It was repaired and given to the Trust in 1906 after a local appeal.

WOLFSCOTE DALE and WOLFSCOTE HILL *south of Hartington, just west of Biggin Dale*   An eighty-acre glen and thirty-four acres of the summit of the nearby hill, with wide views.

Winster
Market House,
Derbyshire

DEVON

Arlington Court

7 miles north-east of Barnstaple

Arlington Court (below) was built for John Chichester in 1822 to the design of Thomas Lee, a local architect who was later to design the Guildhall at Barnstaple. Outside it is a plain, rather severe building relieved by a semi-circular porch. Inside most of the rooms are as Lee left them; but in the 1860s the hall was enlarged by removing the rooms in the centre of the north side. At the same time the house was enlarged by the addition of a new wing, the attractive formal garden was laid out, and a handsome stable block was built.

The building contains furniture which was made for it by a Barnstaple cabinet-maker when the house was built, some family portraits, and a water-colour by William Blake, signed and dated 1821. This is thought to have been brought to Arlington by John Chichester shortly after it was painted.

Arlington Court, Devon: the drawing-room

Miss Rosalie Chichester, who bequeathed the estate to the Trust, was born at Arlington in 1865 and lived there until her death in 1949.

It was her great-grandfather, Colonel John Chichester, who built the house. Before him the Chichester family had been in possession of the estate since 1384. It is not known when they first built a house there; but the foundations of what is probably a sixteenth-century building are visible in the park to the south of the present one.

Miss Chichester was an assiduous collector, with a special interest in ships and the sea, and accumulated during her long life collections of model ships, British and foreign shells, pewter, snuff-boxes and other objects. These are on view in the house. She also made the large park an animal sanctuary, and it is now grazed by Shetland ponies and Jacob's sheep. The lake is a haunt of wild fowl and buzzards, and ravens nest in the woods. There is a circular nature walk.

The Trust has now established in the stables a small collection of carriages and horsedrawn vehicles, and has added to Miss Chichester's collection a model of *Gipsy Moth IV*, in which her nephew, Sir Francis Chichester, sailed around the world.

Bideford

BURROUGH FARM, NORTHAM *about 3 miles north of Bideford* Burrough Farm's forty-five acres run down from Northam to low wooded cliffs on the left bank of the Torridge estuary. Cliff and field paths give access to a small cove.

KIPLING TORS *north-west of Bideford at Westward Ho!* Eighteen acres of the gorse-covered hill of *Stalky & Co.* were given by the Rudyard Kipling Memorial Fund.

Bradley Manor

at the western edge of Newton Abbot

Bradley Manor (over) is an interesting example of medieval domestic architecture. Most of the building dates from about 1420, when a thirteenth-century house was altered and enlarged. A chapel was included in these

Bradley Manor, Devon: the east front

enlargements and this remains, together with the Solar, Great Hall and porch. The walls of the house are roughcast and the roof is slate. It is set in a valley of meadow and woodland.

The fifteenth-century building was the work of Richard Yarde, who inherited the earlier house from his grandmother. His descendants sold the property in 1750 and it changed hands again several times. Its style of architecture being out of fashion, the house was converted to be a farmhouse, with poultry kept in the chapel. In 1909 a descendant of the Yardes bought and restored it and in 1938 his daughter gave it to the Trust.

BRANSCOMBE and SALCOMBE REGIS A four-mile stretch from Branscombe to Dunscombe Cliff, south of Salcombe Regis, including cliffs, foreshore and farmland in a wooded valley with footpaths, and, at Branscombe, two medieval farmhouses, a group of thatched cottages, a forge and a bakery.

Buckland Abbey

Buckland Abbey (below) was founded in the thirteenth century as a Cistercian house. During the Middle Ages the monks had wide estates and built a large abbey church, presumably with cloisters, refectory and dormitories to scale. But it is not clear how these were laid out on the site. When the abbey was converted to be a secular dwelling-house after the dissolution of the monasteries, the abbey church became the hall of the new house, the monks' quarters were dismantled, and new kitchen and living quarters were built.

This conversion was carried out by Sir Richard Grenville of the *Revenge*, whose grandfather had bought the property in 1541. The date over the fireplace in the hall—1576—is taken as indicating that he completed the work in that year. But he did not stay at Buckland long. In 1580 he went to live at another of his family's properties and shortly afterwards (1581) Buckland was bought by Sir Francis Drake. Drake was then rising forty, already famous and a comparatively wealthy man. He lived much at Buckland from then on, when not voyaging, but made no changes in the house. He took an active part in Plymouth affairs, as mayor in 1581 and later as M.P. for the city.

Buckland Abbey, Devon

Drake's brother inherited the property and it remained in his family's hands until 1946. They made some alterations to the interior during the eighteenth century and, it is thought, pulled down some part of the monastic buildings which had been left by Sir Richard Grenville. The medieval tithe barn, however, still stands.

The abbey was acquired and repaired by the Trust in 1948 with the help of private donors and the Pilgrim Trust. It has been leased to Plymouth Corporation and is maintained as a naval and Devon folk museum.

Clovelly

Near Clovelly, at the head of the valley down which the village straggles to the sea, is MOUNT PLEASANT, a little field with views over Bideford Bay. It was given in memory of Clovelly men who fell in the 1914–18 war.

Between Clovelly and Hartland Point are THE BROWNSHAMS, two ancient farmhouses in three hundred acres of farm and woodlands, seventy acres of which are a nature reserve.

FATACOTT CLIFF *4 miles north-west of Clovelly* A cliff with adjacent farmland commanding wide sea views.

EAST TITCHBERRY FARM *about a mile short of Hartland Point* A site of 120 acres with a mile of cliff and access on foot to Shipload Bay.

Compton Castle

4 miles west of Torquay

Compton Castle (opposite) was built as a fortified manor, intended to give protection to the food supplies and non-combatants of the neighbourhood, rather than to withstand a full-blooded siege. But it had high walls and portcullises to protect the entrances. This was desirable when it was first built, about 1320, as French raids on places so near to the coast—it is only a few miles inland from Tor Bay—were something to be taken into account. It was reconstructed and enlarged twice in the following two hundred years, but has remained a fortified dwelling-house.

In Queen Elizabeth I's reign the Gilberts, who had acquired the Compton estate by marriage early in the fourteenth century, were much involved both

Compton Castle, Devon

in the defence of the west country against the Spanish and in colonization of the New World. John Gilbert, Sheriff and Vice-Admiral of Devon, was knighted in 1571 and was engaged in organizing the defence of the county. His younger brother, Sir Humphrey Gilbert, was an enthusiastic supporter of the North West Passage idea, and in 1583 sailed as leader of the expedition which led to the colonization of Newfoundland.

Compton remained in the possession of the Gilbert family until 1800 but was in other hands during the nineteenth century. In 1930 it was bought back by Commander W. R. Gilbert, who gave it to the Trust in 1951.

Castle Barton, 51 acres immediately opposite Compton, was added to the property in 1972.

Dartmoor

BRIDFORD WOOD *3 miles north-east of Moretonhampstead* Eighty acres of oak-covered hillside above the River Teign. Seen from Steps Bridge across the river, the woods are a fine feature of the magnificent view, while within the woodland itself are picnic places and over a mile of walks. Devon County Council helped with its purchase and endowment.

GOODAMEAVY *6 miles north-east of Plymouth, 2 miles south of Yelverton* Standing at the south-western corner of Dartmoor, this property covers nearly four hundred acres including Dewerstone and Cadworthy Woods, the Dewerstone Rock and part of Wigford Down. Finds of archaeological interest have been made at the last two places. It is fine walking country and there is access by footpath to the Trust's moor and woods, though not to the

Goodameavy, Devon, looking down the River Meavy

farms. The property was acquired in 1960, partly from the Treasury which had accepted it in payment of death duty, and partly by purchase from two legacies.

HEMBURY and BURCHETTS WOOD *2 miles north of Buckfastleigh* Wood-land rides for nearly a mile on the west side of the Dart valley, with a circular nature walk and an Iron Age hill fort of Hembury Castle, and also the mutilated motte and bailey of Dane's Castle. Just to the south is Burchetts Wood, a further twenty-five acres.

HENTOR and WILLINGS WALLS WARRENS Open moorland on the south-west flank of Dartmoor rising to fifteen hundred feet and containing much of prehistoric interest. It overlooks the River Plym and is crossed by a mile of the Abbots Way (*2,800 acres*).

HOLNE WOODS *3½ miles west of Ashburton* On the west side of the River Dart, 165 acres of woodland mainly of natural oak with footpaths and views.

LYDFORD GORGE *half-way between Okehampton and Tavistock* Part of the Lyd valley with oak woodland and the ninety-foot high White Lady waterfall (*103 acres*). Also Ingo Brake, between the village and the entrance to the Gorge; five acres including a small early Norman fort.

MORETONHAMPSTEAD ALMSHOUSES *at the east edge of the town, on B3212 by the churchyard* These almshouses are built of granite over an open colonnade and have a thatched roof (below). They were built in 1637 and given to the Trust by the Moretonhampstead Almshouse Charity in 1952. They are let and are not open.

Moretonhampstead, Devon: the almshouses

TROWLESWORTHY WARREN Five hundred acres of moorland on the south-west flank of Dartmoor where there are Bronze Age hut circles. Also a small farm, originally the warrener's house, and a circular two-mile nature walk.

WHEAL BETSY *5 miles north of Tavistock* An old engine house and stack of an abandoned lead mine.

WIDECOMBE-IN-THE-MOOR: CHURCH HOUSE A charming arcaded granite building in the style of Moretonhampstead Almshouses (also Trust-owned). It is a fifteenth-century building, given in 1933 by local subscription. Part of it is now used as a cottage, and part as the village hall.

———

DUNSLAND *4½ miles east of Holsworthy* This ninety-acre property was bought by the Trust for the beauty of Dunsland House, a Tudor house enlarged in the seventeenth century. Essential repairs had just been completed, when, in 1967, a disastrous fire destroyed it. The ruins were thought dangerous and have since been demolished.

———

Dartmouth

LITTLE DARTMOUTH *1½ miles south of Dartmouth* This stretch of cliff and farmland forms the western approach to Dartmouth Harbour, running from Warren Point to the harbour entrance. There is access to the beaches at Compass Point and Sugary Cove from the coastal footpath which traverses the 170-acre property and gives many fine views.

———

Exmouth

LYMPSTONE *about 3 miles out of Exmouth* Six acres overlooking the estuary from the east bank of the Exe.

ORCOMBE and PRATTSHAYES *2½ miles east of Exmouth* Covers a mile of cliff and foreshore east from Exmouth promenade, and fields inland (*126 acres*).

HOLDSTONE DOWN *halfway between Combe Martin and Heddon's Mouth* Fifteen acres of moorland and cliff rising to 1145 ft.

———

Honiton

COMBE WOOD *at Combe Raleigh, 1 mile north of Honiton* Eighteen acres of woodland.

LOUGHWOOD MEETING HOUSE *north of the Honiton–Axminster road, south of Dalwood* Built about 1653 by the Baptist congregation of Kilmington, near Axminster. The interior was simply fitted in the early eighteenth century and has remained unaltered. Given by the Devon & Cornwall Baptist Corporation Ltd, who contributed, as did the Historic Buildings Council and Axminster R.D.C., to the cost of repairs.

ROCKBEARE HILL *about 8 miles south-west of Honiton, west of Ottery St Mary* This hill-top of heath and woodland was given as long ago as 1940.

—⊃ ⊂—

Ilfracombe

Most of the coastal land from the western outskirts of the town to the village of Lee, with farmland between the town and Flat Point. There are footpaths. Enterprise Neptune Funds bought part of this land, which totals 444 acres.

BULL POINT $3\frac{1}{2}$ *miles east of Ilfracombe* A spectacular headland of 182 acres, uniting the extensive Morte Point and Woolacombe properties and making the Trust's ownership of the coast continuous for five miles.

DAMAGE CLIFFS *3 miles from Ilfracombe, just west of Lee Bay* Along this stretch of cliff-land are two Bronze Age standing stones. Once a golf course, the cliffs yield good views and there are footpaths.

GOLDEN COVE, BERRY NARBOR *3 miles east of Ilfracombe* Ten acres of wooded cliff-land just west of Combe Martin.

MORTE BAY *3 miles west of A361, running about 3 miles north to south* Nine properties which cover about twelve hundred acres of headland, farmland and sand dunes, several of them gifts of the late Miss Rosalie Chichester of Arlington Court. There is land with commanding views on both north and south headlands—Morte Point and Baggy Point. To the north of Woolacombe is Town Farm, land at Morte Fields and at Combegate Beach, and to the south, sand dunes at Woolacombe Warren where there is surf bathing, and land at Vention and Potters Hill. There are 545 acres of steep land at

151

Woolacombe Barton with a possible Bronze Age standing stone. Also twelve acres to the north of Croyde Beach, forming the approach to Baggy Point from the south.

Killerton

KILLERTON GARDEN 7 *miles north-east of Exeter* Part of the six-thousand-acre Killerton Estate given to the Trust by Sir Richard Acland. The estate is mainly agricultural and woodland and includes the villages of Broad Clyst and Budlake and the hamlets of Westwood and Beare.

The Garden (below), which has been in the making and maturing for a century and a half, is on a fifteen-acre lime-free site on the south slope of Killerton Clump. In addition to the spring and autumn glory of the trees and shrubs, there are sheets of bulbs in spring, and the long herbaceous border is at its best in July and August.

The Garden was laid out in its present form after the Napoleonic Wars by Sir Thomas Acland, tenth baronet. Succeeding generations of the Acland family have contributed to the plantings. The higher slopes of the garden

Killerton Garden, Devon

command fine views of the surrounding country. The Trust also owns Killerton Park. Its 300 acres surround the Dolbury, an isolated hill with an Iron Age hill fort. There is public access at all times.

Knightshayes Garden

2 miles north of Tiverton

An extensive garden, mainly woodland and shrubs with fine specimen trees and formal terraces and hedged areas. Spring bulbs and rare shrubs. The garden has been enlarged during the last thirty years by the owners, Sir John and Lady Heathcoat-Amory, who made the Trust the sole trustee in 1973.

Lundy Island

24 miles west of Ilfracombe

The island is three and a quarter miles long, half a mile wide at its widest point and lies approximately north to south. It is of volcanic origin, 93 per cent granite and 7 per cent shale—the shale being like that at Ilfracombe.

Lundy Island, Devon

About a thousand acres are rough grazing and the remaining two hundred pasture or arable. The whole island is a bird sanctuary and a nesting place for a variety of seabirds. There are no reptiles, but the animal population includes deer, soay sheep, wild ponies and wild goats. Seals breed on the south coast.

There is some evidence of occupation in prehistoric times, while a number of interesting buildings survive from more recent times, including the ruins of a medieval castle, a late Victorian church and the old Trinity House fog signal station with its William IV eighteen-pounders still in position.

Lundy was bought in conjunction with the Landmark Trust, to which it is let, with money left by Mr Jack Hayward in 1969. Boats run from Ilfracombe, and there is sleeping accommodation on the island for visitors.

Lynmouth

To the east of Lynmouth, including Foreland Point, Countisbury Hill and Watersmeet, the Trust holds twelve hundred acres. These cover wooded valley areas south of the East Lyn and Hoar Oak Water; Watersmeet; and to the north, Town Farm at Countisbury and the Iron Age earthwork of Countisbury Camp on Wind Hill; the cliffs above Sillery Sands to Foreland Point at the eastern end of Lynmouth Bay. There are several miles of footpaths. A National Trust Information Point is situated at Watersmeet House.

Lynton

Between Lynton and Combe Martin, to the west, the Trust has a series of interesting properties. Illustrated on page 155 is a view from Trentishoe Common.

WOODY BAY There are cliffs and moorland between Lynton and Heddon's Mouth on the slopes from Wringapeak Point down to Woody Bay (*115 acres*).

HEDDON VALLEY Nearly a thousand acres with fine views leading down from Trentishoe Common to the sea. A two-mile circular nature walk leads to the sea at Heddon's Mouth. Also land at North Cleave with Parsonage Wood, and forty acres of steep oak woodland on the west side of the valley.

Lynton, Devon: a view from Trentishoe Common

THE GREAT HANGMAN *between Combe Martin and Heddon's Mouth*
Cliff and moorland rising to over a thousand feet, with views inland as well
as seaward (*280 acres*).

———⟨⟩⟨⟩———

Plymouth

DRAKE'S ISLAND *in Plymouth Sound, opposite the Hoe* Fortified in the
fifteenth century when it was St Nicholas Island, and garrisoned until after
1945; the Trust leases it from the Crown Estates Commissioner. With

the co-operation of the National Association of Boys Clubs, it is being developed as an Adventure Training Centre. Also has access for day visitors.

PLYM BRIDGE WOODS *5 miles north-east of Plymouth*   A hundred acres of the wooded valley of the River Plym. Also Boringdon Gate Piers, formerly the west entrance to Boringdon, the seat of the Parker family before they lived at Saltram.

Saltram

3½ miles east of centre of Plymouth

Saltram (below), which also presents many other delights, has two particular distinctions; the Saloon and dining-room are among Robert Adam's best work, and the pictures in the house include a splendid collection of Reynolds portraits.

The house was built in the middle of the eighteenth century, altering and incorporating parts of a Tudor house which preceded it on the site. It was given a plain exterior but a very decorative interior. The first part of this building was carried out between 1743 and 1750 by John and Lady Catherine Parker. It is not known whom they employed as architect, but the quality of the decoration of the rooms for which they were responsible shows that they enlisted craftsmen of the highest skill. In 1768 their son John (later Baron Boringdon) engaged Robert Adam to make extensive alterations

Saltram, Devon: the west front

to the east wing. Some further work was carried out in 1818, when the porch was added. There have been no material changes since then.

The various collections in the house—furniture, pictures, pottery and porcelain—are immensely interesting. The John Parker who employed Robert Adam as his architect was responsible for a great part of them. He was probably advised on his choice of pictures by Sir Joshua Reynolds, who was his friend and a frequent visitor to Saltram House. Reynolds's portrait of Parker's two children is still in the position their father chose for it, over the chimney-piece in the morning-room. John Parker kept accounts, though not, unfortunately, in great detail. But they do record purchases from Chippendale and Wedgwood of furniture and vases now in the house.

The house stands in a beautifully landscaped park through which, unfortunately, a new motor road has been built. Park, house and principal contents were accepted by the Treasury in payment of death duty in 1957 and given to the Trust. A hundred-acre farm to the south of the park was added in 1961, and later forty acres to the north, and sixty-six acres including Wixenford Bottom, Sellar Acres woods and the west end of the park, making 498 acres in all.

Saltram, Devon: the Adam dining-room

WELCOME MOUTH *On the Devon–Cornwall border* An acre above Welcombe Mouth.

WEMBURY BAY *5 miles south-east of Plymouth* Land round St Werburgh's church and on the foreshore. Also twenty-seven acres of hanging woodland on the south bank of the Yealm estuary, just west of Noss Mayo.

———⊃ ⊂———

Salcombe

At Salcombe, Trust properties cover about twelve miles of coastline on either side of the harbour.

BEESANDS CLIFF *3 miles north of Start Point* Sixteen acres at north end of Beesands Beach.

BIGBURY-ON-SEA *south of B3392* A viewpoint on Clematon Hill.

BOLT HEAD and BOLT TAIL *between Salcombe Harbour and Hope* Nearly a thousand acres of cliff and farmland extending for about six miles to the west of Salcombe. There is a $1\frac{1}{2}$-mile coastal walk at Bolberry Down, along spectacular cliffs.

PORTLEMOUTH DOWN *on east side of Salcombe Harbour* Three hundred acres extending for about five miles from Mill Bay to Venericks Cove. Cliff walks and views.

PRAWLE POINT and GAMMON HEAD Land at Prawle Point, the southernmost part of Devon, and at Gammon Head, the rocky promontory to the west.

SHARPITOR $1\frac{1}{2}$ *miles south-west of Salcombe* A modern house with six acres of small terraced gardens containing many rare shrubs and tender plants. From the gardens are beautiful views over Salcombe Bay. The house is let partly to the Youth Hostels Association and partly to a local museum. It is not open.

———⊃ ⊂———

SHUTE BARTON *3 miles south-west of Axminster* The remains of a grey stone manor house that was built at intervals from the fourteenth to the sixteenth century; the north-east wing was demolished in the late eighteenth century.

———⊃ ⊂———

SIDMOUTH There are small Trust properties at Peak Hill Field, Pond Meadow and Sid Meadows.

———⊃ ⊂———

TEIGNMOUTH: LITTLE HALDON *3 miles north-west of Teignmouth* Heathland with views (*43 acres*).

—⇌—

TIVERTON: OLD BLUNDELL'S SCHOOL The seventeenth-century Grammar School's north-east façade has been little altered since it was described in *Lorna Doone*. It is now converted to dwelling-houses.

—⇌—

Withleigh

3 miles west of Tiverton in the valley of the Little Dart

There are three properties at Withleigh:

BUZZARDS A mile stretch of the Little Dart, covering about eighty acres of coppice and water meadow, was given to the Trust in 1967 (below). A secluded and undeveloped area, it has many wild flowers. Access is by footpath.

HUNTLAND WOOD Twenty-seven acres of hanging woodland on the east bank of the Little Dart, south of Buzzards.

NETHERCLEAVE Steep pasture fields on the east bank, north of Buzzards (*30 acres*).

Withleigh, Devon: Buzzards

DORSET

Beaminster

WINYARD'S GAP 2½ *miles north-east of Beaminster*   Woodland given as a memorial to men of the 43rd (Wessex) Division in the 1939–45 war. There are two view-points near Beaminster:

CROOK HILL near Winyard's Gap and LEWESDON HILL (894 ft), three miles west of Beaminster, which has views over Devon, Dorset, Somerset and the sea.

Brownsea Island

in Poole Harbour about 1½ miles south-south-east of Poole near Sandbanks

Brownsea Island and its woodlands make a fine contribution to the scenic attractions of Poole Harbour, while visitors to the island are rewarded with magnificent views along the Dorset coast.

It extends to five hundred acres made up of woodland, sandy beach, heath, a marsh area and two lakes. There are several miles of woodland paths and glades, a 1½-mile nature walk and a mile of bathing beach (below). Part of the island is managed as a nature reserve by the Dorset Naturalists' Trust, as there are rare wild flowers in the marsh, the lakes are a sanctuary for wildfowl and there is a heronry. The reserve is open to guided parties at fixed times.

Lord Baden-Powell held the first Boy Scout camp here in 1907. Arrange-

Brownsea Island, Dorset: a view of beach and woods taken from the castle landing-stage

ments have been made with the Boy Scout and Girl Guide Associations for them to hold camps on the island, but there is no other camping. A castle was built on the island in Henry VIII's time; but the present castle is a mainly Victorian mansion completed about 1900.

The Trust acquired the island in 1962 from the Treasury, who had accepted it in payment of death duty. A considerable endowment was needed, and this was raised by a public appeal, to which a number of charitable trusts contributed.

———

BURTON BRADSTOCK *about 2 miles south-east of Bridport* Eighty acres of Burton Cliff, which runs west from Burton Bradstock, rising to a hundred feet before descending to Freshwater Bay. Both riverside and cliff walks.

———

CREECH: GRANGE ARCH *about 3 miles south of Wareham and 3 miles west of Corfe Castle* Also called Bond's Folly after the eighteenth-century Bond who built it so that there should be an architectural feature on the skyline viewed from his house below. Given by Mr J. W. Bond in 1941. (The house still belongs to the family.)

———

Dorchester

There are seven Trust properties within ten miles of Dorchester and they provide a variety of interest.

THE CERNE GIANT *8 miles north of Dorchester and just north of Cerne Abbas* A 180-ft high Romano-British giant cut in the chalk of Giant Hill (*600 ft*).

CLOUDS HILL *9 miles east of Dorchester, 1½ miles east of Waddock crossroads* This is the cottage to which T. E. Lawrence retired when he left the Royal Air Force in 1935 (below). It was given to the Trust in 1937 with some of its contents by Mr A. W. Lawrence, as a memorial to his brother.

Clouds Hill, Dorset

Hardy's Cottage

Higher Bockhampton, 3 miles north-east of Dorchester

Thomas Hardy was born in 1840 in a small thatched house which was built by his great-grandfather and which has been little changed externally. The walls were originally built of a composition of chalk, clay, straw and other materials which were much used in the south-west at that time. To give this weather protection they have been reinforced with brick facing or rendered cement.

Hardy grew up in the cottage, walking to school; first to the village school in Lower Bockhampton and then the three miles to Dorchester. He continued there while a pupil in the office of John Hicks, the Dorchester architect. He was twenty-two when he went to try his luck in London. He returned to the cottage five years later and again worked in Dorchester for a time before going to Weymouth. He continued to visit the cottage both during and after his parents' lifetime, his last visit being in 1926.

The cottage was bought by the Trust in 1948 in accordance with Miss K. Hardy's will. A small collection of items of interest connected with Hardy was given to the Trust in 1965.

Hardy's Cottage, Dorset

HARDY MONUMENT *6 miles south-west of Dorchester*   On a three-quarter-acre plot with views over Weymouth Bay, a monument erected in 1846 to Vice-Admiral Hardy who was flag-captain of the *Victory* at Trafalgar.

SOUTHDOWN FARM *7 miles south-east of Dorchester in Ringstead Bay* About three hundred acres of farmland and adjoining them, between Burning Cliff and Whitenothe Cliff, another hundred acres of cliff. Some of Whitenothe cliff path, a legendary escape route for smugglers, is too dangerous for walking.

TOLPUDDLE: MARTYRS' MEMORIAL *7 miles north-east of Dorchester* A seat commemorates the transported labourers of 1834.

WEST BEXINGTON: LIME KILN HILL *2 miles north-west of Abbotsbury* Some of the former stone workings and thirty-seven acres of rough grazing overlooking the Chesil Bank to the south. There are also views northwards.

Golden Cap Estate

The estate extends for about five miles along the coast between Charmouth and Eypemouth. It is made up of nearly 1700 acres of hill, cliff, farmland, undercliff and beach and is served by fifteen miles of footpath, including a six-mile through-route along the coast.

Much of it is farmed and some of it is leased to the Dorset Naturalists' Trust. There is access to a very large part of the estate and visitors are asked to remember that preservation of wild life, animals and plants is of special importance here. There is access by car to viewpoints on Stonebarrow and Chardown Hills, to the sea at Charmouth, Seatown and Eypemouth, and on foot to the beach at St Gabriel's, from Morcombelake. Hardown Hill looks inland over the Marshwood Vale and south past Golden Cap to the sea. It can be reached on foot from Morcombelake.

The estate has been built up by gifts from a number of donors, mostly to Enterprise Neptune. The larger properties comprising the estate include:

DOWNHOUSE FARM *at Eype, about a mile south-west of Bridport*   This 176-acre farm (over) with thirty-five acres of grazing rights over Eype Down, runs from the undercliff up to Thorncombe Beacon (508 ft). It was given in 1966 by R. C. Sherriff as a contribution to Enterprise Neptune.

FILCOMBE and NORCHARD FARMS   Over two hundred acres of farm and wood land.

Downhouse Farm, near Bridport, Dorset

RIDGE CLIFF and WEST CLIFF *on each side of Seatown* 170 acres of cliff, undercliff and farmland.

STONEBARROW HILL and WESTHAY FARM *2 miles south-east of Charmouth* 274 acres of farm, undercliff and hill.

$\smile \quad \frown$

LAMBERT'S CASTLE HILL *4½ miles east of Axminster* 160 acres embracing the 842 ft hill-top site of an Iron Age fort and round barrow with wide views east to Chesil Bank and west to Dartmoor.

DURHAM

Three of the five properties in the old county of Durham are now in the new county of Tyne and Wear. The remaining properties in the new Durham are:

EBCHESTER *12 miles south-west of Newcastle* Here ten acres of woodland on the right bank of the River Derwent are let to Consett U.D.C. Three acres were given by Ebchester Rowing Club.

MOORHOUSE WOODS *3 miles north-east of Durham* Sixty acres of wood-land on the River Wear.

EAST SUSSEX

Alfriston: Clergy House

4 miles north-east of Seaford just east of B2108

Alfriston's clergy house was bought in 1896, and was the first building to be acquired by the Trust. (The first property acquired by the Trust was Dinas Oleu, a piece of cliff-land in Merionethshire above Barmouth with views over Cardigan Bay, which was given in 1895.)

The clergy house dates from about 1350. It is half-timbered and thatched.

———

Alfriston, East Sussex: the clergy house

Bateman's

half a mile south of Burwash on A265

Bateman's was more than 260 years old when Rudyard Kipling, on a house-hunting expedition, fell in love with the place at first sight. That was in 1902, and he lived there until he died in 1936. During those years he made a lasting impression on the garden, where he planted the yew hedges, created the rose garden, for which he made a delightfully amateurish sketch plan, and made the pond with a concrete bottom for his children and their friends to bathe and boat in.

Inside the house in the first ten years of his residence he wrote *Traffics and Discoveries*, *Puck of Pook's Hill* and *Rewards and Fairies*. Pook's Hill can be seen from the garden, and it needs very little imagination to see how much of the surroundings of Bateman's went into the stories.

Mrs Kipling left the house to the Trust when she died in 1939, and with it the books, pictures and furniture which he had known there. His study is

Bateman's, East Sussex

exactly as he left it. A number of his manuscripts, unpublished early verse, letters and first editions are displayed in another room, together with his plan of the rose garden.

In addition to the appeal of its Kipling associations, Bateman's is of interest as a fine example of the country building of the first half of the seventeenth century. It is a comfortable stone-built house with brick chimneys and has a gable porch over the front door. It was built at a time when the Sussex iron industry was still flourishing, probably for the owner of the forge which then stood by the stream a quarter of a mile away.

BATTLE   A piece of land known as Lake Meadow, opposite the Chequers Hotel. Given to preserve the view to the north.

Bodiam Castle

3 miles south of Hawkhurst

The walls and towers of Bodiam (below) remain almost intact; from across the moat it looks every inch a castle. It is a large rectangular building

Bodiam Castle, East Sussex

about fifty yards long and forty yards wide with forty-foot-high walls and high towers. Within the six-foot-thick walls it is largely in ruins, but enough remains to show the layout of the hall, chapel kitchens, staterooms and living quarters.

So far as is known it has never stood siege; but the building of it, in 1385, was no idle fancy. A few years earlier the French had sacked first Rye and then Winchelsea. The River Rother was navigable up to Bodiam and Sir Edward Dalyngrigge was given royal licence to fortify his manor house at Bodiam 'in defence of the adjacent countryside and for resistance against our enemies'. Sir Edward was an experienced soldier who had campaigned in Normandy and Brittany.

Bodiam has changed owners a number of times. It is referred to in accounts of the Wars of the Roses, Richard III issuing instructions for its seizure, but there is no evidence of what ensued. It was lived in during the fifteenth and sixteenth centuries. It may have received internal damage during the Civil War, but here again there is insufficient evidence to say clearly what happened.

Lord Curzon bought the castle in 1917, carried out repairs, made some excavations to explore its history and wrote a book about it. He left the castle to the Trust in his will.

DITCHLING BEACON *6 miles north of Brighton*   Four acres on the north-east slope with wide views and traces of part of the hill-fort.

Eastbourne

CROWLINK, MICHEL DENE and WENT HILL *about 5 miles west of East-bourne, south of Friston*   Six hundred acres of cliff, down and farmland, including part of the Seven Sisters.

BIRLING GAP   58 acres to the east of the Gap forming the cliff approach to Beachy Head, and land west of the Gap adjoining Crowlink.

EXCEAT SALTINGS *about 2 miles east of Seaford* $4\frac{1}{2}$ acres overlooking the Saltings south of Exceat Bridge, and a small piece of the Saltings on the west bank of the Cuckmere River (no public access).

FAIRLIGHT $4\frac{1}{2}$ *miles east of Hastings* Old Marsham Farm and adjoining Stumblet Wood including fifty-eight acres of cliff-land, with access by footpath only.

———⚬ ⚬———

NAP WOOD *4 miles south of Tunbridge Wells* A hundred acres, mainly oak wood, let in accordance with the donor's wish to the Sussex Naturalists' Trust as a Nature Reserve. A permanent signposted nature walk has been established here.

———⚬ ⚬———

RYE: LAMB HOUSE *in West Street* A Georgian house which was the home of Henry James from 1898 to 1916 and contains some of his relics. Given by his nephew's widow to be preserved 'as an enduring symbol of the ties that unite the British and American peoples'.

———⚬ ⚬———

Sheffield Park Garden

midway between East Grinstead and Lewes, half a mile from Sheffield Park Station, on east side of A275

Sheffield Park Garden is not far from the busy motor roads which take Londoners to and from the south coast. But inside the gardens, beside the

Sheffield Park Garden, East Sussex: the middle lake

water or among the tall trees, the visitor is at all times immersed in a great peacefulness.

The garden layout is on the spacious eighteenth-century scale, covering nearly 100 acres and including five lakes on different levels (page 169). Basically this is the work of Capability Brown, who designed a garden here in 1775 for the first Lord Sheffield. Brown's layout was extended and the trees and shrubs of the present garden planted between 1909 and 1934 by Mr Arthur G. Soames, who bought the estate in 1909. The property also includes sixty acres of park and woodland.

When Mr Soames began his planting he was able to do so against a background of fine mature oaks and sweet chestnuts. He introduced a great variety of trees and shrubs, giving colour and interest to the garden at all seasons. They reach their peak in October and November when maples and tupelo trees add brilliance to the autumn tints of the native trees and, for good measure, autumn gentians and cyclamens are in bloom. The lakes in spring reflect the azaleas and rhododendrons in flower and in summer carry water lilies.

The Trust bought Sheffield Park Garden in 1954 with money from special funds, a public subscription and grants from local authorities. The house at Sheffield Park (built at the time when Brown laid out the gardens) does not belong to the Trust.

TELSCOMBE *3 miles north-west of Newhaven, 1½ miles north of Peacehaven*
Mr E. Thornton Smith, who gave the manor house and gardens to the Trust, also gave ten acres at Knotts Bushes to protect the skyline. This protection has been extended by the acquisition from several donors of protective covenants over nearly eight hundred acres (not open).

WYCH CROSS: THE WARREN 2½ *miles south of Forest Row* 15 acres of woodland.

ESSEX

Trust properties that were in old Essex are now in the new county, except for Eastbury House (Barking) and Rainham Hall (near Barking) which now come into London. There has been no addition by transfer from another county.

Chelmsford

There are two Trust properties about five miles east of Chelmsford.

BLAKE'S WOOD *just south-west of Little Baddow* Eighty acres mainly horn-beam and chestnut. There are public footpaths.

DANBURY and LINGWOOD COMMONS *north and south of A414* Two hundred acres 300 ft above sea level, Danbury Common is mainly open with gorse, thorn and birch, while Lingwood is more wooded. Part of Danbury Common is let to the Essex Naturalists' Trust.

Coggeshall: Paycocke's

on the south side of West Street (A120)

Paycocke's is a two-storey half-timbered house, a fine example of its period and much enriched inside with carving. It was built about 1500 and named for the man who is thought to have built it, John Paycocke. His will, which describes him as a butcher, also reveals that in addition to Paycocke's he had two other houses, in one of which he himself lived. It has been suggested that in addition to being a butcher, or grazier, he had prospered as a clothier—Coggeshall, Colchester and other neighbouring towns having at that time a flourishing cloth trade—and that he built Paycocke's for one of his sons.

Paycocke's, Coggeshall, Essex: looking from the dining-room to the hall

During the seventeenth century and until 1746 the house belonged to the Buxton family, and there is some evidence that they—who certainly were concerned with the cloth trade—may have set up looms in the back of the premises. Their descendant, Lord Noel-Buxton, bought the house back in 1904, made some necessary renovations and gave it to the Trust in 1924.

The house is now furnished with sixteenth- and seventeenth-century oak furniture from the Grigsby Collection from West Drayton. The table in the illustration (page 171) is part of this collection.

—◁—▷—

Colchester

There are two properties near Colchester:

BOURNE MILL *a mile south of the centre of the town*　A fishing lodge of 1591, with stepped and curved gables in the Dutch manner, later converted to a mill.

DEDHAM: BRIDGES FARM 5 *miles from Colchester*　This farm stands just west of the village and was given mostly in 1951 (*79 acres*). Not open.

—◁—▷—

Hatfield Forest

3 miles east of Bishop's Stortford

The Trust's Hatfield Forest property, near Bishop's Stortford, measures roughly a mile by a mile and a half and covers just over a thousand acres of woodland and open chases (the wide grass rides between coppices). There is also a lake (opposite) which provides boating and fishing, and a nature walk.

Hatfield was a part of the Royal Forest of Essex from King Harold's time and during the Middle Ages was subject to the Forest Laws. A map of Essex made in 1594 shows Hallingbury and Hatfield Forests as one, and as about the same size as now. It was in private hands during the eighteenth and nineteenth centuries. The lake was made about 1760 and deep drains, which still exist, were laid in the forest in the 1850s. Some ornamental planting was carried out, as witness a group of horse chestnuts near the lake.

Although there was felling of older trees in the 1920s, there are some particularly fine old hornbeams and coppices of oak, hornbeam and other trees. Since 1961 the Trust has been able to adopt a programme of replanting. There are fallow deer, but the red deer were killed off during the 1914–18

172

Hatfield Forest, Essex: the lake

war. The bird population includes nightingales and many green wood-peckers. The main part of the property was given to the Trust in 1924 by Mr E. North Buxton, gifts of additional land being made at later dates by his sons and by other donors.

RAY ISLAND About a hundred acres of unspoilt saltings in the tidal creek between the mainland and West Mersea. An Enterprise Neptune purchase which is let to the Essex Naturalists' Trust. It is cut off at high tide but at other times, to quote the Trust's regional agent, access is by Wellington boot.

RAYLEIGH MOUNT *6 miles north-west of Southend* A mound on which stood an eleventh-century castle. Excavations were carried out in 1959–61.

SAFFRON WALDEN: SUN INN This building, part of which is a fifteenth-century hall house, was the headquarters of Cromwell and Fairfax in 1647. It is now a shop.

GLOUCESTERSHIRE

Trust properties that were in the old county of Gloucestershire are now in the new county, with the exception of Dyrham Park, Horton Court and the Bristol Properties. These have been transferred to the new county of AVON. There has been no addition by transfer from another county.

Ashleworth Tithe Barn

about 6 miles north of Gloucester, 1½ miles east of Hartpury

A stone-roofed fifteenth-century tithe barn, 120-ft long, with two projecting porch bays and queen-post roof timbers (opposite).

Bibury: Arlington Row

on the south side of A433

This row of seventeenth-century stone cottages, once a wool factory, was acquired in 1949, and is not open (opposite). Rack Isle, a four-acre field

Ashleworth Tithe Barn, Gloucestershire

Bibury, Arlington Row, Gloucestershire

opposite, was given to the Trust in 1956. It is bounded by water on three sides and was used as a drying ground when wool was a cottage industry in Bibury.

———◦———◦———

CHEDWORTH ROMAN VILLA *3 miles north-west of Fossebridge, on the Cirencester–Northleach road, A429*   The villa is sited in six acres of woodland and was discovered in 1864. It is very well preserved, with mosaic pavements and a museum.

———◦———◦———

Chipping Campden: Market Hall

in Chipping Campden on B4081 opposite the police station

The Trust had this charming Jacobean building's open arcade re-roofed in the early 1950s (below). It was bought in 1944 with the help of the Midland Counties Trust Fund, Campden Trust and others.

The Trust also owns thirteen acres of meadow in Chipping Campden between the churchyard and the station, known as the Coneygree; and at Dover's Hill, on the right of the Weston-sub-Edge road (B4035), 180 acres of a natural amphitheatre where Dover's games were held from 1612 to 1852.

Chipping Campden, Gloucestershire: the market hall

CRICKLEY HILL: THE SCRUBBS *6 miles east of Gloucester, north of A417.*
Part of an Iron Age fort stands on this thirty-six-acre site, which gives views
over the Severn valley.

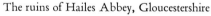

FROCESTER HILL and COALEY PEAK *near Nympsfield, between Stroud
and Dursley* A botanically important site which also provides good views
over the Severn to the Welsh mountains; it rises to 778 ft.

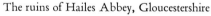

Hailes Abbey

2 miles north-east of Winchcombe, a mile east of the Broadway road (A46)

The abbey is in ruins but enough remains standing, as indicated by the
photograph below, for the visitor to reconstruct in the mind's eye some
idea of the beautiful Cistercian building.

The abbey was founded in 1246 by King John's second son, Richard
Earl of Cornwall, in fulfilment of a vow made when he escaped shipwreck
on the Scillies. He endowed the abbey liberally.

The ruins were given to the Trust in 1937 with neighbouring meadowland. It is under the guardianship of the Department of the Environment.

The ruins of Hailes Abbey, Gloucestershire

There is a museum containing rare armorial tiles, bosses found in the ruins, maps, plans and other objects connected with the abbey.

Hidcote Manor Garden

at Hidcote Bartrim 4 miles north-east of Chipping Campden

'By that time I had become so wildly intoxicated by the spilling abundance of Hidcote that I was no longer in any mood to worry about exact naming, but only in the mood to enjoy the next pleasure to be encountered'—thus the late Lady Nicolson (Vita Sackville West) in the Trust's guide-book. Many a less learned gardener has had the same feeling on a visit to Hidcote.

It is a modern garden, planned and planted—apart from a cedar tree and some beeches—since 1905. That was the year in which the late Major Lawrence Johnston acquired the manor-house and the surrounding fields. The garden he made is formed of a series of small gardens divided by hedges of different species. These contain a variety of trees, plants and shrubs, including many rarities, their arrangement being as Lady Nicolson described it.

Hidcote Manor Garden, Gloucestershire

The garden was given by Major Johnston to the Trust in 1948. It is preserved under a joint arrangement between the Trust and the Royal Horticultural Society. This arrangement was applied first to Hidcote and later to Nymans and a number of other gardens belonging to the Trust.

—————

MAY HILL *9 miles west of Gloucester, a mile north of A40*   The Trust owns 130 acres on this hill from which there are wide-ranging views over ten counties.

—————

PAINSWICK: LITTLE FLEECE *on A46 north of Stroud*   This small Cotswold town house is thought to have been built in the seventeenth century, and is now a bookshop.

Snowshill Manor

3 miles south of the west end of Broadway

Snowshill is a stone-built sixteenth-century Cotswold manor-house (page 180) to which alterations and additions were made in the early parts of the seventeenth and eighteenth centuries. By 1919 it had been in use as a farmhouse for 140 years, and was in need of much repair. The late Mr Charles P. Wade bought it, carried out the necessary repairs, made the present very agreeable garden and amassed the immensely varied collections which are to be seen in the house today. Mr Wade gave house, contents and the small terraced formal garden to the Trust in 1951. He was an architect and artist-craftsman with a special curiosity concerning craft tools and the products which earlier generations made with them. He tried his own hand at using period tools. He lived in Snowshill without electric light and slept there in a Tudor bed.

His intense interest in collecting led him to seek not works of art but bygones of almost every description from this and other countries. In the Music Room, which he panelled himself, he put coaching horns, eighteenth-century hurdy-gurdies, guitars, cellos, bassoons, drums, hautboys, barrel organs, harps and lyres. In other rooms the exhibits include ship models, lacquer cabinets, clocks, navigational instruments, lacemakers' lamps, spinning-wheels, hand-shuttles, bicycles and children's toys.

—————

Snowshill Manor, Gloucestershire

Stroud

There are eight properties within about four miles of Stroud, including land on several commons, woodland, high ground and features of archaeological interest.

HARESFIELD BEACON and STANDISH WOOD *on the north edge of the Cotswolds*   This includes woodland and views over the Severn and there is also a Neolithic long barrow and an Iron Age promontory fort (*350 acres*).

MINCHINHAMPTON COMMONS *to the south*   This is the largest site near Stroud (*580 acres*); the earthworks here include Amberley Camp and Minchinhampton Bulwarks, probably first century A.D.

RODBOROUGH COMMON *to the south*   240 acres including part of the site of a first-century enclosure.

STOCKEND and MAITLAND WOODS *to the north*   Land on Scottsquar Hill (*60 acres*).

The other four Stroud properties consist of four to ten acres each on four commons south of the town: Besbury, Hyde, Littleworth and St Chloe's Green and Watledge Hill.

———— ⊃ ⊂ ————

Westbury Court Gardens

9 miles south-west of Gloucester on A48 at Westbury-upon-Severn

This is a formal water garden laid out 1696–1705 and retaining today the main features that can be seen in a Kip engraving of 1712. Other such gardens of the period were altered to suit eighteenth-century tastes. It has canals, lawns, yew hedges, statuary, and red brick garden pavilions.

In 1954, it was in a state of neglect, canals silted and walls decaying. The Gloucestershire County Council bought it with a view to preservation, pulled down the 1890 mansion house adjoining, built a home for the elderly near its site and in 1967 gave the garden to the Trust. The Trust launched an appeal that raised a substantial sum (including an anonymous gift of £20,000) and the Historic Buildings Council made a grant towards the cost of the needed restoration. With this money and the help of volunteers necessary work was completed and in 1973 the gardens were opened to visitors.

———— ⊃ ⊂ ————

Wotton-under-Edge

about 9 miles south-west of Stroud on B4058

There are three properties near Wotton:

COOMBE ROAD Some steep pasture land on the northern outskirts of Wotton. No public access.

NEWARK PARK *1½ miles east of Wotton* Six hundred acres of woodland and farmland on a spur of the Cotswolds.

WESTRIDGE WOODS *a mile north-west of Wotton* Thirty acres of woodland.

GREATER MANCHESTER

MEDLOCK VALE *1½ miles north-east of Ashton-under-Lyne* Standing on the banks of the Medlock, this site is described in the Trust's List of Properties as a 'rural oasis in an industrial area' (*5 acres*).
Medlock Vale was formerly in the old county of Lancashire.

HAMPSHIRE

BRAMSHAW COMMONS AND MANORIAL WASTES *10 miles west of Southampton, south of A36* Nearly a thousand acres, including Cadnam and Stocks Cross Greens and Bramshaw, Cadnam, Furzley, Penn and Plaitford Commons. There are barrows on Plaitford and Furzley Commons.

HALE PURLIEU and MILLERSFORD PLANTATION *3 miles north-east of Fordingbridge* A five-hundred-acre area of heath and woodland.

HAMBLE RIVER *at Curbridge 1 mile below Botley* Wood and farmland which was acquired in the 1920s to preserve the beauty of the river (*74 acres*). On the Curbridge Estate are the sites of Roman buildings.

HIGHTOWN COMMON *2 miles east of Ringwood on the west edge of the New Forest* This was given in 1929 by the Commons, Footpaths and Open Spaces Preservation Society as a memorial to their President, Lord Eversley (*30 acres*).

———✏—✏———

Ludshott

Here, where Hampshire, Surrey and Sussex (new West Sussex) come together, there is a complex of Trust properties. In the Hampshire section there are three:

BRAMSHOTT CHASE *1½ miles south-west of Hindhead* Sixty acres by the Portsmouth road.

LUDSHOTT COMMON and WAGGONERS' WELLS *1½ miles west of Hindhead, south of B3002* Six hundred acres, including a number of hammer ponds, forming one of the sources of the River Wey. Bought mainly in 1908 through the efforts of a local committee. In 1919 land at Waggoners' Wells was given as a memorial to Sir Robert Hunter.

PASSFIELD COMMON and CONFORD MOOR *2 miles west of Liphook, astride B3004* 230 acres of common land with some woods.

———✏—✏———

Mottisfont Abbey

4½ miles north-west of Romsey

The house was converted from the twelfth-century priory after the dissolution of the monasteries. Major changes in the eighteenth century included fine decoration of several of the rooms. More recently, Rex Whistler added *trompe l'œil* painting in the drawing-room. The garden contains fine trees with an immense London Plane, copper beeches and cedars. A walled garden has been planted with an extensive collection of old-fashioned roses. The whole estate runs to sixteen hundred acres, including four hundred acres of woodland and most of the village.

———✏—✏———

NEWTOWN COMMON: BARN PLOT *3 miles south of Newbury* Here, on the Whitchurch road, a quarter of an acre was given to the Trust in 1906.

———✏—✏———

SANDHAM MEMORIAL CHAPEL at Burghclere, *4 miles south of Newbury, a half-mile east of the Whitchurch road* This was built in the 1920s by Mr and Mrs J. L. Behrend as a memorial to a relation (Mr H. W. Sandham) who was killed in the 1914–18 war. In 1947 they gave it to the Trust. It was designed with a view to its containing the murals which Stanley Spencer painted there. These were inspired by his experiences of the Salonika front and are considered by many to be his best work.

Selborne

4 miles south of Alton

About 240 acres of the common where Gilbert White made many of the observations for *The Natural History of Selborne* were given to the Trust by Magdalen College in 1932 (opposite). In the 1960s other donors gave part of the Long and Short Lythes—the hanging beech woods overlooking Selborne Stream—and land which provides fine views southwards.

SPARSHOLT: VAINE COTTAGES *3 miles west of Winchester* Two thatched cottages (not open).

Stockbridge

The Trust has about 230 acres here, partly on COMMON MARSH, a quarter-mile south of the village, where the burgesses still graze cattle and horses, and partly on STOCKBRIDGE DOWN a mile east of the village, where there are round barrows, part of Woolbury Camp, an Early Iron Age hill-fort, and other features of archaeological interest. In addition to being a landholder, the Trust was given the lordship of the manor. The manorial courts meet annually in March.

The Vyne

4 miles north of Basingstoke, halfway between Sherborne St John and Bramley

The Vyne has been happy in its architectural history. It was built, in a pleasing red brick, in the early sixteenth century (1500–20). In 1654 the

Selborne, Hampshire

northern side was given a portico (below), the first occasion on which such a feature was used on an English country house. About the middle of the eighteenth century the stone hall and staircase of the Tudor building were ingeniously replaced by a very fine classical staircase (opposite) and hall. The Tudor chapel, substantially unchanged, has carved stalls and quite exceptionally fine Renaissance stained glass.

Eighteenth-century accounts and inventories of the contents of the house list much of the furniture which still remains in the principal rooms.

The grounds contain a lake, extensive lawns, shrubs and herbaceous borders.

The Vyne was built by William Sandys, later Lord Sandys of the Vyne,

The Vyne, Hampshire

The Vyne, Hampshire: the staircase

who held important offices under Henry VIII. His descendant sold it in 1653 to Chaloner Chute, lawyer, M.P. and briefly in 1659 Speaker of the House of Commons. It remained in the possession of the Chute family until Sir Charles Chute, who died in 1956, bequeathed it to the Trust.

It was Chaloner Chute who added the portico, his architect being, almost certainly, John Webb. His grandson, John Chute, who made the eighteenth-century alterations to the interior, was his own architect.

———— ⟶ ⟵ ————

WEST GREEN HOUSE *a mile west of Hartley Wintney* A pretty, early eighteenth-century house.

———— ⟶ ⟵ ————

WINCHESTER: CITY MILL *at the foot of the High Street* Built in 1744 over the river and bought by subscription in 1929. It is leased by the Youth Hostels Association.

———— ⟶ ⟵ ————

WOOLTON HILL: THE CHASE *3 miles south-west of Newbury* Wood and farmland with a chalk stream. Given as a nature reserve (*131 acres*).

———— ⟶ ⟵ ————

HEREFORD AND WORCESTER

Berrington Hall

3 miles north of Leominster on west side of A49

Berrington Hall is a late eighteenth-century house (about 1780) designed by one of the leading architects of that time, Henry Holland Jnr. It stands in a park laid out by Capability Brown. There have been no significant altera-tions to the exterior of the house, and practically none at all inside.

It consists of a rectangular main block, rather austere, with a large portico; and three pavilions to house the laundry and other domestic offices. However, the tone of austerity is not continued inside the house. Here Holland gave the principal rooms splendid fireplaces, beautifully decorated ceilings and fine doors and doorcases.

The site chosen for the house looks down on its own park and beyond that to extensive views of the Welsh hills, many miles away in Brecon and Radnor.

Practically nothing is known of the history of Berrington before Thomas Harley bought the estate about 1775, but there are traces of a medieval house

Berrington Hall, Hereford and Worcester: the drawing-room

about half a mile from the present one. Thomas Harley was a banker and government contractor and was Lord Mayor of London during the Wilkite riots. He spared no expense in the building of Berrington, as the surviving accounts show. Holland's estimate for construction was £14,500, a large one

Berrington Hall, Hereford and Worcester, from the north-west

Clent Hill, Hereford and Worcester

for that time. Brown was paid £1,600. Harley's daughter, who inherited the estate from her father, married the second Lord Rodney, son of Admiral Rodney.

In the dining-room are contemporary battle pictures of Admiral Rodney's engagements. The Rodneys continued at Berrington until they sold it in 1900 to Mr Frederick Cawley (later Lord Cawley). In 1957 it was accepted by the Treasury in payment of death duty and transferred to the Trust with some of the contents.

<hr>

Birmingham

CHADWICH MANOR ESTATE *4 miles north of Bromsgrove, astride the A38 on the south-west edge of Birmingham* Four hundred acres of farm and woodland given to the Trust by members of the Cadbury family. It was the first gift to the Trust of a large open space to be preserved as an agricultural estate. Access is by public footpath only, except at Highfield (870 ft), where there are views to the Malvern Hills. A Country Park is being formed at Holywell Farm.

Clent Hill

3 miles south of Stourbridge

Clent Hill (opposite) is not far from Birmingham, Stourbridge and Kidderminster, and is much visited by townspeople in search of a walk and a good view. It provides wide views of both the Wrekin and the Malvern Hills. The Trust property covers 355 acres of Clent Hill and Walton Hill Commons, including some woodland and enclosed land let for grazing. There are many bridle and foot paths. The property was given to the Trust in 1959, part by the Worcestershire County Council, part by Bromsgrove Rural District Council and part by the Feeney Trustees. No less than twenty local authorities contribute to its upkeep.

COFTON HACKETT *2 miles east of the Chadwich Estate* Forty-four acres of farmland which is not open, but is part of the Birmingham green belt.

FRANKLEY BEECHES *2½ miles north-east of Chadwich* The Trust owns the top only of this 800-ft high hill crowned by beeches which form a prominent landmark. Given by Cadbury Bros (*24 acres*).

GROVELEY DINGLE *east of A441 on the south edge of Birmingham* Wood and farmland, partly a bird sanctuary, but also providing footpaths and views for walkers.

SLING POOL *5 miles north of Bromsgrove, ½ mile east of the Bromsgrove–Stourbridge road* In a valley which runs down from the Clent Hills, four acres with a pool given by Mr Paul Cadbury.

BRADNOR HILL *Half a mile north-west of Kington* Common land on a 1,280-ft hill with a golf course on the summit (*340 acres*).

BREDON TITHE BARN *3 miles north-east of Tewkesbury, north of B4080* This (below) is a fifteenth-century stone barn. It is 132 ft long and has five porches, one with unusual stone cowling. Given to the Trust in 1951.

BREINTON SPRINGS *3 miles west of Hereford, north of the River Wye* Fourteen acres of wood and farmland. Part of this is the site of a medieval village. Excavations at Breinton Camp have shown that it was occupied from the twelfth century into the thirteenth.

Bredon Tithe Barn, Hereford and Worcester

BRILLEY: CWMMAU and FERNHALL FARMS *at Whitney on Wye, on the Radnorshire border between Hay-on-Wye and Kington* 350 acres of farm and woodland with wide views from an ancient castle mound. Also two timber-framed farmhouses; Cwmmau Farmhouse is open on request in the summer.

⤙⟶ ⟞

BROADWAY: CLUMP FARM *A half-mile south-east of Broadway, south of A44* 85 acres of farmland with a public footpath and extensive views over the Vale of Evesham.

⤙⟶ ⟞

BROCKHAMPTON *2 miles east of Bromyard mainly on north of A44* Nineteen hundred acres of wood and farmland typical of Herefordshire. There are two houses: Brockhampton, eighteenth-century Georgian, but modernised, is not open; Lower Brockhampton, a late fourteenth-century half-timbered, moated manor house with a detached fifteenth-century gatehouse, and the ruins of a twelfth-century chapel. The medieval hall is open. There are woodland and lakeside nature walks.

⤙⟶ ⟞

Croft Castle

5 miles north-west of Leominster, signposted from A49

Croft affords a variety of interest and beauty—the castle itself (over) and the little church close by, the avenue of Spanish chestnuts, the trees and waters of the Fish Pool Valley and the Iron Age hill fort on the ridge to the north of the castle.

The castle as seen today consists of the walls and towers of the fourteenth–fifteenth-century castle and an eighteenth-century central structure. It looks very much a castle from the outside. Inside, the hall and gallery were made in the eighteenth century on what had been an open courtyard. The walls of the eighteenth-century 'Gothic' staircase and the ceilings of some of the other rooms have delightful plasterwork. Some of the rooms are lined with panelling brought from other houses. There is an interesting collection of family portraits and Croft family heirlooms, the property of Lord Croft.

The small stone church beside the castle has a bell turret and cupola of the late seventeenth–early eighteenth century. But the church itself is much older: how much older is not known, but it was certainly altered in 1515 or, as the contemporary report says, was 'enlarged or more beautifully made'.

Croft Castle, Hereford and Worcester

The Spanish Chestnut Avenue, about half a mile of 350-year-old trees, is a unique feature of the grounds—indeed there is nothing like it in the British Isles. There are many other fine trees, including Indian cedar, Californian redwoods and immense oaks. The Fish Pool Valley is an excellent example of the late eighteenth-century school of landscaping, which insisted on 'nature's negligent disguise'. It was planted with mixed deciduous trees. The estate includes a nature walk.

Croft Ambrey, the Iron Age hill fort, commands a view of fourteen counties. Recent excavations have established that it was occupied from the fourth century B.C. until the Roman Conquest.

There was a Croft at Croft at the time of Domesday and the family continued there until 1750. A gap followed until they bought it back in 1923. The Trust, aided by a grant from the Ministry of Works, bought it in 1957, Lord Croft and other members of the family providing an endowment for maintenance.

Hanbury Hall

2½ miles east of Droitwich

Hanbury Hall (below) is a fine English country house completed in 1701 and has a painted staircase by James Thornhill, who later painted the cupola in St Paul's Cathedral.

It was built for Thomas Vernon by William Rudhall. Thomas Vernon was a very eminent lawyer and for some years M.P. for the City of Worcester. He made a considerable fortune which he used to increase his family's property and to build Hanbury. His architect, William Rudhall, is not known for any other building. It has been suggested that he may have worked in some capacity for William Talman, the architect of Dyrham, Uppark and other houses of the period, since much of Hanbury is very suggestive of Talman's work.

The building of the house was finished in 1701 and the Thornhill paintings must have been executed a little later. The evidence for this is that he included in his composition political allusion to the trial of Dr Sacheverell, which took place in 1710.

The author of the Trust's guide to Hanbury refers to a painted staircase as having been 'a status symbol for a rich man' of the time. In the one which Thornhill executed for Thomas Vernon, and in addition to the portrait of Dr Sacheverell, the ceiling shows an assembly of classical deities, and the walls the story of Achilles. Thornhill also painted the ceiling of one of the principal rooms in the house.

Hanbury Hall: Hereford and Worcester

The eighteenth-century garden has not survived; but on the west side of the house the orangery still stands. It is contemporary with the house.

Hanbury Hall remained in the hands of Thomas Vernon's family until it was acquired by the Trust in 1953 under the will of Sir George Vernon, the second and last baronet.

———— ◦ ◦ ————

HARVINGTON HALL *4 miles south-east of Kidderminster* A moated sixteenth-century house, which the owners, the Roman Catholic Archdiocese of Birmingham, frequently open to the public. Mr H. R. Hodgkinson gave the Trust a piece of land to protect the Hall and, with other benefactors, donated some oak furniture, which is now on show in the Hall.

———— ◦ ◦ ————

HAWFORD DOVECOTE *at Hawford Grange, east of A499, 1 mile south of Ombersley* A square timber-framed dovecote of the sixteenth century.

———— ◦ ◦ ————

KNOWLES MILL *1½ miles north-west of Bewdley* Stands in a small orchard.

———— ◦ ◦ ————

Malvern Hills

Part of Midsummer Hill, where there is an Iron Age hill fort, was given by his parents in 1923 in memory of Reginald Somers Cocks who was killed in

Malvern Hills, Hereford and Worcester

the 1914–18 war. The Trust also owns small pieces of land on Broad Down, a mile and a half to the north of Midsummer Hill; at Foxhall on Castlemorton Common on the eastern slope of the Malvern Hills; at Tack Coppice on the left of the bridle road from Hollybush to Chase End Hill; and Pink Cottage on the east slope near Foxhall.

PENGETHLY PARK *4 miles north-west of Ross, north-east of A49* 120 acres of farm and woodland with footpaths.

POOR'S ACRE *6 miles south-east of Hereford, 1½ miles west of Woolhope* Seventeen acres along the roadside in Haugh Wood.

SWAINSHILL: THE WEIR *5 miles west of Hereford* A steeply sloping riverside garden from which are fine views of the River Wye and the Welsh hills. There is an eighteenth-century house, not open, and 430 acres of land, mainly agricultural.

WICHENFORD DOVECOTE *5½ miles north-west of Worcester* A seventeenth-century half-timbered black and white dovecote.

WORCESTER: GREYFRIARS This fifteenth-century timber-framed house, with later additions, was given by Mr and Miss Matley Moore, who also gave three fifteenth- and sixteenth-century houses in Friar Street, which are now let as shops.

HERTFORDSHIRE

Ashridge Estate

3 miles north of Berkhamsted between A41 and B489 and astride B4586

This estate covers about six square miles along the main ridge of the Chiltern Hills and extends into Bedfordshire and Buckinghamshire. It includes five commons, woodlands (over) and the hills up to Ivinghoe Beacon (700 ft), where there is a direction dial to point out the landmarks. The Bridgewater

197

Ashridge Estate, Hertfordshire: a woodland view

Monument (172 steps) which was built in 1832 in memory of the canal-building Duke of Bridgewater, also provides a splendid view-point, and two nature walks start from the monument.

The Trust's Ashridge Committee produces an interesting leaflet for visitors giving notes on natural history and other aspects of the estate.

Ashridge House itself and parts of the park do not belong to the Trust. The Trust's Ashridge property was acquired partly after public appeals in the 1920s and later, and partly by gifts from Dr G. M. Trevelyan, Miss S. R. Courtauld and other donors.

Also near Ashridge are:

HUDNALL COMMON *a mile east of Little Gaddesden (116 acres).*

LITTLE HEATH *1½ miles east of Berkhamsted (20 acres).*

WATEREND MOOR *2 miles north-west of Hemel Hempstead (4 acres)* The village green by the River Gade.

Ayot St Lawrence: Shaw's Corner

at the south-west end of the village, 3 miles north-west of Welwyn

A twentieth-century house which Shaw bought in 1906. He lived there until his death in 1950 and his ashes were scattered in the garden. In addition to the study (over) he had another writing place in a summer-house in the garden. He gave the house to the Trust in 1944 and the contents were acquired under his will.

He was fifty when he went to Shaw's Corner; *Pygmalion* and *Saint Joan* are among the works which date from his time there. The study and summer-house are arranged exactly as he had them. In the hall are his hats and sticks and the piano which he used. In the drawing-room are bronzes by Rodin and Troubetskoy, including busts of Shaw.

BARKWAY: BERG COTTAGE *4 miles south of Royston* A small thatched house, perhaps 1687, not open.

MORVEN PARK *a half-mile north of Potters Bar* A Victorian house standing in some thirty acres, now an old people's home.

Ayot St Lawrence, Shaw's Corner, Hertfordshire: George Bernard Shaw's study

HUMBERSIDE

Formerly part of the East Riding of the old county of Yorkshire.

HULL: MAISTER HOUSE *in the High Street* Rebuilt in 1744, with a superb staircase-hall. Given by the Georgian Society for East Yorkshire and others. Part is open.

ISLE OF MAN

CALF OF MAN This six-hundred-acre island at the extreme south-west of the main island is an important nature reserve (seals and breeding colonies of sea birds) to which there is controlled public access. Fine views from the highest point (421 ft). Let to the Manx Museum and National Trust.

Bembridge Windmill, Isle of Wight

ISLE OF WIGHT

Bembridge

The following properties surround Bembridge:

BEMBRIDGE and CULVER DOWNS A hundred acres on the downs which—rising 340 ft out of the sea—are the prominent feature of the east of the Island.

BEMBRIDGE WINDMILL *half a mile south of Bembridge* A stone tower mill built about 1700, the last remaining windmill on the island. It was last used in 1913 but still retains most of its original wooden machinery, which is of unique interest (above).

The mill was given to the Trust in 1961, and restored by funds raised by the Trust's Isle of Wight Management Committee.

ST HELEN'S COMMON *a mile north-west of Bembridge* Nine acres together with a cottage. Views over Brading Harbour.

ST HELEN'S DUVER *at the mouth of Bembridge Harbour* Thirty acres on a wide spit of sand and shingle, with a variety of flora, and good walks.

⟿ ⟾

Mottistone

4 to 5 miles south-east of Yarmouth

THE MOTTISTONE ESTATE Left to the Trust by the second Lord Mottistone, the estate covers some 630 acres of farm, woodland and most of the village. It runs from the crest of the downs to the sea. There are foot and bridle paths. Mottistone Manor is not open.

SUDMOOR POINT Thirty acres of cliff here link the Mottistone estate with Trust property to the west.

⟿ ⟾

Newtown

midway between Newport and Yarmouth

NEWTOWN RIVER and OLD TOWN HALL The Trust was helped in 1965 by local societies and individuals to buy the whole of the estuary of the Newtown River (opposite), together with four miles of the foreshore of the Solent, Newtown and Shalfleet quays. Mooring and harbour rights belong to the Trust. Eighty acres adjoining the river at Hamstead were given in 1965.

In the days of active coastal trade Newtown was a busy port, but there is no commercial traffic today. It was also a 'rotten borough'.

The eighteenth-century Old Town Hall (opposite) contains copies of documents and of the mace of the borough.

The Trust also owns nine acres of farmland which protect the Hall's amenities on the east, and fourteen acres of land adjoining the creek.

Newtown River,
Isle of Wight

Newtown, Isle of Wight:
the Old Town Hall

NOAH'S ARK   A stone- and tile-built house of about 1700, formerly an inn. Now let as a dwelling house and not open.

OLD VICARAGE COPSE and WALTER'S COPSE   Seven and forty-eight acres respectively, these are parts of the Newtown Nature Reserve.

THE QUAY FIELDS   Twelve acres of pasture within the old borough, leading down to Ducks Cove.

TOWN COPSE *just east of Newtown*   Twelve acres of open woodland sloping down to the Clamerkin Lake—a branch of the estuary. This used to belong to the burghers and was used for centuries as a common source of timber and firewood.

St Catherine's Point

At this, the most southerly part of the island, there are three Trust properties, all bought with Enterprise Neptune funds.

KNOWLES FARM   This covers 170 acres from the cliff down to the fore-shore. There are footpaths across this wild and beautiful spot.

ST CATHERINE'S DOWN   A downland ridge running north from St Catherine's Hill. The views range to both eastern and western extremities of the island and there are bridle and footpaths (*48 acres*).

ST CATHERINE'S HILL   This hill provides fine views over West Wight, and is accessible on foot only (*24 acres*).

SANDOWN: BORTHWOOD COPSE *2 miles west of Sandown*   Woodland remains of the medieval hunting forest that covered much of East Wight (*60 acres*).

Ventnor

LITTLETON and LUCCOMBE DOWNS   The Trust holds fifteen acres on the crest of the ridge on Littleton Down and ninety acres of the high downs behind Ventnor. Access to both these properties is by car as well as on foot. There are views seaward and inland, and a group of eight Bronze Age bowl-barrows on Luccombe Down.

ST BONIFACE DOWN This rises to 764 ft, the highest point on the island. The Trust property consists of 220 acres of fine downland, with access on foot.

West Wight

In West Wight the Trust owns both downland and a stretch of the coast between Brook and Freshwater Bay.

AFTON DOWN *3 miles south of Yarmouth* The Trust's 230 acres provide good views over the island and to the Hampshire coast. The land is let as a golf course, and access is by right of way only.

BROOK CHINE *astride the Military Road at Brook* Forty acres of grazing land and three hundred yards of shore.

BROOK DOWN *adjoins Compton Down on the east* A hundred acres rising to over five hundred feet. Access by rights of way.

COMPTON FARM *adjoining Afton Down on the east* The 240 acres which the Trust owns here include a hundred acres of Compton Down with views over West Wight, and pasture running down to the sea. Access to this part of the property by footpath, but not to the rest of the farm.

HANOVER POINT and SHIPPARDS CHINE *near Brook* This covers a quarter of a mile of coast and low sandstone cliffs with access to good safe beaches (*26 acres*).

TENNYSON DOWN *a mile south-west of Freshwater* Tennyson took his daily walk on these cliffs when he lived at Farringford (*155 acres*). A thirteen-mile nature walk managed by the local council traverses about four miles of Trust land.

KENT

APPLEDORE: ROYAL MILITARY CANAL The canal, which was dug during the Napoleonic Wars and used again as an invasion defence both in 1914 and 1939, runs from Hythe to Rye. The Trust was given the three and a half-mile Appledore to Warehorne stretch in 1936. This can be walked. Also fifteenth-century Hallhouse Farm with six acres of pasture (not open).

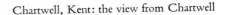

Chartwell

2 miles south of Westerham

The view from Chartwell (below) was one of the things that made Winston Churchill love his house. It stands on the side of a hill with wide-ranging, far-searching views of the weald of Kent and the South Downs. The original house on this site was built in Tudor times, but the present building is largely nineteenth-century. Churchill bought it in 1922 and

Chartwell, Kent: the view from Chartwell

made extensive alterations and additions. Except for the war years he lived there till his death. At Chartwell he wrote and painted, built the brick wall round his kitchen garden and enjoyed the company of his family and friends.

In 1946 a group of his friends bought the house and gave it to the Trust on the understanding that it would eventually be preserved as a memorial to him.

The main rooms today are furnished as they were in the 1930s, except for some pictures and objects which were added after the war. Two bedrooms have been converted for the display of trophies and objects presented to him and of some of his uniforms. His study is furnished and arranged as he last used it. A number of his paintings hang in the house. As the garden and grounds now receive very large numbers of visitors, it has not been practicable to maintain them precisely as they were arranged when Chartwell was a family home. But Lady Churchill's preferences in flowers and colours continue to be observed, and the pool where Sir Winston fed the Golden Orfe, the island he made in the lake and the little brick cottage he built for his younger daughters, remain unchanged.

CHIDDINGSTONE *4 miles east of Edenbridge* A row of sixteenth- and seventeenth-century houses and the Castle Inn. The houses are not open.

COBHAM: OWLETTS *between Dartford and Rochester, a mile south of A2 at the west end of the village* A red brick house of Charles II's reign, given in 1938 with cottages and orchards by Sir Herbert Baker.

COLDRUM LONG BARROW *about a mile east of Trottiscliffe, to the east of A227, and about 2 miles north of Wrotham* A megalithic chambered long barrow from about 2,000 B.C., the most complete survival of the Medway group. Some human skeletal remains recovered here are now in Trottiscliffe church porch.

GOVER HILL *3 miles south-east of Ightham* A hill top covering an acre and a half at the south-west corner of Mereworth Woods.

HARBLEDOWN: GOLDEN HILL *a mile west of Canterbury* Land of two and a half acres given primarily as a children's playground.

Knole, Kent

Knole

at the Tonbridge end of Sevenoaks

Knole (above and page 209)—called 'a whole that is as unforgettable as it is indescribable'—was given its great size and its internal splendour by stages. There was first a medieval house, and its towers remain as reminder of the fact. Then in 1456 this building was enlarged and altered to be an archbishop's palace. Next, Henry VIII, although Cranmer tried to persuade him that it was too small for the King's convenience, took it over and spent money on it without, it seems, ever actually living there. Queen Elizabeth gave it to Thomas Sackville, first Earl of Dorset, and in 1603 and the following years he made extensive alterations and additions, transforming the interior. He introduced the panelling and plasterwork in the Great Hall and other principal rooms, and installed the Great Staircase. At the same

Knole, Kent: the spangled bedroom. The bed dates from James I's time, and its hangings were sewn with glittering metallic spangles

time he laid the foundations of the unique collection of Jacobean furniture which is one of the great distinctions of Knole to this day. The contents of the house, which belongs to Lord Sackville, include seventeenth- and eighteenth-century rugs and tapestries and a large collection of family pictures, among them paintings by Van Dyck, Kneller, Lely and Reynolds.

Knole continued in the possession of the Sackville family (as the surrounding park still does) until 1946 when the house was given by the fourth Lord Sackville to the Trust. Ten years later, twelve acres west of the park were donated to preserve the view from the house.

LOOSE: WOOL HOUSE *3 miles south of Maidstone* A fifteenth-century half-timbered house.

OLD SOAR MANOR *2 miles south of Borough Green (A25) via the A227 and Plaxtol* The solar block of a late thirteenth-century knight's dwelling which is under the guardianship of the Department of the Environment.

OLDBURY HILL and STYANTS WOOD *north of A25, 3 miles south-west of Wrotham* The southern half of an Iron Age hill-fort later used by the Belgae. Excavated 1938 and the subject of much archaeological discussion.

ONE TREE HILL *2 miles south-east of Sevenoaks* Land with good views southwards (*34 acres*).

OTHAM: STONEACRE *3 miles south-east of Maidstone at the north end of the village* A late fifteenth-century half-timbered yeoman's house containing a great hall with kingpost and a small garden.

Quebec House

Westerham

Quebec House (formerly named Spiers) stands at the foot of the hill in Westerham village, now bedevilled by the motor traffic of the A25. It is a square three-storey house of brick and Kent ragstone. Built originally, it seems, in the 1520s, it was made over in the late seventeenth century when the main staircase was inserted. Since various early nineteenth-century alterations were done away with, it must look, apart from the walls round the garden, almost exactly as it did when Colonel Edward Wolfe took a lease of it in 1726. The following year James Wolfe was born in the rectory close by, his mother having gone to stay there while her husband was on service. Spiers was James Wolfe's home until he was eleven, and his younger brother was born there.

Today Spiers has become Quebec House and is dedicated to the memory of General James Wolfe. In the principal rooms paintings, books, letters and objects connected with his career are displayed. These include portraits and busts of the general, his snuff-box and the travelling canteen which he had made for the Quebec campaign.

Quebec House, Kent: the seventeenth-century staircase

The house was given to the Trust in 1918 by Mrs J. N. Learmont of Montreal.

St John's Jerusalem

3 miles south of Dartford on the east side of A 225

St John's Jerusalem was, in the thirteenth century, one of the Commanderies of the Knights Hospitallers of the Order of St John of Jerusalem, and the chapel of their building survives. The rest was probably pulled down when the order was dissolved in 1540.

Abraham Hill, one of the founders of the Royal Society, bought the property in 1665 and lived there till 1721. He rebuilt the house substantially as it is now, though alterations were made in the second half of the eighteenth century when the rooms were decorated with plasterwork.

211

St John's Jerusalem, Kent

It was given to the Trust in 1943 by Sir Stephen and Lady Tallents, together with its large garden, which is moated by the River Darent.

~ ⌐ ⌐

ST MARGARET'S BAY: THE LEAS   Ten acres on the chalk cliffs on the east side of the Bay; given by the local Parish Council.

~ ⌐ ⌐

Scotney Castle Gardens

8 miles south-east of Tunbridge Wells, east of A21

'At Scotney are found, in the happiest combination, a landscape of very great beauty, historic interest and the rarest harmony of buildings, trees and flowers'—so said Marcus Crouch in his book on Kent. A little more specifically, this is a romantic landscape garden surrounding the remains of a moated fourteenth-century castle. The garden was designed in the 1840s by the Hussey family and Mr Christopher Hussey bequeathed it to the Trust in 1970.

Scotney Castle, Kent

Sissinghurst Castle, Kent: the rose garden from the top of the tower

Sissinghurst Castle

about 11 miles east of Tunbridge Wells and 1¾ miles north-east of Cranbrook

The very beautiful garden at Sissinghurst was created by authoress V. Sack-ville-West and her husband Sir Harold Nicolson. It is a post-1930 creation, not a restoration or embellishment of an earlier work. Her own description of their starting-point allows that there were Tudor brick walls to provide the anatomy of the garden, remains of a moat for quiet water and a top spit of quite good soil. But for the rest, the place had been on the market for some years, and the surroundings of the castle used as a dump for old bedsteads and tins which lay in a tangle of weeds.

The general plan of the garden was to make long walks leading to grouped trees or statues; to have small gardens opening off these walks; and in the planting of these small gardens to have an eye to the seasons so that a spring garden is followed by summer gardens, and these in turn by an autumn garden. V. Sackville-West was a poet and brought her gift of poetry to the making of the garden. To this she added a wide knowledge and under-standing of horticulture.

The castle of Sissinghurst was not a medieval castle. There was a late fifteenth-century house, part of which was incorporated in a larger grand Elizabethan house. Queen Elizabeth stayed three days there in 1573. The Baker family who built it lost their fortune in the Civil War, and it suffered progressively from neglect. From 1756 to 1763 it was used to house French prisoners, Edward Gibbon in his capacity of officer in the Hampshire militia being for a while in charge of their guards. The prisoners were over-crowded and badly treated, and damaged the interior. In 1800 much of the dilapidated house was pulled down and the material taken for use elsewhere. After acquiring the property in 1930 the Nicolsons saved much of what little remained and added the minimum of lighting and plumbing needed to make the buildings habitable by modern standards.

Sissinghurst was given to the Trust by the Treasury in 1967, having been accepted in payment of death duty after Lady Nicolson's death. Mr Nigel Nicolson gave funds for endowment and in 1970 some additional land, including a lake.

Smallhythe Place

2 miles south of Tenterden

Smallhythe Place (below) was given to the Trust in 1939 as a memorial to Ellen Terry. The donor was her daughter, Miss Edith Craig, who was also responsible for collecting and arranging the exhibits now to be seen there. These include, in addition to memorials of her mother, many books, pictures and souvenirs of other famous actors and actresses.

Ellen Terry bought Smallhythe Place in 1899 when she was fifty-two, and it was her country home until she died there in 1928. Most of the rooms, including her dining-room, have now been given over to the display of the theatrical exhibits, but her bedroom has been kept as she knew it. Many of

Smallhythe Place, Kent

the dresses she wore on the stage are preserved in the house, with her make-up basket, her books and many of her working scripts.

When making the collection of mementoes of other famous players, Miss Craig cast a wide net to draw in not only English actors from David Garrick to John Gielgud but Duse, Bernhardt and others from continental countries.

Smallhythe Place is a fifteenth-century timbered building with a red tile roof. It was originally connected with a shipyard and still has a dry dock, but after the sea receded it became a farm. The building has been altered at different times but has not lost its original character.

Miss Craig converted the sixteenth-century barn into a theatre where she presented a number of plays and an annual star matinée. The Ellen Terry Theatre Club now presents plays there.

SOLE STREET: TUDOR YEOMAN'S HOUSE *a mile south-west of Cobham* A house of timber construction, restored and given by Sir Herbert Baker.

SPRIVERS *3 miles north of Lamberhurst* A hundred acres of park, orchard and wood. Not open.

Westerham

In the Westerham neighbourhood, and in addition to Chartwell which is two miles to the south, and Quebec House which is at the foot of the main street, the Trust has another six interesting properties furnishing some agreeable views, woodland and a shrub garden. These are:

GRANGE FARM *2 miles to the south at Crockham Hill* A three-hundred-acre farm given to preserve the view from Mariners Hill. Also a stone and tile-hung farmhouse, Close Farm, east of Crockham Hill (not open).

EMMETTS *1½ miles south of A 25 on the Sundridge–Ide Hill road* A hundred acres mostly of farmland, adjoining other Trust property, and containing an impressive four-acre shrub garden. The house is not open.

IDE HILL *2 miles south of Brasted, 2 miles south-east of Westerham* Woodland which overlooks the Weald (*32 acres*).

MARINERS HILL *2 miles south of Westerham*   View of the Weald; part of this property was acquired through Miss Octavia Hill in 1904 and subsequent years (*26 acres*).

PARSON'S MARSH *1½ miles south of Brasted*   Eighteen acres of woodland.

TOYS HILL *2½ miles south of Brasted* (*90 acres*)   Includes Toys Hill Beacon and also Scord's Wood between this and the Ide Hill property (*61 acres*).

———

WROTHAM WATER *1½ miles east of Wrotham*   This Trust property of 260 acres is mainly farmland at the foot of the Downs on the south side of the Pilgrims' Way. Also land joining this property on the north at Great and Little Spratts, and Hognore Farm (*64 acres*) on the lower slopes of the Downs, including the Golden Nob, with access by public footpaths.

———

LANCASHIRE

Where Trust properties are concerned, Lancashire has been pillaged by the new counties. Cumbria has taken those in the north of the county, Merseyside has taken Speke Hall and the Formby sand dunes, and Greater Manchester the farms near Bury and the 'rural oasis' near Ashton-under-Lyne (see note on Medlock Vale). Three properties remain in Lancashire.

GAWTHORPE HALL *between Burnley and Padiham to the north of A 671*   A Jacobean house, substantially altered in the nineteenth century. The Kay-Shuttleworth collection of textiles is housed here and the house is let to Lancashire County Council, which uses it as part of a college of further education.

———

RIBCHESTER *10 miles north-east of Preston*   The Museum of Roman Antiquities; and foundations of the granaries of a Roman fort built around A.D. 80.

———

Rufford Old Hall, Lancashire: the Great Hall

Rufford Old Hall

5 miles north of Ormskirk, east side of A59

At Rufford one sees a composite building. On the one hand there is the medieval Great Hall of the half-timbered fifteenth-century house, on the other the brick-built west wing of Charles II's time, and joining them the section which was reconstructed in the 1820s. The fifteenth-century hall, with its massive movable screen, had few rivals in its own day for the elaborate and pleasing detail of its interior and it has been preserved practically unaltered. Indeed the bulk of the timbering is five hundred years old. When it was found in the late 1950s that despite the use of modern preservatives some parts needed replacement, the new was carefully matched to the old, the craftsmen trimming the timber with hand tools such as the original builders would have used.

In recent years the 1821 wing and part of the Carolean wing have been made a folk museum housing tools, domestic furniture and other relics of village life in south-west Lancashire in earlier centuries. This collection was made by the late Philip Ashcroft, who gave it to the Trust.

When the 1st Baron Hesketh gave the hall to the Trust in 1936, his family had been at Rufford since the thirteenth century and were responsible for the building of both the hall and the later additions.

STUBBINS *5 miles north of Bury, west of Stubbins* This 430-acre property includes eight small farms and is preserved as an agricultural zone.

LEICESTERSHIRE

CHARNWOOD FOREST: ULVERSCROFT *6 miles south-west of Lough-borough* A nature reserve of about eighty acres at one of the highest points in Charnwood Forest. Access by permit from the Leicestershire Trust for Nature Conservation. Also Rocky Field and Rocky Plantation, 20 acres in another part of the forest.

Staunton Harold Church

5 miles north-east of Ashby-de-la-Zouch

Staunton Harold is one of the very few churches that were built during the Commonwealth. Its general appearance outside is that of a Gothic building; but inside the panelling, painted ceiling, pulpit, lectern and pews suggest the seventeenth century, as does the west doorway illustrated on page 221. It has been very little altered, the pulpit retaining even its original cushions and hangings.

There is an inscription over the door reading: 'In the year 1653 when all things Sacred were throughout ye nation Either demolisht or profaned Sir Robert Shirley, Barronet, Founded this church; whose singular praise it is, to have done the best things in ye worst times, and hoped them in the most callamitous. The righteous shall be had in everlasting remembrance.'

220

Staunton Harold Church, Leicestershire

This Sir Robert, whose family had been at Staunton Harold for two hundred years, had succeeded to the baronetcy in 1646. He had been several times imprisoned for complicity in Royalist plots. After the building of the church the authorities ordered him to find the money to raise a regiment. This, they argued, he must be well able to do if he could afford to build a splendid church. He refused and was sent to the Tower, where he died in

1656, leaving money for distressed Royalists. The chapel was given to the Trust in 1954 by his descendant the twelfth Earl Ferrers.

The beautiful silver-gilt communion plate, bearing the date mark 1654, made by a goldsmith at Gloucester, is on loan to the Victoria and Albert Museum.

———⟶ ⟵———

THE THOMAS BALSTON COLLECTION OF VICTORIAN STAF-FORDSHIRE FIGURES *Stapleford Park, 5 miles east of Melton Mowbray* This collection is shown by courtesy of Lord Gretton at Stapleford Park— which is *not* a Trust property.

———⟶ ⟵———

LINCOLNSHIRE

Grantham House

In Castlegate

Grantham House (opposite) stands in the centre of the town, across the road from Grantham church. Its twenty-five acres of garden and grounds lead down to the river and across it to meadows through which there is a public right of way. From this there are views of the beautiful church.

The house and its outbuildings are stone with tiled roofs. It has been altered a number of times and its architectural features date from several different periods. The central hall survives from the original building of about 1380; sixteenth-century windows face the church; the garden front was made over about 1734.

It was built by a family of wool merchants called Hall and was known as Hall Place. It has changed hands several times, the eighteenth-century alterations being made by Anne, Lady Cust, whose son, Sir John Cust, was Speaker of the House of Commons. The house and grounds were given to the Trust in 1944 by the Misses Winifred and Marion Sedgewick.

———⟶ ⟵———

Grantham House, Grantham, Lincolnshire

Gunby Hall, Lincolnshire

Gunby Hall

7 miles west of Skegness on the south side of A158

Gunby Hall (page 223) was built for Sir William Massingberd in 1700 in brick of a beautiful deep plum colour. A north wing was added in 1873 to allow of improved internal arrangements, and this includes a drawing-room which follows successfully the style of the earlier rooms.

Failing any evidence other than the design of the house itself, it is supposed that the architect was a mason or builder who had studied the work of Sir Christopher Wren's school.

Whoever may have designed the house, Tennyson has supplied its apt description in the verse which ends with the line 'A haunt of ancient peace'. Indeed he may well have had Gunby particularly in mind, since there is preserved at the house a copy of the verse written in his own hand, signed and dated 1849.

Among the contents of the house are two portraits by Reynolds and a book of special interest. This is one of the few surviving autographed copies of Boswell's *Life of Johnson*. It was given to Bennet Langton, whose son married the Gunby heiress in 1784.

The delightful walled garden has long borders of roses and flowers.

Gunby was given to the Trust by the Massingberd family in 1944.

Tattershall Castle

3½ miles south-east of Woodhall Spa on the south side of A153

Tattershall (opposite) is a fortified manor-house built about 1440 by Ralph Cromwell, who had become Treasurer of England some years before. It is fully entitled to the name 'castle' not only because it was built on the site of a medieval castle, but also because the defensive features of a castle were included in its design. The introduction of gunpowder had made such castles vulnerable, but Cromwell may have thought it sensible for an un-popular minister in an unsettled time to defend himself at least against less sophisticated attack. The great hundred-foot brick tower of his stronghold still stands.

At the same time he was mindful both of comfort and of the display he thought proper for a great officer of state. The rooms in the four stages of the tower have good windows and fine fireplaces; and from examination of the

Tattershall Castle, Lincolnshire

site and contemporary building accounts it is clear that the castle had spacious, well-equipped kitchens.

Tattershall, like Bodiam Castle in Sussex, was saved from ruin by Lord Curzon. When it came up for sale in 1910 it had been uninhabited for two hundred years and was decaying. American speculators bought it and sold the fireplaces, which were to be sent to America. At that point Lord Curzon stepped in, and saving both castle and fireplaces employed Mr William Weir to restore the castle as far as possible to its original state. In his will Lord Curzon left Tattershall (and Bodiam in Sussex) to the Trust.

─── ⇌ ───

Woolsthorpe Manor

7 miles south of Grantham, just north-west of Colsterworth

Woolsthorpe Manor (opposite), which was given to the Trust in 1943 through the Royal Society and the Pilgrim Trust, who provided funds for its repair, is preserved as a place of historic interest. Isaac Newton was born in this small early seventeenth-century house in 1642. He returned here from Cambridge during the plague years 1665–6 at a time when, in his own words, he was 'in the prime of my age for invention'. He conceived his idea of universal gravitation at this time, and traditionally it was in the garden of Woolsthorpe that he was prompted to it by seeing the fall of an apple from a tree.

─── ⇌ ───

LONDON

BARKING: EASTBURY HOUSE *Eastbury Square off Tudor Road* A red brick manor house of medium size, dated 1572, now in the centre of a modern housing estate. It is let to Barking Corporation and is not open.

─── ⇌ ───

Chelsea: Carlyle's House

24 Cheyne Row, Chelsea

Thomas and Jane Carlyle lived at 24 Cheyne Row from 1834 till her death in 1866; he continued to live there until he died in 1881. It is very fully supplied with their furniture, books, papers and personal relics. The house was given to the Trust in 1936 by the Carlyle's House Memorial Trust

Woolsthorpe Manor, Lincolnshire

which had cared for it during the previous forty years. At the same time the Memorial Trust handed over Carlyle's birthplace, the Arched House at Ecclefechan, to the National Trust for Scotland.

24 Cheyne Row (numbered 5 in Carlyle's time) is a plain, commodious terrace house built in about 1708. Jane Carlyle wrote in a letter soon after moving in: 'We have got an excellent lodgement . . . quite to our humour . . .

Carlyle's House, Chelsea, London: the drawing-room

all wainscotted, carved and queer looking, roomy, substantial, commodious, with closets to satisfy any Bluebeard . . .' Carlyle found the small garden at the back, which he cultivated himself, an excellent place to smoke in.

But it seems not to have been quite commodious enough. In 1852 they took a new, repairing lease and enlarged the library or drawing-room which was on the first floor. And shortly after that they had constructed under Carlyle's own direction the attic study as a soundproof room at the top of the house, with double roof and doors and special ventilation. This was an improvement but not an unqualified success. It cut off the noise of the immediate neighbourhood—the pianos, dogs and parrots that he had found intolerable; but it brought in distant noises, such as train whistles.

Pianos and parrots notwithstanding, it was at 24 Cheyne Row that Carlyle did much of his writing. And during the years of their residence the Carlyles received in the house a great many of the distinguished literary figures of their time: Leigh Hunt, John Stuart Mill, Erasmus Darwin, Emerson, Charles Kingsley, and Tennyson, who once came at two p.m. and stayed till eleven.

CHELSEA: NOS. 97–100 CHEYNE WALK Here in 1674 on the site of Thomas More's garden was built Lindsey House, with a fine seventeenth-century exterior. Though divided into four houses in 1720, it has since been made into two. (Not open.)

Chislehurst

CAMDEN COURT LAND and OAK BANK ESTATE Two strips of land acquired in the 1930s as part of a scheme for preserving Chislehurst Common. The first named is by the roadside and carries some limes; the other is at the top of Station Hill.

HAWKWOOD *between Chislehurst and Orpington* Farmland and woodland adjoining, and to the west of the Petts Wood property (see below). (*230 acres.*)

PETTS WOOD *between Chislehurst and Orpington, on west side of A208* Wood and heath bought after a public appeal, as a memorial to William Willett, inaugurator of Summer Time (*88 acres*).

EAST SHEEN COMMON *adjoining Richmond Park on the north* Given by East Sheen Common Preservation Society in 1908, and managed by the Borough of Richmond (*53 acres*).

HACKNEY: SUTTON HOUSE *Nos. 2 and 4 Homerton High Street* An early sixteenth-century red brick house with panelling from various periods, formerly known as St John's Institute. Access on application to the tenants, the Borough of Hackney.

Ham House: the door on the north front

Ham House

near Richmond, on the south bank of the Thames opposite Twickenham

Ham House demonstrates to us how a rich and influential couple planned, decorated and furnished a grand house in the Restoration period. Some of their decoration has become dulled with time; but it has not been altered and a great deal of their furniture remains. A large proportion of their garden also survives and is being refurbished.

The property belonged in 1672 to Elizabeth, Countess of Dysart in her own right. In that year she married (her second marriage) John Maitland who, as Duke of Lauderdale, was the 'L' in Charles II's Cabal Ministry.

Ham House: the staircase

They enlarged the relatively modest house of 1610, which she had inherited, by enclosing the space between the wings on the south side, thus
doubling the depth of the central block, and building extensions to each side.
Inside they expended much careful planning as well as a great deal of
money. The rooms are surprisingly small but lavishly decorated and furnished.

Chimney-pieces, ceilings, woodwork, and parquetry floors were designed and executed with an eye to their whole effect, and tapestry and other hangings and furniture chosen or made to accord with it. Much of this work was done by Dutch joiners and cabinet makers, and many of the decorative paintings were commissioned from foreign artists. There are a number of portraits in the house, including eight by the most fashionable portrait painter of the time, Sir Peter Lely.

When Elizabeth died Ham was inherited by Lionel Tollemache, Earl of Dysart, her son by her first marriage. It remained in the possession of the Tollemache family until 1948, when they gave the house to the Trust. At the same time Parliament bought the contents and put them in the care of the Victoria and Albert Museum, which now administers Ham on behalf of the Trust.

—◁▷—

Hampstead

on the west side of The Grove

FENTON HOUSE (opposite) stands in about an acre and a half three hundred yards north of Hampstead underground railway station. It is a square brick house with a steeply pitched roof, two storeys and an attic floor, which was built about 1693. Who built Fenton and who was his architect is not known. It changed hands and also names several times during the eighteenth century, being first Ostend House and then Clock House. Finally it became Fenton House after Mr F. I. Fenton, a Riga merchant who bought it in 1793.

The main rooms, which retain their original panelling, are now used to display two collections, one of porcelain and the other of keyboard musical instruments. The porcelain was collected by Lady Binning, who bought Fenton House in 1936 and left both house and collection to the Trust in her will. She died in 1952. Some fine Meissen Italian Comedy figures and groups form the feature of the collection. There is also a representative collection of English porcelain.

The musical instruments now at Fenton House were given to the Trust in 1937 by the late Major Benton Fletcher. There are harpsichords by the leading London and continental makers of the seventeenth and eighteenth centuries, and some spinets. They are in playing order and used by students, as Major Benton Fletcher intended that they should be when he made the collection.

Fenton House, London

SQUIRE'S MOUNT *south-west of Hampstead Heath, between East Heath Road and Cannon Place* A group of late eighteenth-century buildings and one and a half acres of garden (not open).

——— ∽ ⌣ ———

KENSINGTON: NO. 33 KENSINGTON SQUARE Late seventeenth-century house on west side of square—once the home of Mrs Patrick Campbell (not open).

——— ∽ ⌣ ———

Osterley Park, London: the portico on the south front

Osterley Park

just north of Osterley Station, Piccadilly Line

Osterley is almost entirely the work of Robert Adam outside and in: from the great portico (above) to the furniture in the rooms and the design of the elegant gilt brass door handles. But he did not start with an empty field. His task was to remodel an Elizabethan house, and he retained from this the corner towers with their cupolas.

Adam was at work on Osterley between 1761 and 1780. Horace Walpole visited the house twice, and his letters describe the principal rooms almost exactly as they are seen by today's visitors. The decoration of the rooms and the inset paintings are as Adam had them. Much of the furniture which he designed for the house is in its place.

Osterley Park, London: the library

The Elizabethan house at Osterley was built for Sir Thomas Gresham about 1570. It was described as 'a faire and stately building of bricke', and Queen Elizabeth visited Sir Thomas there. Although it changed hands several times during the seventeenth century none of the various owners made any major alterations. In 1711 it was bought by Francis Child (of Child's Bank) and his grandsons employed Adam to design and decorate the present house. The property passed by marriage in 1804 to the Earl of Jersey. It was given to the Trust in 1949 by the ninth Earl of Jersey. The contents belong to the Victoria and Albert Museum, which manages the house for the Trust. In the extensive grounds are an orangery, a temple, and many unusual trees.

RAINHAM HALL *5 miles east of Barking, just south of Rainham Church* Eighteenth-century house built of red brick with stone dressing on symmetrical plan. Contemporary panelling.

ROMAN BATH, NO 5 STRAND LANE *just west of Aldwych Station*
These remains were restored in the seventeenth century, and are of disputed
Roman origin.

SELSDON WOOD *3 miles south-east of Croydon along the Farleigh road* Two
hundred acres managed by the Borough of Croydon.

SOUTHWARK: THE GEORGE INN *on east side of Borough High Street*
Built in 1677 and the only remaining galleried inn in London. Occasional
performances of Shakespeare's plays are held here.

SWAKELEYS *half a mile north of Hillingdon Station* To protect this seventeenth-century house, a quarter-acre spinney was given to the Trust in 1933
together with protective covenants over the house and surrounding estate.

Wandle Properties

The Trust groups under this heading several properties on or near the
Wandle, which provide valuable open space in a densely populated area.
The largest is MORDEN HALL, consisting of the Hall and some cottages,
let to the London Borough of Merton, and 120 acres on the east side of A24,
intersected by the Wandle, with an old snuff mill and a small bird sanctuary.
The others are small parcels of land on the west bank of the Wandle, both
east and west of Mitcham Bridge, and one behind the Royal Six Bells,
Colliers Wood. Also a fragment of the wall of Merton Abbey, running
south from Colliers Wood High Street. Watermeads, twelve acres on the
west bank of the river opposite Ravensburn Park, is used partly for growing
willows.

Westminster

Two properties:

BLEWCOAT SCHOOL *23 Caxton Street* An elegant small building of
1709, now used as a Trust Information Room.

NOS. 40–44 QUEEN ANNE'S GATE Part of a street of Queen Anne
houses and now the Trust's headquarters offices.

MERSEYSIDE

The following properties were formerly in the old county of Lancashire:

Formby

about 10 miles from the centre of Liverpool

The nearest unspoiled coastline to Liverpool and Manchester is the stretch of coast just west of Formby (below). In 1967 the Trust bought four hundred acres of the sand dunes and foreshore with the proceeds of a local appeal made as part of Enterprise Neptune, the Trust's appeal for coastal preservation.

Formby, Merseyside: sand dunes to the west of the town, with marram grass

Speke Hall, Merseyside

Speke Hall

8 miles south-east of Liverpool, just north of the Mersey

Like another most interesting black-and-white house preserved by the Trust (Little Moreton Hall in Cheshire), Speke grew as additions were made to suit the needs and preferences of succeeding generations of one family. The first Sir William Norreys made a start by building the hall soon after 1490. His grandson rendered this more comfortable by adding the screens, about 1524. As his family grew he built the Great Parlour in the West block, and the East block for his domestic staff. His son and grandson both made further

238

additions, but after 1626 there were no more extensions. Between them they made the interior extremely handsome. The hall has a large Elizabethan fireplace with a massive carved oak mantel-beam. Its walls are panelled and contain carved reliefs. The Great Parlour is finished throughout in oak and has an Elizabethan ceiling modelled with a design of fruits and flowers.

Their eighteenth-century descendants allowed irresponsible tenants to neglect the house and serious damage was done to parts of the interior. But it was rescued in 1797 by Richard Watt, a Liverpool man who had made a fortune in Jamaica. He bought the house and spent much care and discrimination as well as money on its restoration. Through provisions in the will of his descendant, Miss Adelaide Watt, it was acquired by the National Trust in 1944. The Trust has leased it to Liverpool Corporation.

———

The Wirral

The Trust has four Wirral properties, acquired between 1916 and 1932, which provide some good view-points.

BURTON WOOD *9 miles north-west of Chester (in Cheshire)*   Twenty acres of Scots pines above Burton village.

CALDY HILL *a mile south-east of West Kirby*   Twelve acres with a view of the Dee.

HARROCK WOOD *4 miles south-west of Birkenhead*   Ten acres of wood and water meadows.

THURSTASTON COMMON *half a mile north of Thurstaston on east of A540* Includes some farmland, playing fields and Irby Heath, and provides views of the Dee estuary (*170 acres*).

NORFOLK

BALE OAKS *5 miles south of Blakeney*   A group of ilexes close to the church.

———

Blakeney Point

8 miles east of Wells

The north coast of Norfolk between Hunstanton and Weybourne is completely unspoiled and of the greatest interest to scientists. Before the Fishmongers' Company and anonymous donors gave the Trust its thousand-acre Blakeney Point property in 1912, Dr Oliver and others from University College, London, had already done valuable scientific work there over many years. Under the Trust's ownership it became the first nature reserve in Norfolk. It is administered by the Trust.

The area is one of shingle ridges, sand dunes and salt marsh and is subject to rapid physical change. Consequent variations in its plant life and the distribution of animal and insect populations provide unusual scope for ecological studies. Its bird population, in addition to winter and summer

Blakeney Point, Norfolk: the ternery

migrants, includes nesting colonies of tern, oyster-catcher and ringed plover. These properties are maintained as Nature Reserves and students are welcome —about a hundred organized school and college parties visit each year—provided they keep strictly to the rules. The importance of this proviso was highlighted by a note in the Trust's 1967 *News Letter*: 'This is the first time for some years that Sandwich tern have stayed through the season on the Point in any numbers, and the Warden is to be congratulated on achieving this by diligently keeping visitors from disturbing the nests.'

The Trust has published a detailed guide to the Blakeney Point property, together with the Scolt Head property (page 250), compiled by experts in the different subjects which can be studied there.

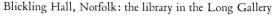

Blickling Hall

a mile north-west of Aylsham

Blickling stands in a lovely setting of lawns and formal garden. It is a fine symmetrical building of mellowed rose red brick with many gables, chimneys and pinnacles. It was built about 1620, on the site of an earlier house, for Sir Henry Hobart, the Lord Chief Justice. The architect was Robert

Blickling Hall, Norfolk: the library in the Long Gallery

Blickling Hall, Norfolk: the south front

Lyminge, who had designed another very famous and not dissimilar Jacobean house, Hatfield House, twenty years before. During the later part of the eighteenth century alterations were made to the north and west fronts, and some changes were made in the interior. As a result the State Bedroom and the Peter the Great Room are now good examples of the style of elegance of the 1780s; but the Long Gallery (page 241) retains its elaborate Jacobean plasterwork ceiling.

Of special interest among the furnishings of the house is the tapestry which gives the Peter the Great Room its name. This was woven in St Petersburg in 1764 and represents Peter the Great at the battle of Poltawa. It was given by the Empress Catherine to John Hobart, second Earl of Buckinghamshire, who was ambassador to Russia from 1762 to 1765.

There is a magnificent formal garden and a landscaped park with a mile-long lake fringed by magnificent trees. The whole estate covers more than four thousand acres, including the park, farms and woodlands.

Blickling passed by marriage last century to the eighth Marquess of Lothian. When the eleventh Marquess, Philip Kerr, died in 1940 while serving as ambassador in Washington, he left the property to the Trust.

BRANCASTER *between Hunstanton and Wells* Two thousand acres of beach, sand-dune, marsh, saltings and four and a half miles of the tidal fore-shore belong to the Trust. The saltings are opposite the Trust's Scolt Head Nature Reserve. Bought with Enterprise Neptune funds. The beach road is submerged at high tide.

BULLFER GROVE $4\frac{1}{2}$ *miles south-west of Holt* Woodland of special botanic interest covering some eight acres.

BURNHAM OVERY *a mile north of Burnham Market* Includes Burnham Overy Water Mill, with maltings, a barn, miller's house and cottages by the River Burn and, on higher ground to the east, a windmill erected in 1816. These properties are now used as dwellings and are not open.

CAWSTON DUELLING STONE *by the old Woodrow Inn on the Norwich-Holt road near Cawston* Inscribed 'H.H.', this stone was placed near where Sir Henry Hobart of Blickling Hall was fatally wounded in a duel in 1698.

Fellbrigg Hall

2 miles south-west of Cromer, off A148

Felbrigg presents two distinct, handsome faces to the outside world—a Jacobean entrance front built between 1600 and 1624 and a west wing which was added in the 1680s. Both remain unaltered. Inside the house, although some of the seventeenth-century plaster ceilings were kept, extensive changes were made in the 1740s. William Windham II, back from the Grand Tour, engaged James Paine to design a new staircase, new dining-room and a library to suit mid-eighteenth-century taste. His son, William Windham III, in the intervals of a busy political life which included some years as Pitt's Secretary for War, made further changes. These provided a

Felbrigg Hall, Norfolk: the west and south fronts

Felbrigg Hall, Norfolk: the cabinet

morning-room and a Great Hall to suit the early 1800s. The furniture and pictures which the Windhams selected to embellish these rooms—including pictures brought back by William Windham II from the Grand Tour—remain to embellish them today.

The walled garden is being replanted, and there is an orangery near the house.

Great Yarmouth: No. 4 South Quay, Norfolk

The house and park are protected from north-easterly winds by a six-hundred-acre Great Wood, which has been carefully maintained and improved since its first planting in the seventeenth century. A circular woodland walk through the Great Wood begins and ends at the Hall.

Felbrigg gets its name from the family that sold the property to the Windhams in the fifteenth century. The Windhams sold it in 1863 to John Ketton
of Norwich, whose grandson, R. W. Ketton-Cremer, left it to the Trust
when he died in 1969.

Great Yarmouth: No. 4 South Quay

For about 350 years, No. 4 South Quay had a succession of owners including mayors and prominent merchants of Yarmouth. It was built from 1590 to
1596 on the site of an earlier building. Its seventeenth-century owners gave
the rooms oak panelling and fine chimney-pieces. The present outside
appearance of the house dates from about 1810. The front was at that time in
need of repair, and the owner encased it in white brick and enlarged the
windows.

It was given to the Trust in 1943 and has been leased to Yarmouth Corporation as a museum. Some seventeenth-century glass panels of ships and
fishing scenes have been incorporated in windows overlooking the courtyard.

Horsey Windmill, Norfolk

HORSEY *about 11 miles north of Yarmouth*   Horsey Mill (page 247) is a fine landmark and vantage point for those who go up it to admire the views to Horsey Mere and out to sea. It was built in 1912 as a drainage mill on the site of an earlier mill. It was struck by lightning in 1943, and although it has been restored it is no longer used for drainage purposes.

The Trust's whole Horsey property extends to seventeen hundred acres and includes farmlands as well as Horsey Mere, marshes and marrams. The mere is accessible by boat, but as it is a breeding ground for marsh birds access is restricted.

The Trust bought the property in 1948 with the help of a public sub-scription and a grant from the Pilgrim Trust.

———⌒   ⌒———

KING'S LYNN; ST GEORGE'S GUILDHALL   An early fifteenth-century building and the largest surviving medieval guildhall in England. It was long put to theatrical use and now after repairs is being so used again. The St George's Guildhall Company hold an annual Festival of the Arts, and concerts during the rest of the year.

———⌒   ⌒———

MORSTON MARSHES *between Blakeney and Stiffkey*   Saltings laced with tidal creeks and backed by scrub-covered grassland. 556 acres forming two miles of the south shoreline of Blakeney Harbour. Bought in 1973 from Enterprise Neptune funds and a local appeal.

———⌒   ⌒———

Oxburgh Hall

7 miles south-west of Swaffham at Oxborough

The house (opposite) was built in 1482, at a time of transition from the fortified manor-house or castle to the later unfortified country house. It still retains the general outline of the original building, although from time to time parts of the house have been damaged and restored or altered, and additions have been made.

The Great Tower, which remains completely unchanged, is a truly impressive sight, rising eighty feet straight from the edge of the moat. The detail of the brickwork is as impressive as the proportions of the tower, and the layman has no difficulty in accepting Pugin's dictum that it is 'one of the noblest specimens of the domestic architecture of the fifteenth century'.

Oxburgh Hall, Norfolk

Inside the tower on the first floor is the King's Chamber, so called because Henry VII lodged there when he visited Oxburgh in 1487. Displayed in this room are some panels of needlework embroidered and signed by Mary Queen of Scots. These are among the very few known examples of her work. They were brought to Oxburgh in 1761 by a daughter of Viscount Montague of Cowdray, who married a Bedingfeld.

The formal parterre garden was created about 1845 by Sir Henry Paston-Bedingfeld, 6th Baronet. The design was taken from one by the eighteenth-century French landscape gardener, Alexandre le Blond, and is called '*Parterre de Compartiment*'.

Oxburgh, which was built by the Bedingfeld family and has been their home for more than 490 years, was given to the Trust by the Dowager Lady Bedingfeld in 1952.

SALTHOUSE BROAD *1½ miles north-east of Cley* Thirty acres of marsh called locally Arnold's Marsh, and let to the Norfolk Naturalists' Trust. An important adjunct to the National Trust's Blakeney Point nature reserve. The salt lagoons are visited by many migrant waders, but the public is requested not to visit this part of the broad.

SCOLT HEAD ISLAND *3 miles north of Burnham Market* Bought for the Trust in 1923 with funds raised by the Norfolk Naturalists' Society, and leased to the Nature Conservancy in 1953. Also see text accompanying Blakeney Point illustration (page 240). (*1,600 acres.*)

WEST RUNTON *between Sheringham and Cromer, south of West Runton Station.* Seventy acres of land including the highest point in Norfolk. Known locally as the 'Roman Camp'. Recent excavations did not confirm this description but found instead evidence of ironworking from A.D. 1000 to 1200. Also thirty-seven acres of Beeston Regis Heath acquired in 1971. This open and wooded heathland gives fine views of the coastline and includes most of the ridge between the 'Roman Camp' property and Brittons Lane.

NORTHAMPTONSHIRE

BRACKLEY PARK *about half-way between Oxford and Northampton, A43* Three acres of land on the east side of Brackley High Street. Managed by the Corporation.

EASTON-ON-THE-HILL *about 2 miles south-west of Stamford on A43* A pre-Reformation priest's house.

Lyveden New Build

4 miles south-west of Oundle

Lyveden New Build (or Bield) (opposite) was, for all its eccentric plan and decoration, evidently intended to be a comfortable family house. It was never finished and has virtually had to fend for itself since building stopped in 1605. The fact that the shell has deteriorated so little is a great tribute to the masons who built it.

[Lyveden New Build, Northamptonshire

If it had been completed, it would have contained the usual kitchen, buttery and servants' quarters in the basement, Great Hall and a parlour on the floor above and Great Chamber and bedrooms on the floor above that. The only odd thing about the domestic layout is the entrances. The front door is six feet above the ground and was to have been approached by a flight of steps; the back door, opening into the basement, was approached by an underground passage.

But Sir Thomas Tresham's main purpose was that the building should be symbolical of the Passion. It is in the shape of a cross with equal arms, a bay window at the end of each arm. Running round the outside are two friezes. On one of these was depicted, among other things, Judas' money bag surrounded by the thirty pieces of silver, the crown of thorns, the sponge, the spear and the seamless garment between three dice. On the other were cut sentences from the Vulgate and other references to the Passion. Sir Thomas also incorporated mathematical arrangements in his plan. The arms of the cross are equal squares which enclose another of the same size, making five equal squares; the bay windows start five feet from the corner of the building and have five faces each five feet in length. The letters of the wording on the frieze are spaced one to a foot, and the length of the lettering to each arm is eighty-one feet, or nine times nine.

So far as is known Sir Thomas never revealed the ideas which prompted such eccentricity in his building. He also had a triangular lodge built at Rushton expressing the doctrine of the Trinity.

Sir Thomas came of a family long established in Northamptonshire, and spent a certain amount of time in prison. Brought up as a Protestant, he became a Roman Catholic in 1580 and fell foul of the religious laws. During his imprisonments he developed his fancies and his mystic ideas, and when at liberty applied them to his buildings. Just after his death his son was involved in the Gunpowder Plot and imprisoned, and later the estate passed into other hands.

Lyveden New Build was bought by the Trust by means of a public subscription in 1922. It has not been restored, but has been given weather protection.

NORTHUMBERLAND

THE ALLEN BANKS *3 miles west of Haydon Bridge* Two hundred acres of hill and woodland where the Allen joins the Tyne, with walks, river scenery and a nature trail. Most of the property was given by members of the Bowes-Lyon family. The property includes the old kitchen garden of Ridley Hall, and some steep woodland on the left bank of the river.

Beadnell Bay

about 7 miles north-north-east of Alnwick

Around Beadnell Bay:

BEADNELL LIME KILNS *a half-mile south-east of Beadnell* A group of eighteenth-century lime kilns by the sea.

DUNSTANBURGH CASTLE and EMBLETON LINKS *9 miles north-east of Alnwick* Five hundred acres of foreshore, including a golf course. Also the ruins of the fourteenth-century castle, which are now under the guardian-ship of the Department of the Environment, and approachable on foot only.

Beadnell Bay, Northumberland

Adjoining Embleton Links is a freshwater pool, Newton Pool, a nature reserve of special ornithological interest (near Newton-by-the-Sea). A grant from the World Wildlife Fund helped to secure this property.

NEWTON LINKS Fifty-five acres of sand dunes and rough grazing in Beadnell Bay south of Long Nanny were bought in 1966 from Enterprise Neptune Funds.

Farne Islands

The Farne Islands are about ten miles south of Berwick-upon-Tweed, a mile and a half to five miles off the coast. According to the state of the tide there are fifteen to twenty-eight or more of them. The largest (the Inner

253

The Farne Islands, Northumberland: guillemots on Staple Island

Farne) is sixteen acres in extent at low tide, much of it bare rock rising to seventy or eighty feet. Its cliffs are similar to those in the photograph above, of guillemots on Staple Island. A nature trail is in operation on the Inner Farne.

The islands are a breeding-place for seals and a host of sea birds: eider-duck, guillemot, puffin, fulmar, petrel and another fifteen or more species. Access is allowed, except that landing on some of the islands is forbidden during the breeding season. Visitors are required to keep strictly to the rules which have been made to preserve the islands as a bird sanctuary.

The known history of the islands begins in the seventh century when St Aidan was a visitor, and later St Cuthbert established his hermit cell on the Inner Farne. On this island are remains of a fourteenth-century chapel. There have been lighthouses since Charles II's time, and the Longstone Lighthouse (not Trust owned), built in 1826, was the home of Grace Darling.

Acquired after a public appeal in 1925.

——⇒ ⇐——

LADY'S WELL: HOLYSTONE *7 miles west of Rothbury* Traditionally associated with St Ninian.

——⇒ ⇐——

Lindisfarne Castle

The castle stands on Holy Island, just off the Northumbrian coast between Berwick and Bamburgh. Holy Island came into history in the seventh century when it was the seat of a bishopric. In the eleventh century there was a Benedictine monastery here.

The castle came afterwards. It was built in Edward VI's reign as a defence against the Scots. With the accession of James I its point was lost, and after a successful siege by Parliamentary forces during the Civil War it was neglected until 1903. In that year it was taken in hand by Sir Edwin Lutyens, commissioned by Mr Edward Hudson. Lutyens converted the Tudor castle into a dwelling house.

Lindisfarne (page 256) was given to the Trust in 1944 by Sir Edward de Stein and his sister.

——⇒ ⇐——

The Roman Wall

4 miles east of Haltwhistle

The Trust preserves Housesteads, one of the seventeen forts that were spaced along Hadrian's Wall (page 257); and about three and a half miles of the wall. It also owns Hotbank and Highshield Farms, and Crag Lough, which total nearly twelve hundred acres.

Housesteads (that is its modern name: it was Borcovicium in fifteenth-century lists) was built at the same time as the wall, A.D. 122–30. It housed an infantry unit a thousand strong and had temples, shrines, a bath-house and quarters for women and children. In the museum, which contains antiquities found near by, there are models of what it was like in full occupation. Today's visitor can admire the wonderful views from the site or, if imaginatively inclined, gaze at them through the eyes of a Roman sentry.

Lindisfarne Castle, Northumberland

The Roman Wall, Northumberland, seen from Cuddy's Crag near Housesteads

ROS CASTLE *12 miles north-west of Alnwick* A hill top with wide-ranging views and traces of a possible Iron Age earthwork, given as part of a memorial to Lord Grey of Fallodon.

ST AIDAN'S and SHORESTONE DUNES *2 miles south-east of Bamburgh* Sixty acres of sand dunes with views of the Farne Islands.

Wallington

at Cambo, 12 miles west of Morpeth

Wallington (page 258) is built on a site where previous owners had erected a medieval castle and then, in extension of it, a Tudor house. Both of these were pulled down to make way for another house in 1688. They provided some of the stone from which it was built and its cellars are the foundations of the medieval building. The builder was Sir William Blackett of County

Wallington, Northumberland

Durham, who had inherited and made a lot of money from mines and shipping and bought the Wallington estate to provide himself with a place in the country. He already had a large town house in Newcastle. He built the present square house at Wallington—120 ft square—but left it fairly spartan inside. His son put in the staircase and brought in Italian craftsmen to do the fine plasterwork in the principal rooms. He also built the stables and clock tower. It seems that he first intended the clock tower to be a chapel, for thus it appears on the plans.

Then in the eighteenth century the Trevelyans came to Wallington from Cornwall on the marriage of a Trevelyan to a Blackett heiress. At that time the centre of the square of which the house consists was still a courtyard. But in the following century, when Pauline, Lady Trevelyan, made Wallington a salon which attracted such writers and artists as Swinburne, Ruskin and Millais, Ruskin suggested that the courtyard be roofed. This was done and the former courtyard became a picture gallery.

The extensive grounds contain a nature walk, fine historic terraced gardens, a portico, and a walled garden with a conservatory containing magnificent fuchsias.

In 1942 Sir Charles Trevelyan, who had been President of the Board of Education in the first Labour Government, gave the house, its contents and the grounds to the Trust. Codger Fort on the eastern edge of the estate was added in 1972.

WYLAM-ON-TYNE *8 miles west of Newcastle* The mid-eighteenth-century cottage where the inventor George Stephenson was born (not open).

NORTH YORKSHIRE

Beningbrough Hall

5½ miles north-west of York, 3 miles west of Shipton

Viewed from the outside, Beningbrough has the taciturnity that is popularly supposed to be characteristic of Yorkshire people. Also, a Yorkshireman might add, it is solid, dignified and spiced with a touch of unconventionality. It is a compact building made of small bricks (9 in. × 2⅛ in.). There are two storeys and an attic floor with eleven windows at each level. Steps lead up to the doors on both the main entrance and the garden front (below). The porches above these doors carry beautifully executed stonework.

The house was built about 1716. There is no solid evidence of who may have been the architect; but some unusual detail in the design is to be found

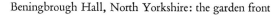

Beningbrough Hall, North Yorkshire: the garden front

elsewhere in buildings designed by Thomas Archer, so it has been suggested that he made rough plans and a local builder worked from them. Certainly there were at that time some excellent builders and wood-carvers in York and some very fine work was put into Beningbrough—notably the staircase. The wide treads of this are parqueted and the balustrade, with its slim uprights, looks as though it had been wrought in iron. In the Drawing Room, Saloon and State Bedroom is a wealth of delightful and most expertly executed wood-carvers' decoration.

When the Trust acquired the property in 1958 (from the Treasury which had accepted it in payment of death duties) it was empty of furniture. But gradually this state of affairs is being remedied.

BRAITHWAITE HALL *1½ miles south-west of Middleham* The seventeenth-century hall, which is now a farmhouse, and 750 acres of moor and farmland.

BRANSDALE *6 miles north of Helmsley* In a beautiful valley between high moors are eighteen hundred acres of farmland. Accepted by the Treasury in payment of death duties and given to the Trust.

BRIDESTONES MOOR *12 miles south of Whitby* Nine hundred acres of moor and farmland with a four-mile nature walk. The Bridestones are strange-shaped masses of rock left by the erosion of softer surrounding rock. Three groups of barrows on Grime Moor were probably excavated *c.* 1850.

BRIMHAM MOOR AND ROCKS *8 miles south-west of Ripon* Four hundred acres of moorland with many fantastically-shaped rock formations.

Hudswell

CALFHALL, ROUND HOWE and BILLYBANK WOODS *between Richmond and Hudswell, just south of A6108* Ninety acres of woodland situated on the south bank of the Swale.

HAG WOOD *2 miles west of Richmond* A further forty acres of woodland.

MALHAM TARN *6 miles north-east of Settle* The Tarn House, the Tarn and three farms covering three thousand acres between Ribblesdale and Wharfedale. The Tarn and some land have been let to the Field Studies Council, but there is public access to the south shore of the Tarn and to some of the unfenced farmland. A nature trail follows the path around the north-east and northern edges of the Tarn.

MOULTON HALL *5 miles east of Richmond* A house that was rebuilt about 1650, and has a fine carved wood staircase.

MOUNT GRACE PRIORY *6 miles north-east of Northallerton* Remains of the fourteenth-century Priory, which are under the guardianship of the Department of the Environment, and are the most important Carthusian ruins in England.

NUNNINGTON HALL *4½ miles south-east of Helmsley* Mainly late seventeenth-century manor house, but west wing was begun in 1580. Panelled hall and staircase.

RIEVAULX TERRACE AND TEMPLES *2 miles north-west of Helmsley* The half-mile terrace and the two classical temples (one at each end) look down on the ruined medieval abbey (not under Trust ownership) far below and beside the river. The whole scheme is one of the most remarkable pieces of eighteenth-century landscaping. For good measure, the Ionic temple was given a painted ceiling and elegant furniture, which are still there. Terrace, temples and adjoining woodland were bought by the Trust in 1972 after a public appeal.

RIPON: SANCTUARY CROSS *at Sharow, three-quarters of a mile north-east of Ripon.* The stump of the only surviving cross marking the limit of Abbey sanctuary.

SALTWICK NAB *a mile east of Whitby* A small piece of cliff-land, which includes a rocky nab jutting out into the sea.

SCARTH WOOD *8 miles north-east of Northallerton* This wide stretch of moorland near the Cleveland Hills provides good views towards the Pennines (250 acres).

STAINFORTH BRIDGE 2½ *miles north of Settle* A seventeenth-century single span bridge over the Ribble.

⟜ ⟝

Treasurer's House, York

at the north-east corner of the Minster

The Romans had a building on the site, but there is no evidence to show exactly what it was, and Treasurer's House, as an official residence for the Treasurer of the See of York, starts with William the Conqueror and ends with Henry VIII. William appointed a canon of Bayeux to be Archbishop of York and the new archbishop built houses for various officers of the diocese, including the Treasurer. In 1547 the last Treasurer handed over his dignities and the key, saying that as the diocese had been plundered of its treasure it had no further need of a Treasurer.

Since then the house, which has been much altered, has changed hands many times, and a variety of people of interest have owned or been connected with it—Protector Somerset, Lord Fairfax (the Civil War general), Mathew Robinson (the father of the bluestocking Elizabeth Montagu) and Lawrence Sterne, who was a frequent visitor when the house belonged to his uncle.

Treasurer's House, York: the drawing-room

In 1896 it was in use as three dwellings. Then a new owner (Mr Frank Green of Nunthorpe Hall, who gave the house to the Trust thirty-four years later) undertook extensive alterations. He opened up windows which had been bricked up, and within the hall removed a seventeenth-century upper floor.

Above ground, the house as it stands today is largely the house as it was rebuilt in 1620. Beneath is part of the undercroft of the house of the time of Edward I, the eleventh-century house having, probably, been destroyed by the fire that wrecked most of the town in 1137. The interior decoration ranges over the seventeenth and eighteenth centuries and includes some interesting fireplaces and painted ceilings. The furniture and paintings are to match, as they include seventeenth-century portraits, eighteenth-century landscapes, Jacobean tables and George II mirrors (opposite).

Wensleydale

EAST SCAR TOP FARM *a mile south-east of Bainbridge* Three hundred acres running up to 1500 ft at Addleborough and giving a view of the whole dale.

NOTTINGHAMSHIRE

Clumber Park

2½ miles south-east of Worksop

Clumber Park, a fine and extensive piece of late eighteenth-century landscaping, was made from a part of the old forest of Sherwood and some adjoining heathland. It covers 3,800 acres, of which about 2,000 are woodland, and contains Hardwick village and farm, an eighty-acre lake and a three-mile-long lime avenue (page 264). Before the park was laid out the land was described as 'a black heath, full of rabbits, having a narrow riving running through it with a small boggy close or two'. When the Dukes of Newcastle had the park made they also had built a mansion, with terraces and fountains to grace it, by the lake. This has been demolished, except for one small portion now used as a restaurant, and the chapel and the stables. Clumber was acquired by the Trust in 1946 through public appeal and the sale of timber, and with the help of eight local authorities. Two nature walks now exist in the park.

Clumber Park, Nottinghamshire: the lime avenue

Clumber Chapel was designed by one of the architects of the Gothic revival, G. F. Bodley, and has been described as Bodley's 'cathedral in miniature'. It was built by the seventh Duke of Newcastle (between 1886 and 1889) as his private chapel and for the use of the people of Clumber Park. It is in the Decorated style of the fourteenth century. Its tower and spire rise to 180 feet. It contains some beautifully carved limewood statues of the evangelists, saints and archangels; stained-glass windows by C. E. Kempe; and some fine quality metalwork, much of which was wrought by blacksmiths on the estate. Services are held in the chapel on Sundays in the summer.

COLSTON BASSETT: THE MARKET CROSS *10 miles south-east of Nottingham, 5 miles south of Bingham* This dates from the eighteenth century, though the base is medieval. It was given to the Trust by the Society for the Protection of Ancient Buildings.

OXFORDSHIRE

The new county of Oxfordshire now contains a large proportion of the National Trust properties formerly in the county of Berkshire.

Abingdon

RUSKIN RESERVE, COTHILL *3 miles north-west of Abingdon* Four acres of marshy woodland let to the Nature Conservancy.

───◁ ▷───

PRIORY COTTAGES, STEVENTON *4 miles south of Abingdon* Former monastic buildings converted into two houses, one of which is open. The Trust has protective covenants over some other medieval buildings in Steventon.

───◁ ▷───

Ashdown House

3½ miles north of Lambourn on the west side of B4000

Ashdown House, as shown in the illustration below, is unusually tall and narrow for a country house, rising to four storeys. It is also unusual, being built of chalk—chalk blocks with stone quoins.

Ashdown House, Oxfordshire

It was built about 1665 by the first Earl of Craven, but it is not known for certain who was his architect. Lord Craven dedicated it to James I's daughter Elizabeth, Queen of Bohemia. He devoted himself to her service throughout her life and spent much of his considerable wealth in supporting her interests. Unfortunately she did not live to see Ashdown finished.

The rooms are well proportioned, but very little of any original decoration remains. The staircase occupies about a quarter of the floor space in the house and rises to the attic. The roof is a good viewing point.

The garden consists of a box parterre laid out in the style of the seventeenth century. There is a fine lime avenue.

Ashdown was given to the Trust in 1956 by Cornelia, Countess of Craven.

———

ASTON WOOD 1½ *miles north-west of Stokenchurch* A hundred acres of beechwood astride the Oxford–Wycombe road (A40). Mainly the gift of Sir Edward Cadogan.

———

Buscot

THE BUSCOT ESTATE *between Lechlade and Faringdon* The estate runs to nearly four thousand acres of farm and woodland and includes the village and Buscot Park. It was given to the Trust by Mr E. E. Cook. Buscot Park, which was built in 1780 in the style of Adam, and altered at later times, now contains the Faringdon Collection of paintings, furniture and porcelain. It has an extensive garden with avenues, and a water garden designed by Harold Peto.

THE OLD PARSONAGE Built in Cotswold stone in 1703, and given separately by Mr P. F. C. Stucley. He expressed a wish in his will that it should be let, preferably to a United States citizen engaged in literary, artistic or academic studies.

COLESHILL *adjoining and south of Buscot* The Coleshill estate is another bequest from Mr E. E. Cook. There are about 3,600 acres of farm and woodland (with access in some parts) together with Coleshill village, which has buildings of Cotswold stone and tile. Badbury Hill has an Iron Age hill fort.

———

COOMBE END FARM 2½ *miles north of Pangbourne* A partly seventeenth-century farmhouse and two hundred acres, at the southern end of the Chilterns.

———

Great Coxwell Tithe Barn, Oxfordshire

Great Coxwell: The Great Barn

about 1½ miles south-west of Faringdon

This is a stone-built Cistercian barn with stone-tiled roof that dates from the early thirteenth century. The Trust carried out extensive repairs in the 1960s. Professor Walter Horn of the University of California, in a long report on his study of the barn, quotes William Morris's description of it as 'the finest piece of architecture in England'. He also makes his own comment on the interior: that it displays 'one of the most magnificent medieval frames of roof supporting timber'. The barn is 152 ft long by 43 ft wide and at the ridge is 48 ft high. It was acquired by the Trust in 1956 under the will of Mr E. E. Cook.

Greys Court

3 miles west of Henley-on-Thames

Today's visitor sees a substantially late sixteenth-century house but with some agreeable later alterations. It faces the tower of a medieval house and, spaced at a discreet distance, stables, a well house and other outbuildings

267

which are of a somewhat earlier date than the present house. Perhaps a rather confusing complex architecturally, but it is nevertheless very gracious and acceptable.

Interspersed among these buildings are delightful gardens of roses, old varieties of wisteria, shrubs, a multitude of other flowers and some old-established trees.

The family who built the second house were Knollys, one of whom, a cousin of Queen Elizabeth, was for many years Lord Treasurer of the Royal Household.

The property was given to the Trust by Sir Felix Brunner, Bt. in 1968.

The Carlisle Collection of miniature rooms is now housed in the Cromwellian Buildings.

IDSTONE *a mile south-west of Ashbury which is 5 miles west of Swindon* A small seventeenth-century house with nineteenth-century additions. It is called Trip-the-Daisy, having once been a public house that was named after a successful greyhound.

Watlington Hill, Oxfordshire

KENCOT MANOR FARM *5 miles south of Burford* A small early seven-teenth-century house in two and a half acres (not open).

———

SOUTH LEIGH *2½ miles east of Witney* Two seventeenth-century cottages (not open).

———

STREATLEY *north of the town* Downland on LARDON CHASE and on LOUGH DOWN which forms part of the same hill top and has views over the Chilterns and the Thames. (On Oxfordshire–Berkshire border.)

———

Watlington Hill

a mile south-east of Watlington

Watlington Hill (opposite), in the Chilterns, part open down and part coppice, commands fine views of Oxfordshire. The Trust was given over a hundred acres of the hill in 1941 and 1957 by the Hon. Lionel Brett, now the fourth Lord Esher, and his father and mother who also gave 150 acres of beech woods surrounding Watlington Park, a mile to the south.

———

SALOP

Attingham Park

4 miles south-east of Shrewsbury on the north side of A5

At Attingham (pages 270–1) the house and park result from two exercises in late Georgian elegance. First, the building of the house by the first Lord Berwick and the architect George Steuart; second, the planning of the park and additions to the house by Nash and Humphry Repton for the second Lord Berwick. George Steuart was commissioned to design a house that would, among other things, look impressive when seen from the road beyond the park. So Attingham, which was built with exceptional speed between 1783 and 1785, has giant columns to the portico of the main block, and extends for nearly four hundred feet between the pavilions at either end.

Attingham Park, Shropshire

Nash's contribution to the house was to fill in part of the courtyard to make the picture gallery (opposite). In doing this he made use of a building technique which in 1807 was a novelty—the glazed roof of the gallery has a frame of cast iron.

The internal decoration of the house is most impressive, with its elegant chimney-pieces, pier-glasses, scagliola columns in the hall and expert

Attingham Park, Shropshire: the picture gallery

plasterwork in the ceilings of the principal rooms. These rooms also contain pictures and furniture of interest.

Two important Roman roads cross the estate which occupies part of the site of Viroconium.

Attingham was left to the Trust by the eighth Lord Berwick, who died in 1947. Most of the house has been leased to the Shropshire County Council as a College of Adult Education.

⟶ ◦ ◦

CRONKHILL *between Atcham and Cross Houses* The first Italianate villa to be built in England. Designed about 1803 by John Nash. Access by appointment only.

⟶ ◦ ◦

Benthall Hall

4 miles north-east of Much Wenlock

From the outside, Benthall is a good example of sixteenth-century domestic architecture. It is built largely of brick faced with ashlar stone, and with its

Benthall Hall, Shropshire: the early seventeenth-century staircase

gables and moulded brick chimney-stacks makes a pleasing appearance. Records of its building have been lost, but it was probably first built in about 1538 and then altered later in the century. These alterations may have been prompted by a desire to provide hiding-places for priests, for the house contains several. There is no history of these having been used, but the Benthall family were Roman Catholics.

Improvements were made inside the house in the seventeenth century: the dining-room was panelled and a fine staircase (opposite) installed, its large newel posts carrying carvings of grotesque heads.

Benthall stands high above the River Severn within a mile of the Severn Gorge. During the Civil War it was first held for two years for the King by Lawrence Benthall, then surprised and taken by Parliamentary forces, who used it as a base from which to prevent supplies being carried by river to the Royalists in Worcester and Bridgnorth. The house does not seem to have suffered during these military operations, but outbuildings were destroyed.

In 1844 the house was sold to a neighbouring estate and occupied till 1934 by various tenants. One of them, the botanist George Maw, author of *The Genus Crocus*, planted many rare plants in the garden, and some of his uncommon crocus plants naturalized and still flower there. In 1934 a descendant of the builders bought back the house, and in 1958 she gave it to the Trust, other members of the Benthall family providing endowment.

———— ⇀ ⌐ ————

HOPESAY HILL *3 miles west of Craven Arms*   A hundred and thirty acres let as a sheep walk. There is a footpath.

———— ⇀ ⌐ ————

The Long Mynd

15 miles south of Shrewsbury

The modern wayfarer on these magnificent and ancient moorlands can, like those before him, enjoy superb views to the Black Mountains in Breconshire, or across Salop or the Cheshire plain. The Portway, the track which runs the length of the crest of the Long Mynd, is believed to be older even than the barrows which stand beside it.

The Trust owns 4,500 acres here (page 274) which was bought by public subscription in 1965. A further 650 acres to the south of it, Minton Hill, were added shortly afterwards.

———— ⇀ ⌐ ————

MORVILLE HALL *3 miles west of Bridgnorth*   An Elizabethan house with eighteenth-century additions. Access is by appointment.

———— ⇀ ⌐ ————

The Long Mynd, Shropshire: above Carding Mill valley looking north-east

SHREWSBURY: TOWN WALLS TOWER *south side of the town* The last remaining watch tower, overlooking the Severn. Built in the fourteenth century. Not open.

———⊶ ⊷———

Wilderhope Manor

7 miles south-west of Much Wenlock, a half-mile south of B4371

Wilderhope (opposite) is a limestone building of about 1585 with contemporary plaster ceilings, standing on the southern slope of Wenlock Edge in remote, wooded country. It was built by a local family called Smallman who occupied it until 1742. It later changed hands a number of times but was not enlarged or altered to any extent. At the time that it was given to the

Wilderhope Manor, Shropshire

Trust (1936) by the W. A. Cadbury Trust, extensive repairs were carried out. It has been leased to the Youth Hostels Association but is open to visitors.

In 1971, Mr and Mrs John Cadbury gave the two-hundred-acre Wilderhope Manor Farm.

SOMERSET

Trust properties formerly in the north of Somerset are now in the new county of Avon.

AXBRIDGE: KING JOHN'S HUNTING LODGE *corner of the Square* A merchant's house of about 1500 and now a local museum.

Barrington Court, Somerset: the south front

Barrington Court

3 miles north-east of Ilminster, east end of Barrington

Architectural historians point to Barrington (above) as an exceptionally fine example of English domestic architecture of the sixteenth and seventeenth centuries and, since it was built so early in the period (in 1514–20) it is probably a prototype. Its general plan, so far as domestic arrangements are concerned, follows that of the traditional medieval manor-house; but all the defensive features of a fortified manor-house were omitted. The experts see some French influence in the beautiful spiral chimneys and the sculptured finials which top the vertical lines of the building and provide decorative features of the exterior.

That there should be a trace of French influence about these details is not surprising. The man who had Barrington built, the second Lord Daubeney, had soldiered in France and had very likely been in Paris while his father was ambassador there. The house is made of the local golden stone from Ham Hill. Adjoining it is a brick stable block built in 1670. The extensive formal gardens were laid out by Gertrude Jekyll.

Barrington has had its ups and downs in the hands of a number of different owners. During the nineteenth century it was a farmhouse and

276

allowed to become dilapidated. It was bought for the Trust in 1907 and after the 1914–18 war the late Colonel A. A. Lyle, whose son now rents and maintains it, rehabilitated the house and installed oak panelling and other interior fittings which he had obtained from derelict houses.

BLACKDOWN HILLS *2 miles south of Wellington, a half-mile east of the Wellington–Hemyock road* Sixty acres giving clear-weather views across the Bristol Channel of the Welsh hills. Also, half a mile west of this, is the Wellington Monument, an obelisk of 1817 commemorating the duke's exploits.

BREAN DOWN—see AVON

BROOMFIELD HILL *6 miles north of Taunton (110 acres).*

BRUTON DOVECOTE *about half a mile south of Bruton* A sixteenth-century roofless dovecote.

CHEDDAR CLIFFS *8 miles north-west of Wells.* The Trust has been acquiring land here at intervals since 1910 and its holdings now amount to about 320 acres. Some of this land is on the north side of the gorge and some on the west side. Part is managed by the Somerset Trust for Nature Conservation as land of special scientific interest, and there is a circular nature-walk at the head of the Gorge.

COLERIDGE COTTAGE: NETHER STOWEY *8 miles west of Bridgwater.* This is where Coleridge wrote 'The Ancient Mariner'.

EBBOR GORGE *3 miles north-west of Wells* A wooded limestone gorge in the Mendip Hills. Most of this was given by Mrs G. W. Hodgkinson in memory of Sir Winston Churchill. It is leased to the Nature Conservancy, and there is access by footpaths, and two nature walks.

Selworthy, Somerset: looking south towards Dunkery

Exmoor

HOLNICOTE ESTATE and DUNKERY *east and south of Porlock* The Trust's vast estate here includes nearly seven thousand acres of the Moor, Dunkery and Selworthy Beacons, four miles of coast, thirty farms and the greater parts of nine villages and hamlets, including the picturesque village of Selworthy (above)—twelve thousand acres in all. There is a three-mile circular nature walk at Cloutsham.

LAND BY TARR STEPS $1\frac{1}{2}$ *miles south-west of Winsford Hill* The old clapper bridge does not belong to the Trust, but two acres nearby on the left bank of the Barle were leased to the Trust in 1918.

WINSFORD HILL AND SOUTH HILL *between Exford and Dulverton*
About 1400 acres of moorland including the Caratacus Stone and a group
of Bronze Age barrows.

———

Glastonbury

GLASTONBURY TOR *just east of Glastonbury* The trust owns the top
sixty acres of this famous hill where a church tower—the remains of a
fifteenth-century church—stands. There are views over the Vale of Avalon.

WEST PENNARD COURT BARN *3 miles east of Glastonbury* A fifteenth-
century barn with a roof of interesting construction.

———

Lytes Cary

2½ miles south-east of Somerton, west of A37

Lytes Cary (page 280) is a stone-built manor-house with an added appeal to
those interested in the history of gardening.

The house was not built all at one time but grew over quite a long period.
The principal features are the fourteenth-century chapel adjoining the house,
the Great Hall of about 1450, the Great Chamber of 1533 which has a fine
plasterwork ceiling, and the Great Parlour which has early seventeenth-
century panelling.

The house was built by the Lyte family, who owned the property from the
thirteenth century until the eighteenth.

Henry Lyte, who took over the house when his father retired to London
in 1558, made a botanic garden here and in 1578 published his *Niewe
Herball*, a translation from the Flemish which became a best-seller in the
following thirty years. No trace of his botanic garden has survived, but during
the last sixty years a beautiful garden in the Elizabethan style with lawns,
clipped hedges and topiary has been established in its place. The Lytes
sold the house about 1760, and during the nineteenth century it came to be
neglected. But it was bought and restored in 1907 by Sir Walter Jenner
(son of the Victorian physician), who laid out the present garden. He died
in 1948 leaving the property to the Trust in his will.

———

Lytes Cary, Somerset

MARTOCK: THE TREASURER'S HOUSE *between Ilminster and Ilchester a mile north of A303* Formerly the dwelling of the Treasurer of Wells Cathe-dral. A small thirteenth- or fourteenth-century house, well preserved. Access is to the fine medieval Great Hall and kitchen only.

———— ⌒ ⌒ ————

Montacute

in Montacute village, 4 miles west of Yeovil, north of A3088

Montacute (opposite) is an outstandingly good example of an Elizabethan house, and the few changes made since it was built have not altered its character.

Montacute, Somerset: the west front

It is a tall, symmetrical house in Ham Hill stone with large windows, and makes a brave show—as it was intended to do. The interior is decorated with plaster friezes, heraldic glass and handsome chimney-pieces.

The architect has not been definitely identified, but a good deal of evidence points to William Arnold, a Somerset mason, who later designed Wadham College, Oxford, and had a hand in the building of several houses in the west country.

In 1590, when the house was built, the Montacute property belonged to Sir Edward Phelips, a local man whose family had acquired it after the dissolution of the monasteries. He had the money and the ambition to build a fine house. He had already made money at the Bar, and went on to be Speaker of the House of Commons and Master of the Rolls.

Montacute remained in the possession of the Phelips family until 1931, when they sold it, and it was given to the Trust by Mr E. E. Cook through the Society for the Protection of Ancient Buildings.

In 1931 it was very sparsely furnished, but in recent years, handsome additions have been made with gifts and loans of paintings, tapestries and furniture.

There is a fine formal garden with ancient yew hedges and shrub borders. The property includes part of the village, and three hundred acres.

———

MUCHELNEY: PRIEST'S HOUSE 1½ *miles south of Langport* A fourteenth-century stone-built house with a large Gothic hall window.

———

The Quantocks

Besides Coleridge Cottage (q.v.) the Trust has four small properties here. There are fine views from two of these—the sixty acres of moorland on LONGSTONE HILL, *west of Holford*, and SHERVAGE WOOD *two miles west of Nether Stowey* with 130 acres of oak and woodland. At WILLOUGHBY CLEEVE ½ *mile west of Holford* there are eighty acres of wood, farm and moorland and, at HOLFORD FIELDS *3 miles west of Nether Stowey*, twenty acres of pasture and orchard.

———

Sedgemoor

In this area the Trust has five excellent viewpoints and a windmill.

BURROW MUMP 1½ *miles north-east of Athelney Station*   Land on an isolated hill giving views all round. Given as a 1939–45 war memorial. On the summit is an unfinished eighteenth-century chapel built on the site of a small Norman castle.

COCK HILL *half-way between Bridgwater and Glastonbury* Three-quarters of an acre of the crest of the Polden Hills.

HIGH HAM: THE MILL *2 miles north of Langport* An early nineteenth-century thatched windmill, in use up till 1910.

IVYTHORN and WALTON HILLS *a mile south of Street* Ninety acres of high land and wood.

RED HILL *3 miles west of Langport*   Land on a hill top on the south edge of Sedgemoor, giving fine views of Glastonbury Tor.

TURN HILL *4 miles north of Langport*   Looking across the battlefield of Sedgemoor to the Quantocks.

Stoke-sub-Hamdon Priory

between Yeovil and Ilminster, 2 miles west of Montacute

Stone buildings of the fourteenth and fifteenth centuries. They were the residence of the priests of a nearby chantry. The hall of the chantry house is open.

Tintinhull House

5 miles north-west of Yeovil on the eastern outskirts of Tintinhull

Tintinhull House is a fine, small house in a beautiful, formal garden. The layout of the latter was begun after 1900, and from 1933 onwards the late Captain F. E. Reiss and Mrs Reiss developed and improved it. It is a small garden where carefully placed trees and hedges provide a variety of delightful garden views. It contains a wide assortment of plants chosen and planted to ensure that every area is beautiful throughout the year.

Tintinhull House, Somerset: the west front

The house is of dressed Ham Hill stone with a roof of local stone tiles. It was built about 1600 but around 1700 was given a new, more charming and elegant west front, with a pediment.

Mrs Reiss, who died in 1961, had given Tintinhull to the Trust in 1953.

———

WELLS: TOR HILL *just east of the city and east of the Shepton Mallet road* There are views from here of the cathedral and surrounding country.

———

SOUTH YORKSHIRE

Derwent Estate

13 miles west and north-west of Sheffield

A six-thousand-acre estate in the Peak District National Park. Some of the estate is in Derbyshire. Deeply undulating moorland rising to 1,775 ft. Given by the Treasury, which had accepted it in lieu of death duty.

———

STAFFORDSHIRE

Originally in Staffordshire, Wightwick Manor is now in the new county of West Midlands (see page 322).

DOWNS BANK *1½ miles north of Stone, south-east of Barlaston* Moorland with a stream, given as a war memorial in 1946 after a local appeal (*160 acres*).

———

HAWKSMOOR *1½ miles north-east of Cheadle* 270 acres of woodland, open space, and Eastwall Farm beside the River Churnet. The local management committee has established three separate nature walks on the property.

———

KINVER EDGE *4 miles west of Stourbridge* Two hundred acres of heath and woodland given as a family memorial in 1917. The site of an Iron Age pro-

284

montory fort, there are also cave dwellings which were inhabited in the seventeenth century and up to 1900.

LETOCETUM *at Wall, on the A5, 2 miles south-west of Lichfield* The remains of a Roman posting station on Watling Street near the intersection with Ryknild Street. The bath house now belongs to the Trust and has been excavated. There is a museum and the site is under the guardianship of the Department of the Environment.

MANIFOLD and HAMPS VALLEYS: *see under Derbyshire: Dovedale illus-trations and accompanying text.*

In addition to property noted in the Derbyshire entry referred to above, the Trust has another Manifold Valley property at Apes Tor, the north entrance to the Gorge. This rockface forms part of Ecton Hill and is of particular geological interest. A nature trail is in operation in the Staffordshire part of the property.

Moseley Old Hall

4 miles north of Wolverhampton between the Penkridge and Cannock roads west of A460

Moseley Old Hall (page 286) is one of the houses in which Charles II hid while he was a fugitive after the battle of Worcester. It stands on the edge of Cannock Chase and was then very isolated. The King arrived from Boscobel early on 8th September 1651 and stayed till the evening of the 9th. He was received by Lord Wilmot, who was in hiding, Thomas Whitgreave, to whose family the hall belonged, and John Huddlestone, a priest who was living there in the guise of tutor to Whitgreave's nephews. There are three accounts of his visit, one given by the King himself to Pepys and the others written by Whitgreave and Huddlestone. Whitgreave's loyalty was rewarded in 1666 by the grant of an annuity.

The hall was built in 1600, a black-and-white building of oak beams and plaster. In 1870, when the timber was in need of extensive repair, it was encased in brick. Inside there is oak panelling, and in the King's Bedroom the four-poster bed in which Charles slept. By the fireplace in this room is the secret hiding-place in which, at a pinch, two people can crouch.

Moseley Old Hall, Staffordshire

The Whitgreaves let the hall as a farm during the nineteenth century, and it continued as one till 1940. In that year Mr Wiggin bought it and began much-needed renovation. He died before he could complete the task, but his holding operation made preservation possible. His widow gave the hall to the Trust in 1962. The Wolverhampton National Trust Centre and Staffordshire County Council have provided funds for maintenance by appeal and grant. The King's Bed, which had remained in the hall until 1935, was bought by the late Sir Geoffrey Mander and returned to the hall when the renovations had been finished. More recently the garden has been remade to a seventeenth-century pattern and stocked with plants in cultivation in that century.

Shugborough

5½ miles south-east of Stafford on A513

Shugborough (opposite) grew to its present size and was given its splendidly decorated principal rooms in three stages. First, William Anson built a square three-storey block in the 1690s; this forms the centre of the building.

Shugborough,
Staffordshire

Shugborough,
Staffordshire:
the dining-room

Then in the eighteenth century two immensely knowledgeable patrons, employing distinguished architects, made extensive additions and alterations. First, in the middle of the century Thomas Anson added to the house and employed James Stuart to erect the remarkable buildings in the park. In the 1790s Thomas William Anson (later created Viscount Anson) employed Samuel Wyatt to make further alterations and additions.

The principal rooms contain a variety of interesting French and English furniture, china, busts, tapestry and paintings.

The Thomas Anson who made the mid-eighteenth-century additions at Shugborough was the elder brother of the famous Admiral Lord Anson. The admiral was a wealthy man and probably helped to finance his brother's projects. Dying childless, he left his brother his heir. So it is fitting that one of the garden monuments can be taken as commemorating the admiral. It is a Chinese garden house built from sketches brought back by one of the officers who accompanied him on his eventful four-year voyage round the world. It is one of the major focal points of the extensive grounds which include a Victorian-style rose garden, and beautiful trees and shrubs. The grounds are enclosed by an arm of the River Trent.

The house, park and contents were accepted by the Treasury in part payment of death duties on the death of the fourth Earl of Lichfield, and in 1966 were transferred to the Trust. They have been leased to the Staffordshire County Council, who have now established a county museum in the stable block.

SUFFOLK

BUNGAY: OUTNEY COMMON   In the loop made by the River Waveney are six 'goings' or rights of pasturage on this five-hundred-acre common.

—⊃ ⊂—

BURY ST EDMUNDS: ANGEL CORNER *on Angel Hill*   An eighteenth-century house in which the Gershom-Parkington collection of clocks and watches is housed.

—⊃ ⊂—

DUNWICH HEATH *about half a mile from Dunwich, south of the road from Westleton*   Two hundred acres of cliff and heath with a mile of beach. Bought in 1968 with money given to Enterprise Neptune by the H. J. Heinz Company Ltd.

—⊃ ⊂—

Flatford Mill

10 miles south-west of Ipswich, a mile south of East Bergholt

Flatford is the mill depicted in Constable's 'Hay Wain' and other of his pictures. The mill, millhouse and Willy Lott's cottage were built in the eighteenth century and belonged to his father. Constable himself worked in the mill for about a year.

The Trust bought the mill in 1943 but was reimbursed some years later by a benefactor.

The mill, some land, and a nearby half-timbered building of the fifteenth century are let to the Field Studies Council and used by them as a Field Study Centre.

Flatford Mill, Suffolk

Ickworth

3 miles south-west of Bury St Edmunds on west side of A143

Ickworth (pages 291–2) was built on a most unusual plan. Generous in size, the central portion is a lofty rotunda, and curved corridors lead from this to the two wings. The height of the rotunda is a hundred feet and the length of the whole building two hundred yards.

This plan was devised by a remarkable man, Frederick Augustus Hervey, Bishop of Derry, who became Earl of Bristol in succession to his brother in 1779. He was an enthusiastic traveller and collector of works of art—such a well-known traveller that many of the Hotels Bristol in continental countries are named after him. It was his intention that one wing should contain pictures, the other sculpture, and that the rotunda be used as living quarters. But he did not live to finish the house (he began it in 1794 and died in Italy in 1803) and his son, who finished the building, changed the internal arrangement. He made the East Wing his residence and furnished the rooms in the rotunda as entertaining rooms.

Although the marble group which the earl-bishop commissioned from Flaxman stands in the entrance hall, his art collection did not all find its way to Ickworth. He had assembled much of it in Rome, and this was confiscated after 1798 when the French invaded Italy. But other members of the Hervey family, both before and since his time, accumulated furniture, porcelain and, notably, silver of the highest quality; so Ickworth, as he intended, houses magnificent collections. The paintings include a Velasquez portrait of a son of Philip IV of Spain and family portraits by Reynolds, Gainsborough, Angelica Kauffmann and other famous artists. Among the subjects of these portraits are the famous beauty and wit, Molly Leppell, who was the bishop's mother, and Lady Elizabeth Foster, later Duchess of Devonshire, who was his daughter.

The house stands in a setting of magnificent beeches, cypresses and cedars.

It was acquired by the Trust in 1956, having been accepted by the Treasury in part payment of death duties.

KYSON HILL *three-quarters of a mile south of Woodbridge* Four acres of parkland overlooking the River Deben.

Ickworth, Suffolk: the north portico

Ickworth, Suffolk: the dining-room

Lavenham: the Guildhall

in the Market Square

Lavenham Guildhall (below) was built in the 1520s by the Guild of Corpus Christi. This was a trade guild, concerned with the wool trade which had flourished in Suffolk for two centuries, but also concerned to celebrate the festivals of the Church. On feast days they processed from their fine half-timbered hall to church or—as, for example, at Corpus Christi—held their celebration in the hall.

But the guild did not long survive the suppression of the religious houses, and before the end of the century their Guildhall had become parish property.

Through most of the seventeenth century it was used as the town hall. Thereafter it became at different times a prison, a workhouse and a wool store.

Although the inside suffered from these vicissitudes and not much of the original panelling and carving has survived, the outside remains a good example of the rather ornate style of half-timbered building in fashion under Henry VIII.

It was rescued in 1887 by Sir Cuthbert Quilter, who undertook the repair

The Guildhall, Lavenham, Suffolk

of the building, and in 1951 his son, with the aid of the Lavenham Preservation Committee, gave it to the Trust.

Funds for upkeep were raised by a local appeal supported by the Pilgrim
Trust, and it is now used by Lavenham for public meetings and other social
activities.

—◦ ◦—

Melford Hall

3 miles north of Sudbury in Long Melford

In the Middle Ages Melford (below) belonged to the abbots of Bury St
Edmunds. After the dissolution of the monasteries it was granted to William
Cordell, a local man who became Speaker of the House of Commons and
later Master of the Rolls. He built virtually a new house, though incorporating in it some parts of the old one. When exactly it was built and who
was employed on the work is not known. But presumably it was finished by
1578 because in that year Cordell entertained Queen Elizabeth at Melford
and did so, according to contemporary accounts, most sumptuously.
Although the inside has been much altered since her visit, the outside must

Melford Hall, Suffolk

have appeared to Elizabeth very much as the attractive brick manor-house one sees today.

The internal changes and additions were made at two different periods. In the 1730s and 40s the Elizabethan screens in the hall were replaced by Doric columns, a large staircase was introduced and the hall redecorated. At this period the Blue Drawing Room was given a carved wood chimney-piece and an ornamented ceiling of mid-Georgian style. Then in 1813 a library was added, fitted with Regency bookcases and furnished with chairs and tables designed for the room.

The contents of the house, which are varied and interesting, reflect something of its history and that of the families who have been its owners. The andirons in the Hall probably belonged to the earlier monastic house, perhaps to the twelfth-century abbot. William Cordell had them remounted and added his crest. Beside them are two Nonsuch chests, so called because of the illustrations of Nonsuch Palace which decorate them; reputedly a gift to her host from the visiting Queen Elizabeth. Other rooms contain fine furniture and family portraits of the Parker family. The house was bought by Sir Harry Parker in 1786 and remained in the ownership of the family until 1960, when it was accepted by the Treasury in part payment of death duties and given to the Trust. Sir Harry devoted himself to the administration of the estate. His father, brother and nephew, all named Hyde Parker, were all admirals of gallantry and distinction. In the Library are paintings of their actions, executed by Dominique Serves, marine painter to George III, and charts used by them in engagements in which they took part. The second Admiral Hyde Parker was knighted for forcing the boom in the attack on New York in 1776. Later he was in command at the battle of Copenhagen, and it was to a signal from him that Nelson turned a blind eye.

THORINGTON HALL *2 miles south-east of Stoke-by-Nayland* An oak-framed gabled house of about 1600, though extended later. There are also some farm buildings (not open).

295

SURREY

ABINGER HAMMER *about 4 miles west of Dorking on A25* The two properties here are Piney Copse, a four acre wood left to the Trust by E. M. Forster, and Abinger Roughs, just north of the A25; 270 acres on a wooded ridge with Hackhurst farm adjoining.

⟶ ⟞ ⟝ ⟵

BLACKHEATH *a half-mile south of Chilworth Station, south of A25* Twenty acres of heather and pine.

⟶ ⟞ ⟝ ⟵

BOOKHAM and BANKS COMMONS *2½ miles west of Leatherhead* An area of richly wooded common, of particular ornithological interest. It includes a cottage and roadside verges in Little Bookham, and manorial rights in Great Bookham Common (*450 acres*).

⟶ ⟞ ⟝ ⟵

Box Hill

a mile north of Dorking

The Trust has been accumulating parts of Box Hill (opposite) since 1914 when the late Mr L. Salomons, who then lived at Norbury Park near by, made a gift of 230 acres, including the summit. A number of other donors have made gifts at various dates since, and in 1974 the Trust owned 840 acres of the down and woodland of the hill and holds protective covenants over another 280 acres. (See note in Introduction.)

It is a fine picnic place and much used as such—so much used, in fact, that after a sunny week-end there may be several tons of litter for the Trust to clear.

The hill is of great interest to students of natural history, partly because it is an area of chalk down where the plant life is not disturbed by agricultural activities. Juniper Hall (on the westward slope of the hill near Mickleham) is let to the Field Studies Council.

There has been some speculation as to when box trees first grew on the hill. It was at least as early as 1655, which is the date of a note about them in John Evelyn's diary. The wooded western flank, where on the most steeply sloping parts only box and yew can maintain a hold, is exceptionally

Box Hill, Surrey

beautiful. Seventy acres of Mickleham Downs, adjoining the Box Hill
property, were given by Lord Beaverbrook in 1938; and West Humble
Chapel, a ruined twelfth-century chapel near Box Hill Station, was given in
the same year by Cubitt Estates Ltd.

CHURCH COBHAM: CEDAR HOUSE *on north side of A245 overlooking
the Mole* A fifteenth-century building altered and enlarged in the seventeenth and eighteenth centuries. It is let.

Clandon Park, Surrey: the entrance hall

Clandon Park

Clandon was built about 1730 by the Venetian architect Leoni for the second Baron Onslow. It is constructed in red brick, the west front faced in stone. The only change made to the exterior since it was built was the addition in 1876 of a porch to the front door. The original magnificent plasterwork, for which Clandon is famous, decorates the ceilings of the two-storey entrance hall (opposite) and of other rooms. Changes were made in the decoration of some of the rooms in the latter part of the eighteenth century, during the period when the Adam style was in fashion, and gilt mirrors, cut-glass chandeliers and flock wallpapers were introduced.

The rooms contain fine eighteenth-century furniture, French and English, Mortlake tapestry and some interesting portraits. Among these are portraits of three members of the Onslow family who have been Speakers of the House of Commons.

The Lord Onslow who employed Leoni to build the present house had married a wealthy heiress, the daughter of a well-known Jamaica family. It was her money which helped her husband to carry out his building plans. A full-length portrait of her hangs in the Palladio Room.

Clandon was given to the Trust in 1956 by the Countess of Iveagh, a daughter of the fourth Earl of Onslow.

Between 1968 and 1970 the house was redecorated under the direction of Mr John Fowler. This redecoration was made possible by a gift from Mr Kenneth Levy of £75,000 on the occasion of the Trust's 75th anniversary. At the same time the very remarkable collection of furniture and china bequeathed to the Trust by Mrs David Gubbay was installed at Clandon.

The park does not belong to the Trust and is not open.

ESHER: CLAREMONT *on the south edge of Esher on the east side of A3* Fifty acres of garden originally landscaped around a lake by William Kent about 1730, and part of the grounds of Claremont House (which is not a Trust property). Managed by Esher U.D.C.

FRENSHAM COMMON *about half-way between Farnham and Hindhead, astride the A287* Nine hundred acres of heathland including Frensham Great Pond and some large bowl-barrows. Part of this is now a County Park.

Godalming

EASHING BRIDGES *3 miles west of Godalming* A medieval bridge in two parts over the River Wey.

NOS. 116–122 OCKFORD ROAD *in Godalming* Given in 1925 to show how old cottages could be modernized.

HAMBLEDON *3 miles south of Godalming* Some land near the church and Glebe House (not open).

HYDON'S BALL and HYDON HEATH *3 miles south of Godalming* Heath and woodland with views from the 593-ft summit (*125 acres*).

SANDHILLS COMMON ½ *mile west of Witley Station* Eleven acres of common.

WINKWORTH ARBORETUM *3 miles south-east of Godalming on the east side of B2130* A hillside planted with rare trees and shrubs and maintained by the Surrey, Hambledon and Godalming Councils (*95 acres*).

WITLEY AND MILFORD COMMONS *about 3 miles south-west of Godalming between A3 and A286* Common acquired in the 1920s (*240 acres*).

Guildford

SHALFORD MILL *1½ miles south of Guildford* An eighteenth-century water mill on the Tillingbourne. Given by Ferguson's Gang, anonymous bene-factors who also gave property in the Isle of Wight and elsewhere.

WEIR HOUSE *on the Wey at Millmead* Probably built in the middle of the eighteenth century and added to in the nineteenth century (not open).

HACKHURST DOWN *a half-mile north-east of Gomshall & Shere Station* Thirteen acres on the south slope of the North Downs with views over the Tillingbourne Valley. Managed in conjunction with the Surrey Naturalists' Trust as part of a nature reserve.

HASLEMERE: SWAN BARN FARM *on the east edge of Haslemere* Seventy acres of farm and woodland.

Hatchlands

just east of East Clandon, north of the Guildford–Leatherhead road

Hatchlands is a mid-Georgian house, and its interior decoration is among the earliest work known to have been done by Robert Adam after his return from Italy. His drawings (e.g. below) for this, dated 1759 and entitled *Designs for Admiral the Hon. E. Boscawen*, are in the Soane Museum.

There is no record of who designed the building, but it is known from their correspondence that the admiral and his wife had been making plans for some years to build a house at Hatchlands. It had a very unusual internal plan. The main block was partly divided into two storeys, partly into three and partly into four, with staircases arranged to make this multiplicity of floors a workable proposition. Perhaps the late Mr Goodhart-Rendel was right when he described this plan in the Trust guide-book as '. . . a very ingenious piece of packing which I like to think was the work of the admiral himself, aided by his talented and adorable wife'. The admiral received a substantial sum of money for defeating the French at Louisberg in 1758. He used this for building the house, and it is described in the epitaph his wife wrote as 'a seat he had just finished at the expense of the enemies of his country'. But the admiral did not live long to enjoy his new house, dying of fever there in 1761. His widow sold the property some years later and it changed hands again in the nineteenth century. Internal and external alterations have been made at various dates. Robert Adam's work remains in the drawing-room, library and morning-room.

Hatchlands was given to the Trust by the late Mr Goodhart-Rendel in 1945.

———— ◁ ▷ ————

Hatchlands, Surrey: Robert Adam's drawing for one of the chimney-pieces

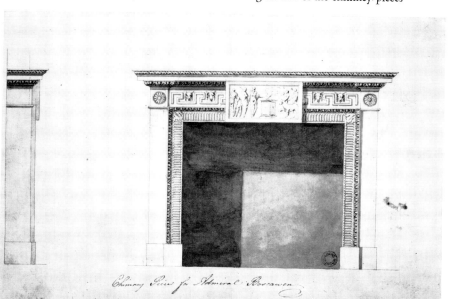

Chimney Piece for Admiral Boscawen

Headley Heath

4 miles south of Epsom and 3½ miles south-east of Leatherhead

Headley Heath (below) is near the north-east side of Box Hill, on the north downs; an open space of nearly five hundred acres with wide-ranging views. There are rides as well as footpaths. Here, as in many other parts of the country, the Trust receives much welcome help in maintenance from volunteers. The photograph below was taken when Surrey Scouts and Rangers, in conjunction with the Council for Nature's Conservation Corps, were making a carefully planned assault on the birch scrub which had become a threat to the heath.

The heath, including the lordship of Headley Manor, was given to the Trust, with some wayside strips in Headley village and Heath Plantation, twenty-three acres to the south, between 1946 and 1952.

Headley Heath, Surrey: Surrey Scouts and Rangers clearing birch scrub

Hindhead, Surrey: looking north from Gibbet Hill

Hindhead

12 miles south-west of Guildford

Gibbet Hill, from which the photograph above was taken, is to the east of Hindhead village. It is nearly nine hundred feet high and a good viewpoint, with a two-mile nature walk.

The Trust owns a thousand acres of connected common, heath and woodland in this area. The greater part of it was given in 1906 by the Hindhead Preservation Committee, and other donors added further land at later dates. These later properties include Nutcombe Down, Tyndall Wood and Craig's Wood, totalling a hundred acres of heath and woodland; thirty acres of woodland at Polecat Copse; five acres at Stoatley Green near Haslemere Station; a hundred acres of wood and heath at Woodcock Bottom; Stony Jump, thirty acres of heather-clad hill; and Whitmore Vale, fifty acres of wood, heath and pasture running down to Whitmore Bottom.

303

HOLMWOOD COMMON *a mile south of Dorking* Six hundred acres, much of it wooded. Given by the County Council and other local councils, with funds for maintenance.

———

Leith Hill

north-west of A29, west of A24, south of A25

The top of Leith Hill is four and a half miles south-west from Dorking Parish Church as the crow flies. At 965 ft it is the highest point in the south-east of England and the Tower, which Richard Hull built in 1766, puts it well over the thousand-foot mark. It is a splendid viewing point as he intended. In addition to a few acres here on the summit, the Trust owns, within two and a half miles of the Tower, the woods of Leith Hill Place (the house is not open), woodland at Friday Street, and 250 acres of the heath and woodland just north of the summit, including Mosses Wood, and Duke's Warren which contains a source of the Tillingbourne.

———

Limpsfield Common

south-east of Limpsfield

350 acres of common land given to the Trust by Major R. H. Leveson-Gower, the Lord of the Manor, in 1972. He had told local residents that he would make the gift to any competent body acceptable to them. They agreed on the Trust and launched an appeal which in nine months received £72,000 for an endowment fund. The property includes West Heath, The Chart, Little Heath and Moorhouse Bank Common, and lies on the green-sand ridge south-west of Oxted, extending to the county boundary.

———

LITTLE KINGS WOOD *on south escarpment of North Downs above Gomshall* Sixty acres of mixed woodland. No road, but footpaths and the North Downs Way on the northern boundary of the property.

———

NETLEY PARK *at east end of Shere, on both sides of A25* Two hundred acres going up nearly to the ridge of the Downs. A farm, woodland and a house which is let to the Holiday Fellowship.

Polesden Lacy

3 miles north-west of Dorking, 2½ miles south of Bookham Station

Polesden Lacey stands in the beautiful surroundings of its own lawns, trees and garden with views of the fine woods on Ranmore.

From 1906 until she died in 1942 the house belonged to the Hon. Mrs Ronald Greville, who entertained many distinguished guests there. She completely redecorated the interior of the house and furnished it with fine collections of pictures and furniture, some of which she had inherited from

Polesden Lacey, Surrey: from the east

her father but most of which she collected herself while at Polesden. There is much variety in the style of decoration chosen for the different rooms. The drawing-room sparkles elegantly, with a gilded ceiling brought from an Italian palazzo; the corridor around the central courtyard is panelled in Jacobean style; the library is neo-Grecian. The contents of the rooms, too, are varied. They include interesting pieces of French furniture of the Louis XV and Louis XVI periods, Flemish and Italian seventeenth-century chairs, Chippendale chairs, Dresden and Fürstenberg china, Chinese seventeenth- and eighteenth-century porcelain and pictures of English, Dutch and Italian schools. In sum, the gardens, house and collections at Polesden fulfil completely the wish that Mrs Greville expressed when she bequeathed the property to the Trust, namely that the grounds should be open to the public and that the house should become a museum and picture gallery.

Polesden Lacey, Surrey: the drawing-room

The house which Mrs Greville acquired in 1906 had been built in 1824 on the site of an earlier house destroyed by fire. The main part of the south front, with its fine colonnade, remains as in 1824. But the entrance front was altered and given its cupola later in the century.

For a few years around 1800 Richard Brinsley Sheridan lived at Polesden in the house that was later burned. He made an important contribution to the charms of the present Polesden by completing and lengthening the long terraced beech walk from which there are views to Ranmore woods. The fine formal layout includes a rose garden, herbaceous borders and trees and spacious lawns.

RANMORE COMMON *2 miles north-west of Dorking* Common land adjoining the southern boundary of the Trust's Polesden Lacey estate. It amounts to 420 acres and is partly wooded. Next to it, on the southern slopes of the North Downs, the Trust has another 245 acres, known as Denbies.

Reigate

On the North Downs immediately above Reigate, there are a number of small properties amounting together to about 150 acres of down, copse and beechwood on the escarpment and on the top of the Downs. There are views and good walking. Other properties near Reigate are:

BLETCHINGLEY: SANDHILLS ESTATE *3 miles east of Reigate* Farm and woodland south of the village (*430 acres*).

BROCKHAM: THE BIG FIELD *4 miles west of Reigate* A fifty-acre field given anonymously and primarily for recreational use.

GATTON *1½ miles north-east of Reigate* Two hundred acres on the north slopes of the North Downs, on the west side of Gatton Park. Half woodland and half park.

HAREWOODS *5 miles south-west of Reigate, 2½ miles south of Bletchingley* A two-thousand-acre estate of farms and woodland which includes Outwood Common. Limited access by public footpaths.

PARK DOWNS *about 5 miles north of Reigate, a mile south-east of Banstead* Common rights over a seventy-acre open space, which belongs to Banstead U.D.C., were conveyed to the Trust in 1914.

SIX BROTHERS FIELD *about 5 miles north-east of Reigate, between Merstham and Caterham, just south of Chaldon* Land given in memory of William and Andrew Harman by their four brothers and used as a sports ground.

The River Wey Navigation

from Guildford to the Thames at Weybridge

This fifteen and a half mile stretch of the Wey was originally made navig- able by Richard Weston (grandson of the builder of Sutton Place, on the river) and others, who opened it in 1653. The necessary cutting and deepen- ing and the provision of twelve locks is said to have cost them £15,000. There were teething troubles. For one thing the builders failed to compensate all the landowners through whose property they cut, and the landowners retaliated by damaging locks and breaking down banks. Also, the operators quarrelled about sharing the profits. But these troubles were overcome and a substantial barge traffic was established. The owners were in trouble again during the eighteenth century, this time with the water mill owners, who interfered with barge traffic. But an agreement was finally achieved, and by 1831 more than 30,000 tons of freight were carried in one year from the Thames into the Wey. Loads included corn, coal, slate and hemp. For return trips there were flour, malt, hay, cheese, and gunpowder from Chil- worth. Barge traffic continued to be quite substantial until the end of the

The River Wey Navigation, Surrey: a view near Send

First World War, but now the Navigation is much used by pleasure craft, which have many delightful stretches on which to ply.

The property was given to the Trust in 1964 by Mr Harry W. Stevens. His family had bought control in 1902 and he himself had been sole proprietor for twenty-four years from 1940.

GODALMING NAVIGATION *4½-mile stretch between Guildford and Godal-ming* This was made navigable about a hundred years after the Guildford to Weybridge stretch. It carried farm produce and flourished in the first part of the nineteenth century when the Basingstoke Canal was linked to the Wey. It is used only for pleasure craft now and was given to the Trust in 1869 by Guildford Corporation.

The towpath along the whole stretch of the River Wey Navigation provides good walking.

Runnymede

half a mile above Runnymede Bridge, on the south side of A308

At Runnymede the Trust owns practically the whole of the meadows where Magna Carta was sealed, a hundred acres on Cooper's Hill slopes over-looking the meadows, and the lily pond (page 310). The Kennedy Memorial is on land adjoining the Trust property.

The meadows were given by Lady Fairhaven and her sons in memory of her husband in 1931, and the Cooper Hill Slopes by Egham Urban District Council in 1963.

THURSLEY *2 miles north of Hindhead* Eight acres protecting the church, a memorial to the poet John Freeman, who is buried there.

Woldingham

SOUTH HAWKE *1½ miles south of Woldingham* This four and a half acre open stretch, 750 ft up on the North Downs, was acquired in 1920. In 1958 Sir Adrian Boult, to protect this land with its views, gave protective cove-nants over fields to the north.

HANGING WOOD On a south slope of the North Downs, four and a half acres with fine views, given by Surrey County Council.

Runnymede, Surrey: the lily pond with Cooper's Hill in the background

TYNE AND WEAR

Three of the five properties which were in the old county of Durham are now in the new county of Tyne and Wear.

——•——

GIBSIDE CHAPEL *6 miles south-west of Gateshead* An eighteenth-century chapel, built as a family mausoleum in Palladian style by James Paine. Given to the Trust in 1965 by Lord Strathmore.

——•——

310

Penshaw Monument

half way between Sunderland and Chester-le-Street east of A183

This Doric temple (below) was erected in 1844 as a memorial to John George Lambton, first Earl of Durham, Governor General of the British provinces in North America in 1838 and author of the Durham Report.
Given to the Trust in 1939 by the fifth Earl.

Washington Old Hall

5 miles west of Sunderland

Washington Old Hall (page 312) is a small manor-house of the early seventeenth century in which were embodied parts of an earlier house which had

Penshaw Monument, Tyne and Wear

Washington Old Hall, Tyne and Wear

stood on the site. The original house was built in the twelfth century and from 1183 until 1613 was the home of George Washington's ancestors.

Washington is an old village in the northern industrial and mining area of County Durham, the surrounding country now very built up. In its centre is a village green and, just off the square below the church, which is on a little hill, stands Washington Old Hall.

It was rescued in 1936, when it had become dilapidated, by a committee formed for the purpose. With help from both sides of the Atlantic it was restored and furnished, and in 1956 transferred to the Trust. Let to the Washington Urban District Council, it is used by the people of Washington as a community centre. A small formal garden was laid out in 1970.

Charlecote Park, Warwickshire: the house with the gatehouse in the foreground

WARWICKSHIRE

Charlecote Park

4 miles east of Stratford-upon-Avon

Charlecote Park is the place where Shakespeare reputedly poached deer. His subsequent appearance before the magistrate, the story continues, gave him the model for Mr Justice Shallow in *King Henry IV* and *The Merry Wives of Windsor*. The Sir Thomas Lucy to whom this tradition applies built Charlecote in 1558 and entertained Queen Elizabeth to breakfast there in 1572 on her way to Kenilworth. Falstaff's comment to Shallow—''Fore God you have a goodly dwelling and a rich'—applies very well to the house Sir Thomas built.

Since his time it has been enlarged and a good deal altered both inside and out; but the general outline of the Elizabethan building remains. The gate-

313

house (page 313), which guards the approach to the front, was built a little earlier than the house itself and has remained unaltered. The plum-red brick in which it was made has mellowed beautifully.

The park, which still harbours the descendants of Sir Thomas's deer and with them Spanish sheep imported in the eighteenth century, was laid out in its present form by Capability Brown.

There are a number of interesting family and other portraits in the house, including a contemporary picture of Queen Elizabeth I.

The late Sir Montgomerie Fairfax-Lucy gave Charlecote to the Trust in 1945.

Coughton Court

2 miles north of Alcester on the east side of A435

The principal architectural feature of Coughton (below) is the gatehouse, a formidable and solidly proportioned stone building of the early sixteenth century. We do not see it today exactly as it was first built because the stone

Coughton Court, Warwickshire

wings adjoining the central portion were added in a 1780 version of Gothic, probably in place of some earlier work, but they contribute satisfactorily to the impressiveness of the whole frontage.

The other parts of the house are in contrast, consisting of Elizabethan half-timbered upper storeys on ground storeys of brick. Two wings of this construction are set at right angles to the gatehouse and form a court behind it. Originally they were joined by a third wing and the court was entirely enclosed.

Inside the house, the dining-room has exceptionally fine panelling of different periods and an elaborate chimney-piece in marble and timber.

The contents of the rooms belong to Sir Robert Throckmorton, a descendant of the Sir George Throckmorton who built the gatehouse in 1509. They include porcelain, some notable furniture, portraits and an interesting exhibition of Throckmorton family muniments. Among the family portraits is a picture of Sir Nicholas Throckmorton, father of Bessie Throckmorton, who was a lady-in-waiting to Queen Elizabeth and married Sir Walter Raleigh. On the first floor of the gatehouse, in what is now the Drawing Room, the arms of Catesby and others concerned in the Gunpowder Plot are displayed in heraldic glass. The Throckmortons were not directly implicated in the plot, but according to tradition the wives of some of the plotters assembled in this room to await the outcome of the affair.

During the Civil War Coughton was seized by Parliamentary forces, who were in turn bombarded by Royalist forces. How much damage this caused is not known because when the damage was repaired after the Restoration, alterations were made in the interior of the house. In 1688 it was in trouble again. The Throckmortons have always been Roman Catholics, and when King James II fled the country a Protestant mob from Alcester destroyed the entire east wing. This was not restored; but towards the end of the eighteenth century the site was cleared and the moat, which till that time had surrounded the house, was filled in.

In 1946 Coughton was given to the Trust by Sir Robert Throckmorton and leased back to him.

———

EARLSWOOD MOAT HOUSE *south of Birmingham, a mile east of Earlswood Lakes Station* A small fifteenth-century timber-framed house with sixty-five acres of pasture and woodland (not open).

———

Farnborough Hall, Warwickshire

Farnborough Hall

6 miles north of Banbury

Farnborough (above) is a trim, classical, mid-eighteenth-century stone-built house which incorporates some part of the late seventeenth-century house which stood on the site. Inside, the hall (opposite) and dining-room have fine stone and marble fireplaces and rococo ceiling and wall decoration; the staircase is lit by an oval dome in which the lights are decorated by a bold wreath of fruit and foliage.

On the great grass terrace, laid out in the eighteenth century, which looks up to Edge Hill three miles away, there are two charming garden temples and an obelisk. The grounds present one of the few remaining examples of unaltered eighteenth-century landscape gardening in the country.

Farnborough Hall, Warwickshire: the entrance hall

Ambrose Holbech bought Farnborough in 1683 and it was probably his grandson, William Holbech, who carried out the remaking of the house between 1745 and 1755. There are no records of the work, but the names of a stonemason and of a plasterer employed by him are known, and it looks as though he acted as his own architect.

The house and grounds were acquired by the Trust in 1960, having been accepted by the Treasury in part payment of death duties. The house is closed to the public at present, but the gardens are open at advertised times.

⌐◦ ◦⌐

Kinwarton Dovecote

1½ miles north of Alcester, just south of B4089

Kinwarton dovecote (page 318) probably belonged to the Abbey of Eves‑ham, which had property where the dovecote stands, near Alcester.

It has been established, from the evidence of the architectural detail of the arch over the doorway, that the Kinwarton dovecote was built about the middle of the fourteenth century. These circular dovehouses were furnished

Kinwarton Dovecote, Warwickshire

inside with an ingenious contrivance called a *potence* (French for gallows). To a vertical beam in the centre of the building several horizontal beams are attached at different heights, and at the extremity of each, close to the wall, is a length of ladder. The vertical beam pivots so that the horizontal beams with their ladders can be moved round the wall, giving access in turn to all the nesting boxes—in this case five hundred of them. Kinwarton is unusual in that this useful piece of equipment has survived. Kinwarton was given to the Trust in 1958. (See also Willington Dovecote, pages 50-1.)

Packwood House, Warwickshire

Packwood House

a mile east of Hockley Heath which is on A34, 1 mile south-east of Birmingham

The main part of the house was built about 1560 by a yeoman who seems to have called it his 'Great Manciant House'. He built a typical mid-sixteenth-century black-and-white house which has since been rendered over. About 1670 his lawyer grandson made the excellent brick-built additions to provide stables and outbuildings. In between those dates, during the Commonwealth, this same lawyer planned and established the extraordinary topiary work in the yew garden (above), representing the Sermon on the Mount: clipped yews stand for the multitude and larger yews for the Twelve Apostles.

The house contains a great deal of interesting tapestry and furniture. This was collected for preservation at Packwood by Mr G. Baron Ash, who gave house and collections to the Trust in 1941.

Stratford-upon-Avon Canal (Southern Section)

The Southern Section of the Stratford Canal (below) runs from Stratford, where it is connected by a lock to the River Avon, thirteen miles north-west to Lapworth, where it links up with the other section of the Stratford Canal. This in turn is linked to the Grand Union. The Trust owns the freehold of the whole of this thirteen-mile Stratford to Lapworth Section and its tow-path. It is open to boats, and as it passes through the Warwickshire country-side presents both those in boats and walkers on the towpath with many pleasing views.

It is also of interest to students of industrial archaeology and to those concerned with the restoration and maintenance of inland waterways. The canal, with its thirty-six locks, twenty cast-iron split bridges and two large cast-iron aqueducts, was a very considerable engineering feat for the period

Stratford-upon-Avon Canal (Southern Section), Warwickshire: volunteers on maintenance work at Lock 22

in which it was built: 1793–1815. It was bought by railway interests in the nineteenth century and its traffic dwindled. By 1930 it was derelict and in 1958 proposals were made for it to be dismantled. The Stratford-upon-Avon Canal Society and the Inland Waterways Association opposed this plan and in 1961 the Trust leased the canal from the British Waterways Board. There followed three years of rehabilitation. This formidable task was carried out by a handful of full-time staff aided by a great many volunteers working at week-ends or during their holidays, by R.E. and R.A.F. units and by men from H.M. prisons. The money needed to finance the work was £61,000. Towards this the Ministry of Transport made a grant of £20,000, and £33,000 was raised by public appeal.

The canal was formally reopened to traffic in the summer of 1964 by H.M. Queen Elizabeth the Queen Mother, President of the National Trust. Volunteers, including young people, continue to give help in maintenance and improvement tasks, as the picture on page 320 shows.

⌐◯ ◯⌐

Upton House

7 miles north-west of Banbury on the west side of A422

Upton House (below) was built in 1695 of the orange-gold local stone, and in spite of some alterations retains outwardly the appearance of a house of the period. The interior has been completely remodelled to display exceptionally fine collections of pictures and porcelain. It is this collection which provides the principal interest of Upton House.

These collections were made by the second Lord Bearsted, who gave them to the Trust with the house and its terraced gardens and water garden in 1948. The pictures, of which there are nearly two hundred, range over a wide variety of schools, British, Dutch, Flemish, French, German, Italian and Spanish, and include works by Pieter Brueghel, El Greco and many other masters. In the porcelain collection there are many very fine English porcelain figures and a number of good Sèvres pieces.

Upton House, Warwickshire

WEST MIDLANDS

One of the properties in this new County was previously in Staffordshire, and one (Knowle) in Warwickshire.

KNOWLE CHILDREN'S FIELD *9 miles south-east of Birmingham*   A three-acre field for games, standing near the church; given in 1910.

~ — ᴅ ~

Wightwick Manor

3 miles west of Wolverhampton just north of A454

As an inscription over the front door records, the house was begun in the year of Queen Victoria's jubilee. Mr Theodore Mander, a Wolverhampton industrialist and mayor of the city, employed as his architect Edward Ould, to build a half-timber house with elaborately carved gables and timbers on a base of red sandstone. They used William Morris wallpapers and materials for the interior decoration. Mr Mander's son, the late Sir Geoffrey Mander, who gave the house and its contents to the Trust in 1937, added nineteenth-century pictures, furniture, books and manuscripts to his father's collection.

Fine craftsmanship went into the making of the house, and its decoration exemplifies the tastes of the period. In addition to the William Morris tapestry and wallpapers, there is much stained glass by C. E. Kempe and tiles by William de Morgan. The very interesting collection of pictures in the

Wightwick Manor, West Midlands: the hall

Great Parlour and other rooms includes drawings and paintings by Burne-Jones, Holman Hunt, Madox Brown, Millais and Rossetti. There are some Chinese vases and books from Rossetti's house in Cheyne Walk and a decorated cupboard and a bed from No. 2 the Pines at Putney, the home of Theodore Watts-Dunton and Swinburne. The gardens contain yew hedges and topiary, terraces and pools.

———— ⊃ ⊂ ————

WEST SUSSEX

All Trust properties formerly in the County of Sussex and west of Brighton are now in West Sussex and one property (at Grayswood Common near Haslemere) formerly in Surrey, is now in West Sussex.

BRAMBER CASTLE *south-east of Steyning* The remains of a Norman castle on a steep escarpment of the South Downs.

———— ⊃ ⊂ ————

Chichester Harbour

The photograph reproduced on page 324 was taken on East Head, West Wittering, a spit of land on the east side of Chichester Harbour entrance. In 1966 the West Sussex County Council gave the Trust fifty acres of the sand dunes and twenty acres of sandy beach here—a mile-and-a-quarter stretch of the coast. This was a contribution to Enterprise Neptune, the Trust's coastal preservation appeal. There is a Nature Walk at East Head.

To the west of Chichester, at Bosham between the church and the creek, the Trust has an acre of land, known as Quay Meadow. Here Harold embarked for Normandy in 1064.

———— ⊃ ⊂ ————

DROVERS ESTATE *astride the Midhurst–Chichester road, north of the Goodwood Estate* A thousand-acre agricultural estate.

———— ⊃ ⊂ ————

DURFORD HEATH *2 miles north-east of Petersfield, south of A3* Seventy acres, mainly heathland.

———— ⊃ ⊂ ————

Chichester Harbour, West Sussex: East Head, inner side of sandbank looking north

Haslemere

GRAYSWOOD COMMON *a mile north of Haslemere* A small property (sixteen acres) on the London road, which a local subscription bought for the Trust in 1909.

To the south of Haslemere are two complexes of property built up between 1911 and 1964 with the help of a number of individual donors, local subscriptions and several local authorities:

BLACK DOWN *to the south-east* This property amounts to about six hundred acres, including five hundred on Black Down itself and its 918-ft summit, the highest point in Sussex. There is a $1\frac{1}{2}$-mile nature trail.

MARLEY Common land and woodland at Kingsley Green Common, Marley Common, land at Marley Coombe, a viewpoint on Marley Heights, and Shottermill Ponds—two hammer ponds.

LAVINGTON COMMON *2 miles south-west of Petworth* Eighty acres of heather and pines.

—————

NEWTIMBER HILL *5 miles north-west of Brighton between Pyecombe and Poynings* 240 acres of down and woodland with views of the Weald and the sea. There are some ancient beeches along Beggar's Lane.

—————

Nymans

4½ miles south of Crawley on the south-east edge of Handcross

The garden (page 326) at Nymans extends to about thirty acres and consists of a series of small, linked gardens which not only show a variety of plants but also are delightfully varied in design. The charm of the whole garden is enhanced by the beauty of the surrounding woodlands. The garden's seasons of special interest are spring and autumn, when its rare trees and shrubs make their displays.

Nymans was the creation of Mr Ludwig Messel, who bought the property in the 1880s, and his son, Lt-Col. L. C. R. Messel, who bequeathed it to the Trust when he died in 1954. Mr Messel's granddaughter, the Countess of Rosse, writing in the Trust's guide-book to the gardens, records his appreciation of the encouragement that he received in the early years from Miss Jekyll, Mr Robinson and others of the famous gardeners of the time.

The estate includes 570 acres of wood and farmland.

—————

Petworth House

5½ miles east of Midhurst, in Petworth

Petworth has a whole string of claims to fame—its pictures, its Grinling Gibbons carving, its long succession of splendid staterooms, its magnificent west front (page 327) and the beautiful park overlooked by the west front.

The making of Petworth has been a long process. The Earls of Northumberland had a house here at least from the thirteenth century onwards and the chapel which they built for it, altered and finely decorated in the late seventeenth century, is still the chapel today.

Nymans, West Sussex: in the walled garden

Petworth House, West Sussex: the west front

Petworth House, West Sussex: the Grinling Gibbons room

Everything else was swept away about 1690 when the 6th Duke of Somerset (who had married a Percy heiress) did a grand rebuilding which included the present splendid west front.

The house is sited on the very edge of the park with its back to the town. On that side there are the stables, lodge and offices. From the park the west front is in view, and quite evidently a triumph of architectural design. The design is a combination of French and English elements. The architect is unknown, although his identity has been the subject of much ingenious speculation by writers on architectural history.

Some of the decoration of the interior was carried out when the house was built and some has been introduced since. Grinling Gibbons worked there while the house was building, putting into the room (page 327) which is named after him a wealth of carving that is widely accepted as being the best he ever did. The staircase had to be repaired after a fire early in the eighteenth century, and is now decorated with murals by Louis Laguerre. The North Gallery was made later in the eighteenth century by the third Lord Egremont to contain his almost unique collection of pictures and the antique sculptures acquired earlier in the century by his predecessors. The Square Dining Room was redecorated early in the nineteenth century and contains carving by Jonathan Ritson, a local man.

In this room are hung some Van Dyck portraits which were transferred from the older house. The Red Room is given over to the paintings of Turner, who was a frequent visitor to Petworth. In the Beauty Room are the contemporary portraits of beauties of the court of Queen Anne which gave the room its name.

The house and park were given to the Trust in 1947 by the third Lord Leconfield. The greater part of the pictures and furniture are on loan to the Trust from the Treasury. The gardens do not belong to the Trust and are not open.

—————

SELSFIELD COMMON *4 miles south-west of East Grinstead*   Seven acres that were acquired in 1912 and are now managed by West Hoathly Parish Council.

—————

Slindon Estate

6 miles north of Bognor Regis

An agricultural estate of 3,500 acres, with woodland, extending to the northern foot of the South Downs. There is access to the park and by footpath only to other parts of the estate, which includes Bignor and Coldharbour Hills and Glatting Beacon, and also the Neolithic causewayed enclosure of Barkhale. There are round barrows and other antiquities and the estate also includes most of Slindon village, with a park containing some notable beeches.

—◁▷ ◁▷—

Standen

2 miles south-west of East Grinstead

An important Victorian house built round a medieval yeoman's house, designed by the architect Philip Webb and thought to be the finest existing example of his work. The house contains original William Morris designed wallpapers and linoleum. It overlooks Ashdown Forest to the south. Bequeathed to the Trust in 1973 by Miss Helen Beale, whose family built it in 1891–4.

—◁▷ ◁▷—

TERWICK ¾ *mile east of Rogate* Ten acres adjoining the church. Partly planted with lupins at the donor's request.

—◁▷ ◁▷—

Uppark

5 miles south of Petersfield, a mile south of South Harting

Uppark (page 330) was built about 1690 by one of the then most successful country house architects, William Talman. From the outside it is a charming Wren-style country house, but inside it is all eighteenth century, an unusually complete preservation of an eighteenth-century interior. The house was completely redecorated and refurnished in 1750–60 by people with taste and the money to indulge it. Their work has been very little touched since then, so that not only their furniture but even some of their fabrics and wallpapers remain in excellent condition.

A part from the intrinsic charms of the house and its contents and their remarkable preservation, there are a number of points of interest in its associations. The builder of the house (Forde Lord Grey of Werke and later Earl of Tankerville) had an adventurous career, being involved in the Rye House Plot and in Monmouth's Rebellion, but contriving to finish up as Lord Privy Seal under William III. There is no record of his building activities except that he employed Talman as architect. But Sir Mathew

Uppark, West Sussex

Fetherstonhaugh, who bought the house in 1747, kept detailed accounts. These deal with the changes he and his wife made when transforming the interior in 1750–60, and identify furniture and china to be seen there today.

Sir Harry Fetherstonhaugh, who succeeded to the estate in 1774, brought the young Emma Hamilton from London to Uppark, and she lived there for a year in 1780–1. He entertained lavishly for a time. The Prince Regent was frequently a guest between 1785 and 1810, and in the Red Drawing-room there is the Carlton House writing-table which he gave to his host. About 1813 Sir Harry had a change of heart or perhaps wished to econo-mize, and withdrew from society. At this point the Duke of Wellington appears briefly on the scene. It was proposed in 1816 that he should be presented with a country house and Uppark was among those offered for his consideration. But when he came to inspect the house and saw that it was up a steep hill, he decided that to live there would entail the expense of frequent replacements of carriage horses, and so withdrew.

During his retirement Sir Harry married his dairymaid. They had no children and after his death (in 1846 at the age of ninety-two) she lived on at Uppark with her sister, carefully preserving all the contents. Her sister lived there till 1895 and employed H. G. Wells's mother as housekeeper. Wells's boyhood recollections of Uppark are given in his autobiography.

Uppark was given to the Trust in 1954 by the late Admiral the Hon. Sir Herbert Meade-Fetherstonhaugh and his son. In the last forty years a great deal has been done to ensure the continued preservation of the fabrics by Lady Meade-Fetherstonhaugh. Her rediscovery of the value of the Saponaria plant has helped this work.

Wakehurst Place

1½ miles north-west of Ardingly

The hundred and twenty acre garden with four hundred acres of woodlands have been leased by the Trust to the Ministry of Agriculture and are adminis-tered by the Director of Kew Gardens. They contain one of the richest collections of trees and shrubs in Britain. The house, late sixteenth century, has been extensively altered (not open). The property was bequeathed to the Trust by Sir Henry Price.

Woolbeding

2 miles north-west of Midhurst

The four hundred acre common at Woolbeding (page 332) forms part of a thousand-acre estate which was accepted by the Treasury in payment of death duty and given to the Trust in 1958.

There is public access to some of the woodlands as well as to the common.

Worthing

Four of the five properties near Worthing have features of archaeological interest.

CISSBURY RING *3 miles north of Worthing* This was the site of a flint-mining industry in the early Neolithic period. The eight-acre property six hundred feet above the sea has wide views seaward. There is an Iron Age hill fort.

Woolbeding Common, West Sussex: a view on the common looking towards Telegraph Hill

HIGHDOWN HILL *3 miles north-west of Worthing* There were a Late Bronze Age Settlement, an Early Iron Age fort and a Saxon pagan cemetery here. Some of the finds are in Worthing Museum.

SHOREHAM GAP *east of Worthing, 2 miles north-east of Shoreham* Six hundred acres of down with a bowl-barrow.

SULLINGTON WARREN *8 miles north of Worthing* Twenty-eight acres with wide views of the North and South Downs, and five bowl-barrows.

WARREN HILL *8 miles north of Worthing, on west of A24* 240 acres, including Washington Common, woods, a farm and cottages, and providing views of the South Downs.

WEST YORKSHIRE
East Riddlesden Hall

a mile from the centre of Keighley on the south side of the Bradford road

East Riddlesden Hall is a late seventeenth-century manor which, apart from having been blackened by industrial grime, looks much as it did when it was completed in 1692. It has some contemporary panelling and plasterwork and now houses a collection of seventeenth-century furniture, portraits and domestic bygones.

The Great Barn—illustrated here below—is much older than the present hall and is one of the finest medieval barns in the north of England. It is 120 feet by 40 feet in area, its oak pillars being on stone bases.

East Riddlesden Hall, West Yorkshire: the Great Barn

Hebden Dale

about 5 miles north-east of Todmorden

The Trust has three pieces of property north of Hebden Bridge; two hundred acres of woods and the Hardcastle Crags on the north of Hebden Water; forty acres of woodland on its west bank, and a hundred acres of farm and woodland to the south. The Slurring Rock Nature Trail takes about an hour and a half to traverse.

MARSDEN MOOR See Wessenden Moor entry (page 336).

Nostell Priory

6 miles south-east of Wakefield on the north side of A638

One of the many remarkable things about Nostell is that one of its two architects employed, James Paine, was only nineteen when he began the work. He went on to be one of the foremost of mid-eighteenth-century architects, but to give him this commission seems an act of great perception as well as boldness on the part of Sir Rowland Winn. Paine and Sir Rowland, who was himself a man of architectural knowledge and taste, spent eight years

Nostell Priory, West Yorkshire

Nostell Priory, West Yorkshire: the Saloon

building and decorating the central block and other parts of a larger plan for a Palladian house. But they did not finish; when Sir Rowland died in 1765 his son (also Sir Rowland) had new ideas and employed Robert Adam to add a north wing, planned to harmonize with the central block. Adam also designed the stable block. Since then the exterior of the house has been little changed.

The interior of the house was also a form of combined operation. The proportion and layout of the rooms come from Paine's design and he was responsible for the decoration of some of them. Adam contributed the larger part of the decoration of the rooms and put into them some of his best work. In the library and other rooms where he needed painted murals or ceilings or stucco he engaged Antonio Zucchi, Angelica Kaufmann and Joseph Rose.

The two graceful staircases, by Paine, have elaborately moulded walls and ceilings and are carried to the top of the house. For the Library Adam designed very elegant bookcases and there are mural paintings of mythological subjects. For the Tapestry Room and for the Saloon he designed beautiful pier-glasses. The Dining Room and the State Bedroom were joint operations. In the Dining Room Paine provided the white marble Palladian chimney-piece and the door cases; Adam added wall panels and a plaster frieze of satyrs' masks and vines. In the State Bedroom the rococo ceiling is by Paine and Adam introduced the Chinese wallpaper.

The furniture is as remarkable as the interior decoration. Much of it is by Thomas Chippendale, some of the pieces being to designs by Adam and intended for the places they still occupy. Thus the Chippendale side tables in the Saloon were designed by Adam as part of the decoration of the room.

In addition to family portraits the rooms contain paintings by Jakob van Ruysdael, Van Dyck, Hogarth and other famous artists. The second Sir Rowland kept detailed accounts, which have been preserved. His Chippendale accounts are shown to visitors.

The extensive gardens have fine rhododendrons and a Gothic garden-house.

The original Nostell Priory was a house of Austin Canons, founded in the twelfth century, and the friars continued there until the dissolution of the monasteries. It then passed through several hands and was bought in 1654 by Rowland Winn, a London City alderman with estates in Lincolnshire. It continued in the possession his family until 1954, when it was given to the Trust by the trustees of the estate and the present Lord St Oswald (Rowland Winn). The pictures and furniture are the property of Lord St Oswald.

—◁ ▷—

Wessenden Moor

about 8 miles south-west of Huddersfield, south of Marsden

The illustration on page 337 shows the view from Wessenden Head looking northwards across the Trust's Marsden Moor property. This amounts to nearly 5,700 acres of open moorland, the southern part being in the Peak

Wessenden Moor, West Yorkshire: seen from Wessenden Head

District National Park. It stretches from Buckstones Moss, astride A62, to Wessenden Moor, north of A635, and includes Holme and Binn Moors. Given in 1955 by the Treasury, who had accepted it in payment of death duty.

WILTSHIRE

Avebury

6 miles west of Marlborough a mile north of A4

Around 1800 B.C. Avebury (page 338) was a religious or ritual centre, visited by people from all over Britain and very probably from Europe. It is one of the most important Early Bronze Age monuments in Europe.

Avebury, Wiltshire: part of the Great Stone Circle, looking south across the ditch to the outer bank

A ditch and outer bank enclosed an area five hundred yards in diameter. In this were erected over a hundred local stones to make an outer circle and two inner circles. From the south-east entrance to the circle an avenue of stones stretched for a mile and a half towards the south-east.

In the last three hundred-odd years excavations have been made. Finds from these excavations are in a museum near by. This, with the circles, is under the guardianship of the Department of the Environment.

Earlier generations have viewed the circles quite differently. Some stones were buried during the fourteenth century, apparently because the Church wished to put a stop to surviving heathen rituals there. The eighteenth century had a more utilitarian view and broke up some of the stones to build part of the village of Avebury.

The property was bought by the Trust in 1943 with the help of the Pilgrim Trust and Mr I. D. Margary. It includes, in addition to Avebury, Windmill

338

Hill, a mile and a half to the north-west, where there are Early–Middle Bronze Age barrows.

—⮕ ⬅—

CLEY HILL *3 miles west of Warminster* A chalk hill 800 ft high, on which stands an Iron Age hill fort containing two bowl-barrows.

—⮕ ⬅—

Dinton

DINTON: PHILIPPS HOUSE *9 miles west of Salisbury, on the north side of B3089* The architect of Philipps House (below) was Jeffry Wyatville, known as the architect who gave Windsor Castle its Gothic look. But at Dinton he was starting from scratch and designing a new house for a site which had been cleared of its earlier building. He produced a design in the neo-Grecian style, a two-storey building with a portico to set off its main frontage. The staircase hall and some of the principal rooms are good examples of the style in which he built.

The house was built between 1805 and 1815 for the Wyndham family, who owned the property from 1689 until 1916. It was given to the Trust with two hundred acres of parkland in 1943 by Mr Bertram Philipps, who bought it in 1916. It is now let to the Y.W.C.A. as a holiday home.

In addition to Philipps House the Trust owns Hyde's House, an early eighteenth-century house near the church in Dinton. It is not open. Also, a quarter of a mile east of the church, Little Clarendon, a stone Tudor house, and a seventeenth-century building called Lawes Cottage, once the home of the composer William Lawes.

Dinton, Wiltshire:
Philipps House

Great Chalfield Manor, Wiltshire

DINTON PARK *9 miles west of Salisbury* (see also Dinton: Philipps House. An Iron Age hill fort stands in the two-hundred-acre Park.

———

FIGSBURY RING *4 miles north-east of Salisbury* An Iron Age hill fort which was excavated in 1924. Finds are in Devizes Museum.

———

Great Chalfield Manor

2½ miles north-east of Bradford-on-Avon by B3109

Great Chalfield (opposite) was built around 1480. It has never been altered or enlarged, most of the original building has survived and it provides a good impression of late Gothic domestic architecture. It was built by Thomas Tropnell, a local landowner who managed to improve his fortunes during the Wars of the Roses.

The property has changed hands by inheritance and purchase a number of times. Like other buildings of this style, it went completely out of fashion for a long period. But in 1840, before it had become too dilapidated, detailed plans for restoration were made for the then owner, who died before he could carry them out. These plans, made by a pupil of Pugin, were used when restoration was carried out in 1910. The property was given to the Trust in 1943 by Major R. Fuller.

———

GREY WETHERS *3 miles west of Marlborough* Twelve acres of farmland at Lockeridge Dene, south of the A4, and nine acres at Piggle Dene, north of the A4. On both properties are Sarsen stones (sandstone boulders) which are known locally as Grey Wethers.

———

HOLT: THE COURTS *3 miles east of Bradford-on-Avon* The house has a richly decorated façade of about 1700. It is not open, though the attractve gardens are. They contain topiary, a lily pond and an arboretum.

———

Lacock Abbey

3 miles south of Chippenham, just east of A350

Lacock Abbey (page 342) presents four architectural styles. Parts of the thirteenth-century nunnery remain. These were preserved when other parts

341

were converted to a Tudor dwelling-house in 1550. Alterations were made in 1754 in a Gothic style. Further changes were made in 1828. The different parts of the abbey—each of which is an interesting example of its own style and period—combine today to make the whole building one of romantic beauty.

The Tudor house was built by Sir William Sharington. He had travelled in Italy, and in his Lacock building introduced the new Italian architecture to England. For the eighteenth-century additions, Sanderson Miller was the architect. The grounds have some remarkable trees, and thousands of crocuses in spring.

Sir William Sharington died childless, and the abbey was inherited by his niece Mrs John Talbot. It remained in the possession of the Talbot family until it was given to the Trust, together with nearly the whole of Lacock village, by Miss Matilda Talbot in 1944. Fox Talbot, pioneer of photography, made his experiments at Lacock.

Lacock Village

3 miles south of Chippenham just off A350

When Miss Matilda Talbot gave Lacock Abbey to the Trust in 1944 she gave also the greater part of the village of Lacock (opposite). As landlord, the Trust is concerned to preserve the appearance of the village. But the buildings are let as private dwellings or as shops and business premises, and are not open to visitors.

Every century from the thirteenth to the nineteenth has made contributions to the building of the village, each in its own characteristic architectural style. But there is here a neighbourliness about their contributions, and the

Lacock Abbey, Wiltshire: the west front

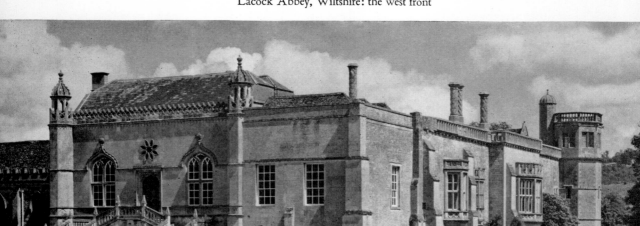

Lacock Village, Wiltshire

sum of their efforts is a very beautiful village. As well as a diversity of architecture, there is a diversity of building materials to be seen. Some of the buildings are half-timbered with brick or other infilling, others are in the local Corsham stone, and some are brick built.

On the edge of the village is one of its finest buildings, a fourteenth-century tithe barn.

The village has not been dependent solely on agriculture. From the fourteenth century until the Industrial Revolution, while the West Country wool trade flourished, Lacock and other villages had a prosperous cottage industry.

PEPPERBOX HILL *5 miles south-east of Salisbury* A seventeenth-century folly, The Pepperbox, some open down with juniper bushes, woodland and views.

Salisbury

JOINERS' HALL *in St Ann Street* The building retains a sixteenth-century timbered façade. Not open.

MOMPESSON HOUSE *Choristers' Square* This was built about 1700 and is one of the finest houses in the Cathedral Close with original panelling and plasterwork.

STONEHENGE DOWN *1 to 3 miles west of Amesbury* Stonehenge itself, which is looked after by the Department of the Environment, does not belong to the Trust. Fourteen hundred acres of the surrounding farmland do, however, and on this land are the Stonehenge Cursus, contemporary with the earliest Stonehenge work, and barrows of the Early and Middle Bronze Age.

Stourhead

at Stourton, 3 miles north-west of Mere

Stourhead gardens have been called 'Henry Hoare's Paradise' after the Henry Hoare who created them, a grandson of the founder of Hoare's Bank. For his gardens (opposite), one of the achievements of eighteenth-century garden

Stourhead, Wiltshire: a view in the gardens

design, he planted a valley with trees, dammed a stream to make lakes and built temples and a grotto. In the design for the garden he was trying to transfer into an actual garden landscape the picturesque scenery shown in paintings by French landscape painters. He was before his time in abandon- ing the formal style of layout, which was still popular, for the more natural- istic style which is today associated particularly with Capability Brown. (Hoare began Stourhead gardens in 1740, and Brown did not set up as a consultant till 1749.) It is not known whether Hoare employed any architect or designer. According to his grandson, writing some years afterwards, he was his own designer. During the nineteenth century further plantings were made, and the gardens are now brilliant in spring with azaleas and rhodo- dendrons. The many fine and rare trees are particularly beautiful in the autumn.

Henry Hoare inherited Stourhead in 1725 from his father, another Henry. Both Henrys were most assiduous in their attention to the business of their bank, and the making of Stourhead, great though their interest and study in the arts, was a spare-time occupation.

Henry Hoare the first, like his son, had been an innovator. On buying the Stourhead estate, in 1717, he had built one of the first houses in the new Georgian style. He employed as architect Colen Campbell, who designed the Palladian building which is the central block of the present house. The wings were added about 1800 by Richard Colt Hoare to house his collection of pictures, statuary and books. These wings were furnished in Regency style, and the furniture which the younger Thomas Chippendale made for them is still there.

The central block was gutted by fire in 1902, but the furniture was saved and put back after the interior had been restored in an exact copy of the original decoration. The statuary and pictures in the house—apart from the many family portraits, which are by painters of note—are mainly the collec- tion made by Richard Colt Hoare and show the tastes of a wealthy, travelled connoisseur in the last part of the eighteenth century.

Stourhead was given to the Trust in 1947 by Sir Henry Hoare, the sixth baronet.

STOURHEAD ESTATE   The estate includes the villages of Stourton and Kilmington, three hundred acres of woodland and King Alfred's Tower.

WHITE SHEET DOWNS *on Stourhead Estate, 3 miles north-west of Mere* Part of a Neolithic causewayed enclosure and half an Iron Age hill fort known as White Sheet Castle.

WARMINSTER: BOREHAM FIELD *south of the Salisbury road* A six-acre field with a right of way.

Westwood Manor

1½ miles south-west of Bradford-on-Avon off B3109

Westwood Manor (below) is a stone house in a modern topiary garden in the beautifully situated village of Westwood, which stands on high ground between two river valleys: those of the Avon and the Frome. It was built towards the end of the fifteenth century and retains some late Gothic windows. Alterations made in the sixteenth and seventeenth centuries included the embellishment of the interior with panelling and some fine Jacobean plasterwork.

In the Middle Ages Westwood belonged to the priory at Winchester, which leased it to tenants. At the dissolution of the monasteries it was used to endow the Dean and Chapter of Winchester, and continued to be leased to tenants until sold to a private owner by the Ecclesiastical Commissioners in 1861.

The house was altered and decorated by a succession of tenants. During the sixteenth century the property was rented by the Horton family, who were

Westwood Manor, Wiltshire

very prosperous clothiers. The property continued to be an agricultural holding. During the eighteenth and nineteenth centuries, when this style of building had little appeal for those wanting a country house, it seems to have served purely as a farm. By 1911 much of the panelling had been covered by wallpaper and the Great Parlour partitioned for use as an apple store. The late Mr E. G. Lister bought it and restored it to its earlier state with knowledge and discretion. On his death in 1956 he left the house with his collection of furniture to the Trust.

—◦ ◦—

WHITE BARROW *7 miles north-west of Stonehenge* A Neolithic earthen long barrow.

—◦ ◦—

WIN GREEN HILL *5 miles south-east of Shaftesbury* At 911 ft the highest point in Cranborne Chase, with views to the Isle of Wight and the Quantocks. There is a bowl-barrow, and nearly a mile of the Ridgeway is included in the boundary (*38 acres*).

—◦ ◦—

CLWYD

The properties now in Clwyd are among those formerly in Denbighshire.

Erddig

1½ miles south-west of Wrexham

Erddig was given to the Trust in 1973 by Mr Philip Yorke, whose family had lived there since 1735. It has been described by the Trust as having 'an almost legendary reputation among connoisseurs'. That is easily understand-able. The bare record of its architectural history shows that it was built in 1684 complete with a formal garden of yew walks, terraces and canals; was enlarged and splendidly decorated inside around 1720; was further enlarged, on the advice of James Wyatt, in 1774 at which date the park was land-scaped. The Dining Room was remodelled by James Hopper in 1827. Since then there have been no major changes. What is more, nothing has been taken away—except a beautiful eighteenth-century State Bed, which in 1973 was on temporary loan to the Victoria and Albert Museum. So, for example, the carved and gilt mirrors, which were a feature of the 1720 decoration, remain in place. So too the family coach, portraits of the family, and, in the Servants' Hall, a series of portraits of family servants. There is a very full collection of wills and documents explaining and dating the stages in the building of the house, and identifying architects and craftsmen employed. These documents will be of immense help in planning the restoration work needed. This is considerable and is expected to take several years. In the 1940s there were coal workings under the house and resulting subsidence has caused damage. Until extensive repairs have been carried out it will not be open to the public.

GLYN CEIRIOG *8 miles north-west of Oswestry* Five acres of meadow and a mile of the Glyn Valley tramway, now a public walk.

GRAIG FAWR: DYSERTH *2 miles south of Prestatyn* Sixty acres, comprising a limestone hill, a smallholding and a site of particular scientific interest; rich in fossils and botanical specimens, and a much-visited viewpoint.

———— ⌁ ————

LLANGOLLEN: VELVET HILL Fine views from this hill above the road from Llangollen to the Horseshoe Pass (*76 acres*).

———— ⌁ ————

DYFED

In Dyfed now are all the Trust properties formerly in Cardiganshire, Carmarthenshire and Pembrokeshire. They preserve a wealth of beautiful and varied coastline, some medieval buildings, some farmland, a nineteenth-century folly and a gold mine.

From Carmarthen Bay westward round to St David's Head and then north-east to Cardigan are the following coastal properties:

TREGONING HILL Cliff-land with views over Carmarthen Bay, on the east headland of the Towy estuary.

LYDSTEP HEADLAND *about 4 miles south-west of Tenby* Fifty acres on the headland.

MANORBIER *about 5 miles south-west of Tenby* Fifty acres on Manorbier Cliffs with views.

KETE *about 6 miles west of Milford Haven* Land of 168 acres with a mile of coast west of Dale. There are views of the coast and Skokholm and Skomer Islands.

MARLOES *about 7 miles west of Milford Haven* (opposite) Situated on the south arm of St Bride's Bay, near the island of Skomer. Here the Trust has three farms which together make up about 520 acres, and there is a 2½-mile nature walk.

SOLVA *about 3½ miles east of St David's* There are two properties to the east of Solva and one to the west. At Newgate there are 180 acres with views; just east of Solva harbour 270 acres with one and a half miles of coastline, which includes two bathing beaches; and Morfa Common, between Solva and St David's, which is rough coastal land and a view-point.

Marloes Beach, Dyfed: looking from east to west

PORTH-CLAIS *about 1½ miles south-west of St David's* Cliff-land at Porth-Clais, Porthlysky and Treginnis Uchaf.

PENCARNAN *about 2 miles west of St David's* Cliff-land at Pencarnan and at Rhosson and Trefeiddan, just to the south.

ST DAVID'S *2 miles north-west of St David's* 234 acres of cliff and farmland with views over Strumble Head to the east. Also rights or part ownership over a further 312 acres of coast and cliff.

MWNT *4 miles north of Cardigan* A hundred acres of coast land, part of which was bought with Enterprise Neptune funds.

PENBRYN *7½ miles north-east of Cardigan* Llanborth Farm (*95 acres*) with coastline and access to Penbryn beach.

LLANGRANOG *about 9 miles north-east of Cardigan* A two-hundred-acre farm just north-east of the village at Lochtyn, bought with Enterprise Neptune funds. It provides a mile and a half of cliff, splendid views, two beaches and an island.

CWMTYDI *2½ miles south-west of New Quay* Caerllan Farm of seventy acres with half a mile of coastline on the east side of Cwmtydi inlet.

⟶

Inland properties:

CILGERRAN CASTLE *3 miles south of Cardigan on a rock above the left bank of the Teifi* A thirteenth-century ruin under the guardianship of the Department of the Environment.

DOLAUCOTHI *halfway between Lampeter and Llanwrda by A482 at Pumpsaint* This is a 2,500-acre estate of farm and woodland, which was given as a memorial to the Johnes family, to whom it belonged from Henry VII's reign, and in particular to Lt-Gen. Sir James Hill-Johnes, V.C. The property includes part of Pumpsaint village and a gold mine which has been worked on and off since Roman times.

PAXTON'S TOWER *south of Llanarthney, which is a mile south of A40, and 7 miles to the east of Carmarthen* A folly built in 1811 as a memorial to Nelson. There are fine views.

PONTERWYD *12 miles east of Aberystwyth* Bryn Bras, a 230-acre sheep farm above the gorge of the Rheidol.

TENBY: TUDOR MERCHANT'S HOUSE *on Quay Hill, opposite Bridge Street* A fifteenth-century merchant's house, given by Tenby Corporation. Part is used as a Trust information centre.

⟶

GWENT

Now in Gwent are all the Trust properties formerly in Monmouthshire. There are no others.

BETWS NEWYDD *4 miles north of Usk, 3 miles south-west of Raglan* A twenty-five-acre hill top with views of the Usk valley.

⟶

Stourhead Park, Wiltshire: the Temple of Flora, and the lake in Autumn

Culzean Castle, Ayrshire: Robert Adam's staircase

THE KYMIN *a mile east of Monmouth*   This eight-hundred-foot hill provides views of the Wye and Monnow valleys. There are two Trust buildings: a pavilion (1794) and a Naval Temple (1802) built by local gentlemen. Nelson on a visit congratulated them on this monument to the English Navy.

———

SKENFRITH CASTLE *6 miles north-west of Monmouth*   Ruins of a Norman castle which show clearly its original plan. Also a thirteenth-century curtain wall with towers. Under guardianship of the Department of the Environment.

———

SKIRRID FAWR *3 miles north-east of Abergavenny, east of A465*   Two hundred acres of the 1596-ft summit, with views of the Black Mountains, the Usk valley, and the Sugar Loaf (see below).

———

The Sugar Loaf

$1\frac{1}{2}$ miles north-west of Abergavenny

The Sugar Loaf (below) rises to 1,950 feet and there is a track to the summit. About two thousand acres of the hill, which commands views of the Usk valley, were given to the Trust in 1936 by the first and second Viscountess Rhondda as a memorial to the first viscount.

The Sugar Loaf, Gwent: seen from Hatteral Hill on the Black Mountains

GWYNEDD

In Gwynedd now are all the Trust properties formerly in Caernarvonshire, Anglesey and Merioneth; also Bodnant Garden, formerly in Denbighshire.

They include some buildings of historical interest, but their outstanding contribution to the Trust's work is the preservation of the natural beauty of some 46,000 acres of the mountainous country of North Wales and of its coastline. After Cumbria (which embraces the Lake District) this is the largest acreage belonging to the Trust in any county in the United Kingdom.

Aberdaron

The Trust has two coastal properties just south-west of Aberdaron with views of Bardsey Island and, given good visibility, all down the coast of Wales to St David's.

At BRAICH-Y-PWLL (below), the most westerly point on the mainland of North Wales, the Trust holds 120 acres, including Mynydd Gwyddel and part of Mynydd Mawr. At an inlet below Mynydd Mawr, medieval pilgrims embarked for Bardsey. There is a holy well and the site of a chapel.

On PEN-Y-CIL, about a mile to the south-east, the Trust has thirty acres of cliff-land given by its North Wales Centre as a contribution to Enterprise Neptune.

Braich-y-Pwll, Gwynedd, the westernmost point of North Wales

Aberglaslyn Pass, Gwynedd

Aberglaslyn

south of Beddgelert

The Trust owns a one and a half mile stretch running south from Beddgelert
along both sides of the pass (above) and covering about five hundred acres.

From Pont Aberglaslyn there are exceptionally fine views to the north. The property was acquired by purchase and by gifts from several donors between 1935 and 1958. The old copper-mine workings are dangerous and should not be explored.

⌐○ ○⌐

ABERSOCH *6 miles south-west of Pwllheli*   Nineteen acres of thorn scrub and bracken-covered sand hills between the Llanbedrog road and the sea.

⌐○ ○⌐

Bodnant Garden

8 miles south of Llandudno on A496, entrance by the Eglwysbach road

The garden at Bodnant was begun in 1875 against a background of large native trees, many of which were then eighty years old, and in a setting which enhances immeasurably the beauty of the garden as it is seen today. It covers nearly a hundred acres on a south-westerly slope looking down to the River Conwy and across to Snowdon. On the upper part of the slope are terraces (opposite) and lawns; lower down, in the valley formed by a tribu-tary of the river, there is a less formal layout known as the Wild Garden. There is a great variety of plantings, the guide-book making special mention of formal rose and flower borders, conifers, rhododendrons, azaleas, mag-nolias, camellias, primulas and gentians. Among the rhododendrons are a great many of the Chinese species sent over by Dr E. H. Wilson in the early 1900s and by other collectors. Hybridization of rhododendrons has been carried out at Bodnant for a long time. Hybrids have also been brought from other gardens.

The gardens were begun by Mr Henry Pochin, and when he died in 1895 his daughter, the first Lady Aberconway, continued his work. Her son, the second Lord Aberconway, took over while still a young man. He gave the gardens to the Trust in 1949 and his son, the present Lord Aberconway, continues their development on behalf of the Trust. Like his father before him Lord Aberconway is President of the Royal Horticultural Society. In their work at Bodnant the Aberconways have had the support of two head gardeners of great knowledge and skill, the late Mr F. C. Puddle and his son, the present head gardener, Mr Charles Puddle, M.B.E.

⌐○ ○⌐

CADAIR IFAN GOCH *about 3 miles north of Llanrwst*   A rocky view-point on the east side of the Conwy valley.

⌐○ ○⌐

Bodnant, Gwynedd: view from the terraces

CAE GLAN-Y-MOR *on the Menai Straits between Telford's road bridge and Stephenson's railway bridge* Seven acres given to preserve the view over the Straits and the Snowdon Range.

—⚬ ⚬—

CEMAES BAY *north coast of Sir Fôn (Anglesey)* Fifty acres on the east side of the bay.

—⚬ ⚬—

CEMLYN *about 2 miles west of Cemaes Bay, Sir Fôn (Anglesey)* Agricultural land with about two miles of coast and three hundred acres. A bird sanctuary, part let as a nature reserve (*320 acres*). Visitors are asked not to disturb the wildlife or nesting birds.

⌒ ⌒

COEDYDD MAENTWROG (FFESTINIOG WOODLANDS) *about 8 miles east of Criccieth, near Maentwrog* Two hundred acres of oak woods in the valley of the Afon Dwyryd. It was bought with the help of the North Wales Naturalists' Trust and let as a nature reserve to the Nature Conservancy.

⌒ ⌒

Conwy

ABERCONWY *at the junction of Castle and High Streets* One of the surviving medieval houses, now let as an antique shop.

SUSPENSION BRIDGE The bridge (below) was built by Telford in 1826 and is preserved as one of the outstanding monuments of the Industrial

Conwy, Gwynedd: the suspension bridge in August 1967, after removal of the catwalk

Revolution. (Telford's Menai Bridge antedates it by a few months but has been altered since its building.)

Conwy Suspension Bridge was handed over to the Trust in 1966 with the balance of accumulated tolls by Conwy Borough Council, and this endowment was supplemented by a public appeal.

———

CREGENNAN *about 5 miles south-west of Dolgellau, east of Arthog, on A493* Seven hundred acres of farm and mountain land with two lakes and fine views. Given by Major C. L. Wynne-Jones in memory of his two sons killed in the 1939–45 war.

———

DERLWYN *6 miles north of Dolgellau* A hundred acres of rough moorland and part of a small lake.

———

DINAS GYNFOR *on the north coast of Sir Fôn (Anglesey)* Four acres on this cliff which is the most northerly point in Wales. Also part of an Iron Age hill fort.

———

DINAS OLEU *above Barmouth* Four and a half acres of cliff-land over-looking Cardigan Bay, given in 1895 by Mrs F. Talbot. This was the Trust's first property.

———

DOLMELYNLLYN *about 4 miles north of Dolgellau to the west of A487* A twelve-thousand-acre estate with pasturage on Y Garn, sheep walks on Y Llethr (2,475 ft), Rhaiadr Ddu, a spectacular waterfall on the Gamlan, two hotels and some cottages in Ganllwyd.

———

DOLOBRAN and BRAICH-MELYN *8 miles east of Dolgellau, north of A458* Two mountain farms, good examples of early Welsh farmhouse architecture. Given by Squadron Leader J. D. K. Lloyd and Dr W. E. B. Lloyd as a memorial to the men of Bomber Command.

———

GAMALLT *3 miles north-east of Ffestiniog* Three hundred acres of moorland and part of two lakes. Access on foot only.

359

HAFOD LWYFOG *5 miles north-east of Beddgelert* Three hundred acres overlooking Llyn Gwynant, given by Mr Clough Williams-Ellis.

Harlech

There are two properties near Harlech:

ALLT-Y-MOR *a mile south of Harlech on the Barmouth road* One and a quarter acres with paths to the sea.

COED LLECHWEDD *north of Harlech below the Caernarvon road* Eleven acres with views over the bay.

LLANRWST: TU HWNT I'R BONT *1 mile north of the town* A fifteenth-century stone building; once a courthouse, it is now a shop and tea-room.

LLEDR VALLEY: RHIW GOCH *on the road from Betws-y-Coed to Dolwyd-delan* 160 acres with view over the valley.

MORFA BYCHAN *a mile south-west of Portmadoc* Eighty-five acres of golf course and sand dunes with about half a mile of seashore.

PENARFYNYDD RHIW 244 acres of agricultural land and rough cliff-top grazing, giving magnificent views of the Lleyn coast to Bardsey Island in the west and Cader Idris in the east. 190 acres will be open to public access.

Penrhyn Castle

a mile east of Bangor

Although there has been a fortified building on the site at least since the fifteenth century, the present castle is less than 150 years old. It was built at a time when there was a vogue for a 'Norman' style, and in 1827 Thomas Hopper was commissioned to be the architect of a vast building in neo-Norman style. He had already built two castles in this style in Ireland and entered into his task with immense thoroughness, designing the furniture

as well as the interior decoration. The castle is splendidly sited on a ridge at the end of the Menai Strait. with views of Beaumaris Bay, Great Orme's Head, Anglesey and Snowdonia. The rounded arches say 'Norman', but for the detail of the outside and the lavish decoration of the interior Hopper seems to have drawn inspiration also from oriental styles. In all he produced one of the most remarkable architectural ventures of the nineteenth century, and very little indeed has been changed since he finished it.

The castle is built in Mona marble from Anglesey. The furniture, some of elaborately carved wood and some made of slate from the local quarries, is massive (the dining-room table, for example, seats sixty-four), so that it is not dwarfed by the size of the rooms. The lavish decoration includes plasterwork as well as wood, stone and slate carving and stained glass designed by Thomas Willement, designer of much of the glass in the Houses of Parliament. Queen Victoria visited Penrhyn in 1859, and the heavily carved oak bed in which she slept remains in the State Bedroom.

In addition to its original furniture Penrhyn now contains other collections with a diversity of interest. In the Dining Room there is a collection of pictures which includes works by Velasquez and Van Dyck. In upstairs rooms there are eight hundred dolls from all parts of the world and a collec-

Porth Neigwl, Gwynedd: a view from the hill above Plas-yn-Rhiw on the west side of the bay

tion of stuffed animals. In the stables there is a collection of locomotives and quarry rolling stock. The small formal Victorian garden with fountains contains rare shrubs.

The Pennant family acquired the Penrhyn property, part by marriage and part by purchase, in the 1760s. They developed the slate quarries into an important business. The castle and the estate of over forty thousand acres in other parts of the county were accepted by the Treasury in part payment of death duties in 1951 and transferred to the Trust.

Plas-Yn-Rhiw Estate

between Aberdaron and Llanbedrog

The Trust's Plas-yn-Rhiw estate (above) in the Lleyn Peninsula is about 400 acres and largely coastal land. It includes some extremely fine view-points, a small manor house and garden and some traditional Welsh cot-tages. Acquired by the Trust between 1950–66, it was restored and given, piece by piece, by the Misses Lorna and Honora Keating and their late sister, Eileen.

The Estate consists of the following properties:

PLAS-YN-RHIW MANOR HOUSE *4 miles east of Aberdaron on the south coast road* This small manor house, medieval in part with Tudor and Georgian additions, was restored by the Misses Keating after it had been empty for fifteen years, together with a traditional Welsh cottage. They also replanted the garden with sub-tropical shrubs, specie rhododendrons, azaleas and clipped box and yew. There is a fine magnolia mollicemata.

ABERDARON *2 miles to the north-west of Aberdaron* Cliff-land between Mynydd Anelog and Port Orion and, on the south coast between Aber- daron and Rhiw, the sandy beach, waterfall and stream of Porth Ysgo.

FOEL FELIN WYNT (WINDMILL HILL) *north-west of Mynytho* A local landmark (700 ft) with views of the Snowdon range and seawards. The stone walls of the windmill remain standing.

LLANENGAN *on the eastern arm of Porth Neigwl* Seventy acres with extensive views across Cardigan Bay and the Irish Sea.

MYNYDD-Y-GRAIG *on the west side of Porth Neigwl* Land of 190 acres with a restored, traditional Welsh cottage. There are fine views from the summit of the rocks Creigiau Gwineu eight hundred feet above the sea, with an ancient hill fort.

PENRALLT NEIGWL A seventeenth-century farmhouse and cliff-land adjoining Porth Neigwl Rhiw.

TAN-YR-ARDD with PENMYNYDD *on the slopes of Mynydd Rhiw* A traditional cottage and nineteen acres of moorland with views to Anglesey and to Pembrokeshire.

SEGONTIUM *on south-east outskirts of Caernarvon* The remains of a Roman fort and a museum containing relics found on the site. Under the guardian- ship of the Department of the Environment.

YNYSGAIN *a mile west of Criccieth* Two hundred acres of foreshore and farmland with about a mile of coastline, and the mouth of the Afon Dwyfor.

YNYS TOWYN *on the south-east side of Portmadoc* A small rocky knoll with magnificent views of the Snowdon range and the Glaslyn estuary.

Ysbyty Estate

south-east of Bangor, astride A5

The pictures of Tryfan and Glyder Fawr on page 365 were taken on a section of the Trust's Ysbyty estate which lies near Capel Curig. Tryfan and Glyder Fawr are to the south of the road. This section of the estate extends to nearly sixteen thousand acres and embraces some of the finest scenery in Snowdonia, including the peaks illustrated, Carnedd Dafydd, the north-west slopes of Carnedd Llewelyn and the head of Nant Ffrancon pass.

Another large section of the Ysbyty estate (twenty-six thousand acres) lies south of Betws-y-Coed. It includes Tŷ Mawr, birthplace of Bishop Morgan who first translated the Bible into Welsh, the village of Ysbyty Ifan, where there was a hospice of the Knights of St John, and, mainly to the west of the village, some beautiful hills, valleys and moorland with Llyn Conwy, a lake nearly 1,500 feet above sea level.

The whole Ysbyty estate amounts to over forty thousand acres and is the largest owned by the Trust. It was given in 1951 by the Treasury, who had accepted it in payment of death duty.

⟨ ⇒ ⌀ ⟩

WEST GLAMORGAN

In West Glamorgan are all the Trust properties formerly in Glamorganshire.

Gower Peninsula

The Trust's first acquisition in the Gower Peninsula was made in 1933. There have been gifts by various donors at intervals since then and purchases from Enterprise Neptune funds. The largest of these was the acquisition in 1967 of seventeen miles at the western extremity protecting Rhosili Down and beach, Worm's Head, Llanrhidian Marsh and foreshore. Much of this is leased to the Nature Conservancy. In earlier years gifts were made of viewpoints in the south of the Peninsula at Notthill, Paviland Cliff, Pitton Cliff, Port Eynon Point and Thurba Head; also of land in the Bishopston Valley, six miles south-west of Swansea, and at Pennard (page 366), a little further west adjoining Pwll-du Head (see illustration, Three Cliff Bay, page 366). A cliff-top nature walk begins and ends at Rhosili Village.

Tryfan, Gwynedd:
from Helyg

Glyder Fawr,
and
Castell-y-Gwynt
m Glyder Fach:
Gwynedd

Gower Ponies at Pitton Cross

Three Cliff Bay, Pennard, West Glamorgan

Whitford Burrows

in the north-west part of the Gower Peninsula

Whitford Burrows, the little peninsula which juts out northwards at the western end of the Gower Peninsula, is made up of sand burrows and salt marsh. Its plant and bird life is of great interest. Six hundred and seventy acres here were bought in 1966 with money subscribed to Enterprise Neptune, the Trust's appeal for coastal preservation.

POWYS

All the Trust properties formerly in Breconshire and Montgomeryshire are now in Powys.

Brecon Beacons

About nine thousand acres of mountain and farmland, being the main part of this mountain massif in South Wales, now belong to the Trust (below).

Two sandstone peaks face north and slope southwards. The highest point is Penyfan (2,907 ft).

Brecon Beacons, Powys: from the mountain road across Mynydd Illtyd on the north-west

There are widespread views, extending south to the Bristol Channel, northwards (reputedly) as far as Cader Idris sixty miles away, and eastwards to another Trust property THE SUGAR LOAF near Abergavenny in Gwent. The main part of this property was a gift from the chairman of the Eagle Star Insurance Company in 1965. There is access to the whole area, in some parts by public footpath only.

HENRHYD FALLS and GRAIGLLECH WOODS *11 miles north of Neath*
A wooded ravine and the famous waterfalls.

Powis Castle

on the south edge of Welshpool

Powis (opposite) began life strictly as a castle, a thirteenth-century stronghold on the English border commanding the upper end of the Severn valley. Some of that building remains; but a great deal has been added and parts have been altered. It has been in continuous occupation as a dwelling-house, and succeeding generations have made the alterations and additions which were considered comfortable or beautiful in their own day. Thus the sixteenth century added a long gallery, a remarkably fine one with excellent plasterwork. The seventeenth century put in the staircase hall which was decorated a little later with murals by Lanscroon. The formal terraced gardens—four terraces nearly two hundred yards long—were designed to the formal taste of the early eighteenth century and have not been since altered to suit any more romantic idea of layout. They contain a great variety of herbaceous plants and shrubs. On the far hillside are great trees and rhodo-dendrons.

The principal rooms contain paintings, tapestry and a variety of interesting furniture accumulated by successive owners of the castle.

The earliest owners were the Princes of Powis. They allied themselves to the English in the thirteenth century and in 1283 became Barons de la Pole. Their line died out in the sixteenth century and Sir Edward Herbert bought the castle. He was a relative of Lord Herbert of Chirbury, whose papers are preserved at Powis. In 1784 a Herbert heiress married Edward Clive (son of Clive of India), and he later became the first Earl of Powis (of the third creation). The fourth earl gave the castle to the Trust in 1952. Most of the contents, including relics of Clive of India which his son brought to the castle, were accepted by the Treasury in payment of death duty and trans-ferred to the Trust.

Powis Castle, Powys: the east front

⌇

COUNTY ANTRIM

CARRICK-A-REDE *5 miles west of Ballycastle* Thirty acres of cliff-land linked to the island of Carrick-a-Rede by the famous sixty-foot rope bridge.

⌇

COLLIN GLEN *a mile south-west of the Falls Road boundary of Belfast* Thirty-nine acres giving access to the foot of Collin Mountain.

⌇

CUSHENDUN *on the east coast of Antrim* Sixty acres of this charming village and bay at the foot of Glendun.

⌇

FAIR HEAD AND MURLOUGH BAY *3 miles east of Ballycastle* A thousand acres in a beautiful coastal area, of great interest to geologists and botanists.

⌇

GIANT'S CAUSEWAY *9 miles from Portrush* The unique rock formation was given with about a hundred acres of cliff-land by the Ulster Land Fund and Sir Anthony Macnaghten, Bt. in 1961.

⌇

GLENOE *8 miles south-west of Larne* A small glen (two acres), with a water-fall, next to the village.

⌇

NORTH ANTRIM CLIFF PATH A ten-mile right of way from the Giant's Causeway to White Park Bay. The route covers the rocky peninsula on which sit the ruins of Dunseverick Castle—another Trust property. The Trust also owns Dunseverick Harbour.

⌇

TEMPLETOWN MAUSOLEUM *at Templepatrick, between Antrim and Newton Abbey* Built in Castle Upton graveyard, in memory of Arthur Upton, and designed by Robert Adam in 1783.

White Park Bay

on the north coast 1½ miles west of Ballintoy

White Park Bay (below) is a beautiful and almost unspoiled bay facing the north Atlantic. The beach is of the finest white sand and extends about a mile, with several cliff streams cutting across it. In the hilly grassland which fringes the bay, archaeological finds indicate there was a Neolithic settlement here. A nature trail has been devised by the Route Naturalists' Field Club.

The Trust owns about 180 acres in the bay bought in 1938 through the efforts of the Youth Hostels Association and the Pilgrim Trust.

White Park Bay, County Antrim

COUNTY ARMAGH
Ardress House

7 miles west of Portadown on B28

To begin with, Ardress (below) was a simple seventeenth-century manor house, built in 1660 to replace an earlier building which had been destroyed during the Civil War. Then, about 1770, two wings were added and the interior altered to suit the taste of that time. These additions were made so skilfully and sympathetically that the two building styles were joined to make a pleasing, graceful country house. The man who achieved this transformation was the architect George Ensor, who practised for some time in Dublin, where he was Clerk of Works to the Surveyor General. He came to Ardress when, in 1760, he married the heiress to the property. In the design and decoration of the interior of Ardress he was assisted by Michael Stapleton, a most talented and successful Irish stuccoist whose work in Dublin included the plaster decorations in what is now the residence of the President. Many of his original drawings are housed in the National Library in Dublin. Guided by these the Trust has been able to restore the decorative plasterwork in the principal rooms at Ardress to the water-colour tints he indicated.

George Ensor was followed at Ardress by his son, another George Ensor, who did not follow his father's profession but in the intervals of managing the estate wrote on political and religious subjects, and there are a number of

Ardress, County Armagh

his books in the house. Other members of the Ensor family continued at Ardress until 1960 (completing a connection of two hundred years), when it was acquired by the National Trust through the Ulster Land Fund.

BALLYMOYER *8 miles west of Newry*   Fifty acres of woodland, now leased to the Ministry of Agriculture.

CONEY ISLAND: LOUGH NEAGH *at the southern end of the Lough*   An eight-acre wooded island. Excavations have revealed a Neolithic settlement.

Derrymore House

1½ miles north-west of Newry

Derrymore House (below) is a rare survival of the small, thatched country mansion which was popular with the lesser Irish gentry in the eighteenth century. Although there is no certainty as to the date, it seems to have been

Derrymore House, County Armagh

built for Isaac Corry just after 1776. He was Member for the borough of Newry at that time and legal records show that his family had come into possession of Derrymore property a short while before. He was a supporter of the Union of Ireland and Great Britain, and a lifelong friend of Castlereagh. Castlereagh was a visitor to Derrymore.

The house changed hands several times during the nineteenth century and some additions were made. In 1952 the then owner, whose family had not lived in the house, gave it to the Trust. The nineteenth-century additions were demolished and the house regained its original appearance.

COUNTY DOWN

BALLYMACORMICK POINT *on south side of the entrance to Belfast Lough, north-east of Bangor* Forty acres of rough land on the shore of the Lough.

Castle Ward, County Down: the classical front

BLOCKHOUSE ISLAND and GREEN ISLAND *at the mouth of Carling-ford Lough* Two small islands which are important nesting places for terns. Leased to the Royal Society for the Protection of Birds. Access by permit only.

⟶ ⟵

Castle Ward

7 miles north-east of Downpatrick, 1½ miles west of Strangford village

Though Castle Ward (opposite) cannot escape being viewed as an architectural oddity, it can also claim with assurance to be a highly successful one. The first Lord Bangor and his wife, when they came to build, could not agree on an architectural style. So he had one half built in a classical style which conforms to mid-Georgian taste and she did the other in the 'modern Gothick'. The style she chose may well have startled her neighbours because although it had had its following in England for some time (Walpole's Strawberry Hill was built in the 1750s), it was new to Ireland when she chose it in about 1770. It is believed that one obliging architect coped with both their commissions, but unfortunately it is not known who he was. Some alterations were made in the early nineteenth century, but it is clear that the architect did his work well, and having given the house its two distinct faces contrived, within, to provide different rooms in the two different styles. Thus there is a classical hall with a pillared doorway giving access to the Gothic saloon.

The house is set in a lovely park and garden, with giant oaks and beeches. A mild climate has also favoured many foreign growths. Temple Water, an ornamental lake of the eighteenth century, has a collection of wildfowl, and is overlooked by a small temple. A mile-long nature walk traverses the park.

The property was acquired by the National Trust in 1950 through the Government of Northern Ireland.

⟶ ⟵

CLOUGH CASTLE *24 miles south-east of Belfast* A Norman motte and bailey, leased to the Historic Buildings Branch of the Ministry of Finance.

⟶ ⟵

DUNDRUM: MURLOUGH NATURE RESERVE *2 miles north-west of Newcastle* Sand dunes and heath land, run as Ireland's first nature reserve. A nature walk covers dune and shore ecology. Access by permit only (*700 acres*).

KEARNEY and KNOCKINELDER *3 miles east of Portaferry* Forty-three acres of foreshore and village land with some houses at Kearney and adjoining beach land at Knockinelder which together give access to two miles of coastline. Bought with Enterprise Neptune funds.

———

KILLYNETHER *a mile south-west of Newtownards* 43 acres, mainly woodland.

———

LIGHTHOUSE ISLAND, COPELAND ISLANDS *off the mouth of Belfast Lough* A forty-acre island managed by the Copeland Island Bird Observatory.

———

LISNABREENY *2 miles south of Belfast near Newtownbreda* A farm with a glen and waterfall. There is access to the glen, which provides views of Belfast and Strangford Loughs.

———

MINNOWBURN BEECHES *3½ miles south of Belfast* These stand in 130 acres by Shaw's Bridge on the Lagan and Minnowburn rivers.

———

Mount Stewart Gardens

5 miles south-east of Newtownards on east shore of Strangford Lough

The layout of Mount Stewart Gardens (opposite) on the Ards Peninsula embraces both formal terraces and informal lakeside plantings, covering altogether about eighty acres. The estate also contains over three hundred acres of woodland.

In their present form the gardens are the creation of Edith, Lady Londonderry, who began them in 1921. As she wrote many years later, in her introduction to the guide-book to the gardens: 'I soon discovered that the climate was congenial to many half-hardy shrubs and especially to the more tender rhododendron species usually termed greenhouse subjects; acacias, which we call mimosa trees, grow out of doors, Banksian roses and Lapagerias, a rose-red wax-like greenhouse climber. . . . Groves of eucalyptus trees and Cordylines, palm trees and many kinds of bamboos add to the sub-tropical effect of these gardens, as well as the massive ilex trees and enormous tree heaths which give an Italian appearance to the scene.'

Mount Stewart Garden, County Down: the Temple of the Winds

Mount Stewart formal gardens

All the work of making the garden, including the stonework in the Italian garden, was done by local men.

The garden was transferred to the Trust by Lady Londonderry and Lady Mairi Bury through the Ulster Land Fund in 1956.

The Temple of the Winds (page 377) is a charming eighteenth-century building about half a mile from the entrance to the gardens, standing above the lough shore. Its salon has a handsome ceiling and inlaid floor. Its architect is unknown, but was reputedly 'Athenian' Stuart (James Stuart), who designed the Temple of the Winds in another Trust garden, at Shugborough in Staffordshire. It was given to the Trust by Lady Mairi Bury in 1962, when the Ulster Land Fund gave an endowment.

MOURNE COASTAL PATH Running south along the sea at the foot of Slieve Donard, and including the site of St Mary's, Ballaghanery, associated with St Donard.

Rowallane

11 miles south-east of Belfast on the west of A7

The gardens at Rowallane (below), which consist of a walled garden and informal plantings with woodland, rock and stream, cover about fifty acres

Rowallane, County Down: the gardens

and are about sixty years old. They provide splendid displays of colour in the spring and autumn and are of particular interest to specialists for their magnificent collection of rare trees, shrubs, plants and bulbs.

They are the creation of the late Mr Hugh Armytage Moore, who inherited Rowallane in 1903. He began then to plan the garden in a waste land of whins and outcrops of rock.

The gardens were given to the Trust by the Ulster Land Fund, with an endowment.

Strangford Lough

The Trust has leases over the entire foreshore. The Strangford Lough Wild Life Scheme embraces all of the Lough. Shooting is controlled and refuges have been established for bird watching. Visitors should take care not to disturb birds and to use view-points, hides and car parks, where provided. The foreshore is open to the public at all times.

COUNTY FERMANAGH
Castle Coole

south-east of Enniskillen (A4)

Castle Coole (page 380) is a house that was designed and made, inside and out, all at one time, and has not been subjected by succeeding generations to improvements, additions, alterations or any kind of second thoughts. For all this we can be immensely grateful, as it was designed in a grand, late eighteenth-century manner by a most distinguished architect (James Wyatt) for a patron who had the site, the taste, the determination and the money for such an undertaking—Armar Lowry-Corry, M.P. for County Tyrone, who had inherited estates in Tyrone as well as his mother's Castle Coole property. Later he was created Earl of Belmore.

Wyatt's design has great grace and simplicity, and some of the best London craftsmen of the time (1788–99 was the decade during which the house was built) were brought over to carry out the beautiful interior decoration. Indeed some of the furniture was also made on the spot, as in the later stages joiners who had been making the splendid doors, bookcases and shutters were set to making appropriate furniture. Lord Belmore acted as his own contractor and his accounts for the building work have survived. The Portland stone for the

Castle Coole,
County Fermanagh

Castle Coole,
County Fermanagh:
the landing at the top
of the staircase

fabric of the house he had landed at Ballyshannon, then taken by bullock cart ten miles to Lough Erne and finally water-borne again to Enniskillen. It is not known whether the eighty-acre park which provides such a fine setting for the house was laid out by Lord Belmore or by his son. But fairly certainly its splendid beeches and oaks were already well-grown trees when he planned his house. There is also a flock of grey-lag geese.

Florence Court

7 miles south-west of Enniskillen by A4 and A32

Florence Court (below) provides the visitor with much grandeur outside and ornamentation within. It has also provided students and historians with a fine architectural 'Whodunit?'

There is no record of the date of building nor of whom the architect may have been, nor of the craftsmen who created the outstandingly fine plaster-work in the rooms. There has been much comparison of the designs used in the decoration with designs in Dublin houses which can be dated with certainty. As the outcome of all this, the Georgian Society takes the view that 1764 was the date of completion.

Whoever was responsible achieved an east front (the main frontage) of great grandeur. It runs 260 ft, the centre block in three storeys with flanking pavilions joined to it by arched openings. There is plenty of detailed orna-mentation. Inside, all is solid Georgian craftsmanship for staircase, book-

Florence Court, County Fermanagh

Florence Court, County Fermanagh: the entrance hall

shelves and doorcases, and the principal rooms have walls and ceilings decorated with delightful and intricate plasterwork designs.

The family which was responsible for this remarkable house had first settled in Ireland at Enniskillen in the person of Sir William Cole, a Devonshire knight who had fought for Queen Elizabeth in the Low Countries. His great-grandson was the first of the family to build at Florence Court and it was possibly his son who built the present house. The family continued at Florence Court, becoming Earls of Enniskillen in 1789. They gave the house to the Trust in 1953. There was a serious fire in 1955 but fortunately the damage was repairable.

Mussenden Temple, County Londonderry: looking over the mouth of Lough Foyle

COUNTY LONDONDERRY

Mussenden Temple

5 miles west of Coleraine on A2

When it was built Mussenden Temple (opposite) was a summer-house or a cliff-top library, an adjunct to Downhill Castle, which is now in ruins. It was built about 1738 by the Earl of Bristol, who was Bishop of Derry, and named by him for his cousin, Mrs Mussenden. It overlooks the mouth of Lough Foyle and commands views of the Atlantic and the Antrim coastline. The inscription round the entablature is a quotation from Lucretius which has been rendered into English as

'Tis pleasant, safely to behold from shore,
The rolling ship, and hear the tempest roar.

The Temple was given to the Trust in 1949.

Another surviving adjunct of Downhill Castle, Bishops Gate, a gate with lodge which provides the entrance to Mussenden Temple, also belongs to the Trust. It was given by the Ulster Land Fund in 1962.

The Glen nature walk extends for a mile and is of general natural history and geological interest.

ROUGH FORT *a mile west of Limavady* An unexcavated rath or ring fort, surrounded by trees.

Springhill

near Moneymore on the Moneymore–Coagh road (B18)

Springhill (page 384) was built towards the end of the seventeenth century and was originally a fortified dwelling. It was one of the houses designed to suit the needs of those who had come to Ulster shortly after the Plantation of James I, and who had been supporters of Oliver Cromwell. A hundred years later the defensive barriers and fencework which surrounded it were removed to give the house its present accessibility and to open up the views from the house. But the long, low outbuildings for the servants and the

Springhill, County Londonderry

buildings that were laundry, brew-house, slaughter-house and turf-shed remain. Additions were made to the dwelling-house during the eighteenth century and again in 1850.

The Trust was left the property in 1957 under the will of William Lenox Conyngham, a descendant of the Colonel Conyngham who acquired it in the seventeenth century. There is a costume museum and a cottar's kitchen.

—⊃ ⊂—

COUNTY TYRONE

GRAY'S PRINTING PRESS *main street of Strabane* Here, it is said, the printer of the American Declaration of Independence learned his trade.

—⊃ ⊂—

WELLBROOK BEETLING MILL *Cookstown* An eighteenth-century water mill with nineteenth-century modifications for 'beetling', a stage in linen manufacture. The original machinery has been restored to full working order.

—⊃ ⊂—

384

SCOTLAND

❧ ⟿ ⟾ ❧

ABERDEENSHIRE

Aberdeen

PROVOST ROSS'S HOUSE *in the Shiprow* Built in 1593, this house is now the North of Scotland Headquarters of the British Council.

❧ ⟿ ⟾ ❧

Craigievar Castle

26 miles west of Aberdeen, five miles north of Lumphanan

In the scholarly yet racy guide to Craigievar (pages 386–7) which Dr Douglas Simpson wrote for the Trust he describes it as 'the most cultured, scholarly and refined' of all Scotland's many castles, and 'a masterpiece of old-time Scottish architecture'. Less learned visitors also find it easy to agree with these superlatives.

It was finished in 1626 and remains virtually unaltered. It is impressively sited high up on a hillside. The lower walls are solid and plain and above there is a rich array of corbelling, turrets and cupolas. For the most part the design and decoration of the exterior come from native origins but there are also, as the balustrade on one of the towers, elements brought in from abroad. The interior, though largely medieval in its plan, has superb plasterwork, of the style used to decorate Elizabethan houses.

The castle was built by William Forbes, who had made a fortune as a merchant in trade with Danzig. He was a graduate of Edinburgh University and a man of culture. It is not known who assisted him in the design and building of Craigievar, but it is thought probable that he employed a master mason named I. Bel who is known to have worked in Aberdeenshire at the relevant time.

❧ ⟿ ⟾ ❧

Craigievar Castle, Aberdeenshire

Craigievar Castle, Aberdeenshire: the Great Hall

In 1963, following a public appeal, the Trust bought the castle from the trustees of the late Lord Sempill. A start was also made on building up an endowment fund, for which donations are still sought, for its permanent preservation.

Leith Hall

7 miles south of Huntly on A979

Leith Hall (below) is built round a courtyard. It was not designed as a whole but reached its present size and plan by stages as succeeding generations of the Leith family made their additions. The oldest parts are in the north wing and date from 1650. Much of the building was done during the eighteenth century. When James Leith began the Hall which was to be their home for the next three hundred years, the Leith family had been landholders in Aberdeenshire since the fourteenth century. The Hall contains many family and Jacobite relics.

The name of Hay was added to that of Leith when in 1789 General Alexander Leith inherited the Rannes estate from his great-uncle Andrew

Leith Hall, Aberdeenshire

Hay. Andrew Hay had been an ardent Jacobite, 'out' in the '45 rising, and was excluded from the Act of Indemnity. He persisted in seeking a pardon and eventually this was granted. It is on view in the Hall; reputedly the only Jacobite pardon extant. Many of the family soldiered with distinction, notably Sir James Leith Hay, who commanded the 5th Division in the Peninsular War and was buried (in 1816) in Westminster Abbey. Charles Leith Hay, last male representative of the main line of the family, was killed in 1939 while serving as an officer in the Royal Artillery. Leith Hall, with twelve hundred acres of farm and woodland, was given to the Trust by his mother, the Hon. Mrs Leith Hay of Rannes, in 1945.

Pitmedden

14 miles north of Aberdeen

Pitmedden Garden (page 390) near Udny was designed in 1675. At that time the fashion was still for a formal garden, even if it were a large one with a variety of plants. As Miles Hadfield writes in an appendix to the Trust's guide-book to Pitmedden, 'the simple knot had been elaborated into the freely designed baroque parterre'.

Alexander Seton, an eminent lawyer by profession, had studied the gardens at Holyrood House and other great houses. When he came to build a man-sion-house on the site of the old castle of Pitmedden—his family had acquired the estate in 1603—he made his own plan for the garden. His descendants continued in possession of the estate till 1894, when it was bought at auction by Alexander Keith. The garden had not been maintained and had declined to the status of a kitchen garden. Alexander's son, Major James Keith, made improvements and in 1952 gave it to the Trust with sixty-five acres of the estate and an endowment. Since then it has been brought into being again as the garden of parterres and heraldic patterns which Alexander Seton made there.

This reconstruction has required much ingenuity as well as labour. No detailed plan of Seton's garden survived, as many papers were destroyed in a fire at Pitmedden in 1818; but strategically placed, surviving yew trees provided a guide to layout and Seton's garden pavilions were there to be repaired. Miles of box hedge have been replanted: literally miles, as planting in one year alone (1956) amounted to two miles. Colour is provided by thirty thousand annuals, raised under glass at Pitmedden. Of the four par-terres one is now devoted to Alexander Seton and his family and the others are modelled on those of the garden at Holyrood House as shown by James Gordon of Rothiemay, since it is believed that Seton consulted their designer.

Pitmedden Garden,
near Udny, Aberdeenshire

An aerial view of
Pitmedden Garden

ANGUS

Barrie's Birthplace, Kirriemuir

6 miles north-west of Forfar

No. 9 Brechin Road is a modest two-storey house in a corner of the town known as the Tenements. James Barrie was born in it in 1860 and lived there until he was eight. In the small communal wash-house behind the house he staged his first play—reputedly a drama with a finale in which the actors struggled to push one another into the boiler.

Barrie wrote a good deal of his home town. He named it Thrums after the loose threads used by the handloom weavers there to mend broken threads in their looms. His father was a handloom weaver, and at the time of Barrie's birth worked a loom in a downstairs room in the house. As the family grew he moved it to a loom shop. Barrie always held a great love for Kirriemuir, revisited it in the years of his success, and in accordance with his wishes was buried in the cemetery there.

The house and wash-house have been restored and personal possessions and mementoes of the playwright and his family have been collected there.

The house was given to the Trust in 1937 by Mr D. Alves of Caernarvon. He had bought it in that year on hearing rumours that it was to be shipped to America as a Barrie museum and the wash-house taken to London and re-erected in Kensington Gardens.

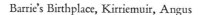

Barrie's Birthplace, Kirriemuir, Angus

Kirkwynd Cottages, Glamis, Angus

Kirkwynd Cottages, Glamis

12 miles north of Dundee

This row of seventeenth-century cottages with stone-slabbed roofs (above) was restored by the Trust in 1957 and converted into a museum. They now house the very fine Angus Folk Collection.

ARGYLE
Gigha Plants
on the Isle of Gigha, west of Kintyre

A collection of valuable plants, including rhododendron hybrids.

These are in the garden of the late Sir James Horlick, who presented them to the Trust in 1962, with an endowment. Under a propagation programme many of the plants are being established in the Trust's own gardens. The Gigha collection is open to visitors during the summer by courtesy of the new owner of the island, Mr David Landale.

Glencoe, Argyllshire, looking south across Loch Leven towards the north end of Glencoe

Glencoe and Dalness

In Glencoe and Dalness the Trust owns 12,800 acres of rugged mountain country. Included in the property are Buachaille Etive Mor and Bidean Nam Bian, which is the highest peak in Argyll (3,766 ft). There is access for walkers and climbers, and the Trust opens an information centre in Glencoe village from May to mid-October. The property was bought in 1935 and 1937 to prevent commercial exploitation, the money for the purchase being provided by the combined efforts of the Scottish Mountaineering, Alpine and other climbing clubs, the Pilgrim Trust and a public subscription.

These Glencoe and Dalness properties make up a rough triangle, each side about six miles long, between the River Etive above Dalness and the

Entrance to Glencoe: Argyllshire, showing Bidean Nam Bean

River Coe above Clachaig. The Trust has published a useful guide to the area, which has a particularly interesting and helpful section on the hill walking for which the area provides the most glorious scope.

The scene of the massacre in 1692 is not on the Trust property.

⌒ ⌒

Isle of Mull

At Burgh, the Trust owns two thousand acres of land known as the 'Wilderness'.

⌒ ⌒

Bachelors' Club, Tarbolton, Ayrshire

AYRSHIRE

Bachelors' Club, Tarbolton

7½ miles north-east of Ayr

Among Trust properties associated with famous Scotsmen there are two associated with Robert Burns—Souter Johnnie's House in Kirkoswald and the Bachelors' Club in Tarbolton. The club, a rural debating society, was formed about 1780, and for their meetings Burns and his friends used the small stone house dating from the seventeenth century which is illustrated above. It is said that Burns became a Freemason here. The Trust acquired the property in 1938. It now contains a small museum of material relating to Burns' life in the area.

Culzean Castle, Ayrshire

Culzean Castle

10 miles south-west of Ayr

The Trust's guide-book to Culzean (above) refers to the castle's 'romantic shell and Georgian interior'. That is a classic example of the understatement which tersely points towards the whole glorious truth.

Culzean stands on the site of a medieval castle. It would be hard to find a more romantic natural setting or more beautiful man-made approaches. The transformation of the old castle and the design and decoration of its 'Georgian interior' was no routine exercise by eighteenth-century craftsmen, but the work of Robert Adam himself.

About 1770, just before the work of transformation began, Culzean belonged to the ninth Earl of Cassillis, whose family (the Kennedys) had played their part in many warlike encounters since medieval times. The ninth Earl's interests lay in peaceful pursuits. He was active in improving standards of farming on his estate, and made some additions to the old castle. His brother, who succeeded him in 1775, employed Adam first to reconstruct

Culzean Castle, Ayrshire: the Round Drawing Room

the old castle internally, then to build a brew-house and later to demolish the seaward side of the castle and built it anew. Adam's brew-house was replaced a hundred years later by the present west wing, which accords satisfactorily with the older parts of the building.

While at work on the castle itself Adam also designed the archway and viaduct at the approach to the castle, and farm buildings in the grounds.

In designing the exterior of Culzean, Adam was concerned to provide his patron not with a strong place capable of withstanding siege, but a romantic, castle-like building of a style then in vogue. He brought to this task both the memory of his youthful study of Scottish traditional styles and all that he had seen of castles in Italy.

For the interior he designed a grand central staircase with elaborate gilt balusters and large columns. This links all the great apartments on the first two storeys.

In the 'Eating Room' (since converted to being the Library), the Round Drawing Room (above) and the Long Drawing Room, he exercised to the full his genius for decoration. Ceilings, fireplaces and mirrors and other fittings are to his design.

In the grounds of the castle, the walled garden was established in the 1780s. This is devoted partly to roses and subtropical plants and partly to flowers, peaches and other fruits. The rest of the grounds were laid out during the earlier part of the eighteenth century. A profusion of flowers border the Avenues; there is a Camellia House and other ornamental garden buildings.

Culzean remained in the possession of the Kennedy family during the nineteenth century, the twelfth Earl of Cassillis being created Marquess of Ailsa in 1831. His great-grandson (the third Marquess of Ailsa) carried out the Victorian changes in the castle and improved the gardens, establishing rare trees and shrubs there. In 1945 the fifth Marquess gave the castle and 565 acres to the Trust.

From 1946 until his death in 1969 a flat in the castle was put at the disposal of Dwight D. Eisenhower as a token of Scotland's thanks for his services as Supreme Commander of the Allied Forces in the Second World War.

In 1971 Scotland's first Country Park, to be run by the Trust in collaboration with the local authorities, was established in the grounds and home farm. Two years later the home farm buildings, also designed by Adam, were restored and adapted to provide reception and information services for visitors.

Souter Johnnie's House, Kirkoswald, Ayrshire: figures of Souter Johnnie and the innkeeper's wife

Souter Johnnie's House, Kirkoswald

4 miles from Maybole

The thatched house now known as Souter Johnnie's House was built in 1785 by John Davidson, the village cobbler of Kirkoswald, and he lived in it for the next twenty years. Burns knew Davidson well and took him as prototype for Souter Johnnie in *Tam O'Shanter*.

The house has been furnished with contemporary furniture, including things used by the Souter's family and a cobbler's chair that was almost certainly his, and with Burns relics.

In the garden are life-size stone figures of Souter Johnnie and other characters from *Tam O'Shanter* which were carved in 1802 and exhibited in various parts of Scotland and England before being brought to the house in 1924.

BUTE

Brodick Castle

Isle of Arran

The delights of Brodick Castle on the Isle of Arran are many and varied. It has a beautiful setting between the bay and the hills and an incomparable garden; its principal rooms contain a wealth of fine furniture, paintings, china and porcelain; and it has a long, eventful history.

The Vikings appreciated the merits of the site and had a fortress here. Robert the Bruce stayed here in 1306 before returning to the reconquest of Scotland. In the fifteenth century the castle was sacked three times, twice by the English. In Covenanting times it changed hands on several occasions. In the Civil War it was held for Charles II until after the battle of Worcester. During the Commonwealth the medieval castle was enlarged, but it was not again to be the scene of violence. Instead the castle was embellished during the eighteenth and nineteenth centuries with the fine collections which it now contains, and during the 1840s was given a new wing. This addition was an ingenious and successful piece of designing by James Gillespie Graham, the architect of a number of Scotland's country houses and of the Tolbooth Spire in Edinburgh. He contrived to make his new wing harmonize very satisfactorily with the exterior of the older building and, at the same time, to provide the more spacious rooms needed as settings for fine furniture and works of art.

Brodick Castle, Isle of Arran: the drawing-room

These enlargements and the accumulation of the contents of the castle were the work of the Hamilton family. Their connection with Brodick began early in the sixteenth century by a marriage with the sister of King James III, and it continued till 1958. They garnered an important contribution to the collections in the castle from the great English collector William Beckford of Fonthill. Beckford's daughter married the tenth Duke of Hamilton in 1810. When her father died she inherited some of his magnificent collection of European and oriental porcelain, Flemish ivories, pastoral paintings by Watteau and other treasures.

The gardens (for all that, there have been gardens at Brodick at least since the eighteenth century) owe their present great distinction and interest to the late Duchess of Montrose (daughter of the twelfth Duke of Hamilton), who began the creation of the woodland garden (opposite) soon after the

Brodick Castle, Isle of Arran: the woodland garden

1914–18 war. She brought the vision and skill of a creative artist to the task, and her garden blooms from early spring to late autumn. She took full advantage of the climate of Arran, which is astonishingly mild and helpful to the gardener, to introduce a variety of shrubs and plants from overseas.

The Trust acquired the castle and grounds in 1958 from the Treasury, who had accepted them in payment of death duty. Endowment towards their upkeep was furnished by public subscription. At the same time Lady Jean Fforde (daughter of Mary, Duchess of Montrose, the creator of the gardens) gave to the Trust eight thousand acres of mountainous country on the island. A note on this property, Goatfell and Glen Rosa, follows.

The Isle of Arran: Goatfell, with Brodick Castle below

Goatfell and Glen Rosa

Isle of Arran

The Trust's Arran property, which extends to eight thousand acres, includes Glen Rosa, Cir Mhor (2,618 ft) and Goatfell (2,866 ft). Here is fine rock-climbing and ridge-walking. Also, which is encouragement to less adventurous spirits, the Trust's Guide to its Brodick and Arran Hills property concludes with the reflection: 'Despite the rugged nature of the Arran Hills they are remarkably safe, being low enough to be climbed quickly but high enough to give that authentic feeling of the wild which is one of the great rewards of hill country.'

Given a clear day these hills command sweeping and impressive views to Ireland, to the Lake District and to the western seaboard of Scotland. Their bird population reads like a catalogue of predators: peregrine falcon, merlin, hen-harrier, buzzard, sparrow-hawk, kestrel and, for good measure, not only the short-eared owl, a daytime hunter, but also the golden eagle. The golden eagle was for a time extinct in Arran but is now re-established.

This property was given to the Trust in 1958 by Lady Jean Fforde at the time when Brodick Castle and the garden which her mother had created there were also acquired.

CLACKMANNANSHIRE

CASTLE CAMPBELL AND DOLLAR GLEN *by Dollar* The late fifteenth-century castle and the wooded glen which provides an attractive walk to it. The castle is under the guardianship of the Department of the Environment.

MENSTRIE CASTLE *in Menstrie* The castle was the birthplace of Sir William Alexander, James VI's Lieutenant for the Plantation of New Scotland, an object furthered by the creation of Nova Scotia baronetcies. The Castle is not Trust property, but the Trust has had rooms in the castle decorated as Commemoration Rooms. The Coats of Arms of a hundred and seven baronets are displayed.

DUMBARTONSHIRE

CUNNINGHAME GRAHAM MEMORIAL *at Castlehill, Dumbarton* A cairn erected on the hill in 1937 in memory of R. B. Cunninghame Graham. It is on the site of the castle where Robert the Bruce reputedly died.

DUMFRIESSHIRE

CARLYLE'S BIRTHPLACE, ECCLEFECHAN *19 miles north of Carlisle* The Arched House, built by Thomas Carlyle's father and uncle (master masons both) in 1791. It now houses some of his letters and belongings. Given by the Carlyle's House Memorial Trust in 1935 when they also gave the house he lived in in London to the National Trust.

The Grey Mare's Tail, Birkhill, Dumfriesshire

The Grey Mare's Tail

8½ miles north-east of Moffat

The Grey Mare's Tail, which is the Tail Burn flowing from Loch Skene just before it enters Moffat Water, is a two-hundred-foot waterfall (opposite). Here the Trust acquired in 1962 a property of rather more than two thousand acres. It harbours rare flowers and, occasionally, some wild goats.

EAST LOTHIAN
Hamilton House

at Prestonpans

Hamilton House (below) was scheduled for demolition in 1937, under a widening scheme, but was later reprieved and acquired by the Trust.

It was built in 1628 by John Hamilton, who is referred to as a prosperous Edinburgh burgess. It has had two tastes of military life, having been used as a barracks while there was the threat of a Napoleonic invasion, and earlier (by repute) occupied by Prince Charles Edward's troops after the battle of Prestonpans.

Hamilton House, Prestonpans, East Lothian

Phantassie Doocot

about 5 miles west of Dunbar

As can be seen in the illustration below, Phantassie Doocot is a highly picturesque building. Its round walls, which are four feet thick at the base, project
upwards to a horseshoe embracing the roof and giving the 'doos' a sheltered
southern exposure. It has been suggested that the builder got his idea for the
design from southern France. It has nesting-places for five hundred birds.
The date of its building is not known, but many 'dowcots', as they were then
known, were built during the sixteenth century, as an Act of 1503 required
lords and lairds to make such provision for food supply. By 1617 so many
had been built that they had become an embarrassment to the authorities.
So, the latter announced that because of 'the frequent building of doucottis
by all manner of personnes', the privilege would be restricted to those owning
a specified amount of land.

Phantassie Doocot,
East Linton,
East Lothian

Preston Mill, East Linton, East Lothian

Preston Mill

about 5 miles west of Dunbar

Preston Mill on the River Tyne is a delightfully picturesque group of buildings and a subject much favoured by artists. It is also still a working mill, being (it is believed) the oldest water-mill in Scotland which is capable of operating. The machinery was renovated for the Trust a few years ago by Messrs Joseph Rank Ltd. In addition to the mill building itself, the photograph on page 407 shows the grain-drying kiln. This is the building with the conical roof, which looks as though it might, perhaps, be an oast house. It is connected to the mill by a stairway. The grain is dried by underfloor heating, and the cowl at the top of the roof turns with the wind to clear the smoke. Its projecting rudder is known locally as the Long Arm of Friendship.

The mill was given to the Trust in 1950 by the trustees of the late Mr John Gray and money for restoration work raised through a public appeal.

EDINBURGH

It seems convenient to note under Edinburgh, rather than under counties, seven properties which are in or near the city.

Nos. 5–7 Charlotte Square

These houses (opposite) are on the north side of a square designed by Robert Adam in 1792. They were completed almost exactly as he intended. It is easy for layman and expert alike to endorse Sir Basil Spence's verdict on one of the finest squares in Europe: 'It is here that we find civic architecture at its best, created by a master.'

Nos 5, 6 and 7 were accepted by the Treasury in part payment of death duty on the estate of the fifth Marquess of Bute and given to the Trust in 1966. No. 5, of which the National Trust for Scotland has been tenant since 1950, is the headquarters of the Trust. No. 6 has been let to a group of distinguished Scots who are collectively the Bute Trustees and have renamed it Bute House. They have adapted it for use both as official residence of the Secretary of State for Scotland and for functions of organizations of national standing. The upper floors of No. 7 are to become the official residence of the Moderator of the General Assembly of the Church of Scotland, and the Trust plans to restore the remainder of the house as a typical New Town residence of Georgian times.

Charlotte Square, Edinburgh

CAIY STONE *Oxgangs Road, Fairmilehead*   A nine-foot monolith of which no history is known.

GLADSTONE'S LAND *in Royal Mile*   Built in 1620 and originally the home of an Edinburgh burgess, Thomas Gledstanes. It has remarkable painted ceilings. Let to the Saltire Society.

STENHOUSE MANSION *off Stenhouse Road*   An early seventeenth-century merchant's house which was adapted by the Trust as a centre for restoration of tempera paintings. Now leased to the Department of the Environment as a restoration centre.

SUNTRAP *No. 43 Gogarbank*   A gardening advice centre, the first of its kind in Scotland. Gives advice and practical instruction to amateurs, Trust members and others. House and grounds given for this purpose by Mr G. B. Boyd Anderson. The gardens have glass-house and outside demonstration units, nursery and garden sections and lecture hall.

LAMB'S HOUSE *Burgess Street, Leith* A five-storey merchant's residence and warehouse of about 1600. Now a Day Centre for Leith Old People's Welfare Council, which helped with its restoration.

———

MALLENY GARDEN *in Balerno* A seventeenth-century house, which is not open, and a garden which is. Interesting plants, including a collection of shrub roses.

———

FIFE

BALMERINO ABBEY *5 miles west of Newport* Ruins of a thirteenth-century Cistercian monastery. Closed to visitors but can be closely viewed.

CULROSS *on the north shore of the Forth* The borough did a prosperous trade in coal and salt during the sixteenth and seventeenth centuries and most of its buildings date from that time. The Trust has acquired and restored a number of properties here, under the 'Little Houses Scheme' (page 441) and according to similar conditions before that scheme came into operation.

'THE PALACE' is a house of about 1600 which retains much of its original interior. It was the Trust's first purchase, made in 1932. Under the guardianship of the Department of the Environment.

ST MUNGO'S CHAPEL Ruins of the Chapel built in 1503 on the traditional site of the saint's birth.

———

Falkland Palace

11 miles north of Kirkcaldy

Although no sovereign has lived at Falkland since Charles II and the Palace has been in the custody of hereditary keepers, it is still the property of the monarch. In 1952 the present hereditary keeper (Major Michael Crichton-Stuart) appointed the National Trust for Scotland to be deputy keeper and made over to the Trust an endowment for future maintenance of palace and gardens.

There were earlier buildings on the site but the Palace, which has been in part restored during the last eighty years, was built in the mid-fifteenth century and enlarged and improved about 1540. It was a hunting palace of many of the Stuarts, including James V and Mary Queen of Scots. James V made the sixteenth-century improvements in the palace in part, it seems, to welcome his French bride. He also had a tennis court built, the second oldest royal tennis court in Britain.

Falkland Palace, Fife:
the Chapel Royal

Falkland Palace, Fife:
seventeenth-century Dutch bed
in the King's Room;
workmanship comparable
to that of furnishing
of Stuart royal bedrooms

In 1650, on practically his last visit to Falkland, Charles II gave new colours to the troops selected to guard him. This is now considered to have been the christening of the Scots Guards. The regiment has retained a connection with Falkland. In 1958 it mounted guard when, on the occasion of the quincentenary of the royal burgh, the Queen visited there.

Misfortune occurred in 1653 when the East Range of the palace was burned, apparently by accident not design, during the occupation of the town and palace by Cromwellian troops.

During the eighteenth century and until 1855 maintenance of the fabric was neglected and the palace became ruinous. The hereditary keeper of that date, on the advice of Sir Walter Scott, began to restore it as a 'romantic ruin'. But in 1877 John Crichton-Stuart, third Marquess of Bute, became hereditary keeper and set about the full restoration of the Gatehouse. His policy has been maintained, and today not only the Gatehouse has been restored but also the finely decorated Chapel Royal (page 411), and the King's Room (page 411) in the East Range has been redecorated and refurnished. Since 1945 the Palace Garden has been re-created.

Beside the Palace Gatehouse is St Andrew's House, once occupied by a member of the royal household. This was restored and given to the Trust in 1952 by Major Michael Crichton-Stuart.

Hill of Tarvit

2½ miles south-west of Cupar

A late seventeenth-century mansion house, remodelled in 1906 by Sir Robert Lorimer and given with its contents and a farming estate. Let to the Marie Curie Memorial Foundation as a nursing home; but part of it is open.

Kellie Castle

3 miles north-west of Pittenweem off A921

The building provides a fine example of the domestic architecture of Lowland Scotland at the turn of the sixteenth century (opposite). But it was not built all of a piece. The first work on the site was about 1360 and changes or additions were made during the next two hundred years. Then between 1573 and 1605 large additions were made which, to quote the Trust's guide book, 'making architectural connexion with the two original towers, so

Kellie Castle, Fife

Kellie Castle, Fife: long drawing-room, originally the Great Hall

wonderfully gave its present unity to the castle'. No architect is named but we can thank—to quote the guide book again—'the imaginative gift of some master builder'.

The interest of the interior includes some fine seventeenth-century plaster work.

The castle came to be neglected in the early nineteenth century but was rescued in 1878 by Professor James Lorimer and in more recent years cared for by his grandson, the sculptor Hew Lorimer.

It was bought by the Trust in 1970 with the help of the Pilgrim Trust, an anonymous benefactor and a grant from the Secretary of State for Scotland. A good start was made towards establishing an endowment fund, but in 1974 the Trust was still asking for additions to the fund.

Kirkcaldy

SAILORS WALK A harbour-side group of seventeenth-century merchants' houses (not open).

The Giles, Pittenweem, Fife: restored under the Trust's Little Houses scheme

Little Houses, Pittenweem and Crail

In 1960 the Trust formed a Little Houses Restoration Fund. This is being used to preserve the charm and individuality which many Scots burghs derive from their domestic architecture. Old houses of interest are bought, reconstructed to modern living standards and sold under safeguards—the proceeds of the sale being then available for another reconstruction. The scheme was selected as one of four restoration projects in Britain for special study during European Architectural Heritage Year, 1975. The illustration on page 414 shows a block of seventeenth-century houses which were in an advanced state of disrepair, now restored and made into family-size houses complying with modern standards of comfort. Similar restorations have been carried out or are in progress in other town; (see 'Little Houses' on page 441, and Dunkeld on page 427).

INVERNESS-SHIRE

Abertarff House

in Inverness

Abertarff House (page 416) is one of the oldest houses in the burgh of Inverness, dating from the sixteenth century.

The Trust received it as a gift from the National Commercial Bank of Scotland in 1963, and during the next three years restored it and improved the interior to modern standards. The restoration work was given a Civic Trust award. The house has been let to An Comunn Gaidhealach (The Highland Association), and is used as its headquarters.

Culloden

5 miles east of Inverness

In the 1930s it was feared that commercial development would encroach on the battlefield and its surroundings. This fear prompted the late Mr Alexander Munro of Leanach Farm to give two pieces of the battlefield to the Trust. Gifts from others (including the late Hector Forbes of Culloden) have followed, and the Trust now has in its care the graves of the Clans,

Abertarff House, Inverness

Culloden, Inverness-shire:
Old Leanach Farmhouse

the Memorial Cairn, the Well of the Dead, the Cumberland Stone and Old Leanach Farmhouse.

Old Leanach Farmhouse, illustrated opposite and a silent witness of the battle, is now a battle museum.

Glenfinnan Monument

about 8 miles west of Fort William

A tall tower topped by a statue of a kilted highlander stands within a grassy enclosure at the head of Loch Shiel (below). On the walls of the enclosure are inscriptions in Gaelic, Latin and English recording that the monument was erected in 1815 by Alexander Macdonald of Glenaladale on the spot where Prince Charles Edward raised his standard on 19th August 1745.

This Alexander was a grandson of the Alexander Macdonald of Glena-ladale at whose house the prince stayed on the night before the raising of the standard.

Glenfinnan Monument near Fort William, Inverness-shire: looking down Loch Shiel

The statue, which is the work of the sculptor Greenshields, does not depict the prince himself but is a figure representative of the men who followed him. There is a staircase inside the tower which gives access to the top platform.

The monument was given to the Trust in 1938 by Sir Walter Blount, the Trustees of Glenaladale Estates and the Roman Catholic diocese of Argyll and the Isles.

The preservation of the monument represents an important side of the Trust's work, namely the preservation of places with historic associations. Other Trust properties in this same category are the Pass of Killiecrankie, Bannockburn Monument and Culloden.

St Kilda

110 miles west of the Scottish mainland

There are two sides to the Trust's preservation work in the St Kilda island group—on the one hand the preservation of the wild life of the islands (page 417), and on the other the study of the way of life established there during the long period of occupation before 1930.

The Trust organizes periodic expeditions to the group, which has been leased to the Nature Conservancy.

The picture (below) shows one of several different styles of cleit construction of which specimens are being preserved. The cleit was a combined store and drying chamber. The turf roof is thick and keeps out rain; the dry-stone walls let through enough wind for drying purposes. A cleit might have contained food, fuel, nets and clothes.

St Kilda, Inverness-shire: a cleit

St Kilda, Inverness-shire: gannets off St Kilda

KINCARDINESHIRE
Crathes Castle

14 miles west of Aberdeen, on the north bank of the Dee

Crathes Castle (below) was built between 1546 and 1596, apart from the east wing, which was added on during the eighteenth century as an enlargement to the building. It has been lived in continuously ever since, and retains not only its original interior decoration but also some of its original furniture.

Crathes Castle, Kincardineshire

It was built by the Burnett family, who had held land here on the River Dee at least since 1323. Shown in the castle today is the jewelled ivory horn reputedly given by King Robert the Bruce to Alexander Burnett in that year, with lands at Crathes and a duty to serve as coroner of the Royal Forest of Drum. It was his descendants who built the sixteenth-century castle, made the eighteenth-century additions to the building, and laid out the fine formal eighteenth-century garden which has been maintained and improved and remains one of the attractions of Crathes. Though mindful of their family home, they were not always a stay-at-home family, and at different times provided Basle with a professor of philosophy and Salisbury with a bishop. During the eighteenth century a William Burnett was successively governor of New York and of New Jersey, Massachusetts and

Crathes Castle, Kincardineshire: tempera painted ceiling, one of the Nine Nobles

New Hampshire, and it is after him that the Burnett Society in America is named. In 1951 the late Sir James Burnett of Leys gave Crathes to the Trust with an endowment.

The castle is a four-storey building with six-foot-thick walls, but is far from being plain and forbidding, since it is topped with square and rounded turrets and has dormer windows and gargoyles.

Inside, apart from the interest of an interior which has been preserved as its sixteenth-century creators made it, there is the very special interest of the tempera painted ceilings (page 421). These were part of the original decoration and the painting is among the most beautiful in Scotland. With the tempera technique (which entails using egg-yolk as a binding agent for chalk colours) the medieval craftsman was able to achieve unusually bright colours. These remain, but the paintings present other problems of preservation, those at Crathes having been subject to a certain amount of flaking. But the Trust (which has similar paintings to care for in the chapel of Falkland Palace, in Gladstone's Land in Edinburgh and at Culross) became engaged on a programme of research and experiment which led to the establishment of a centre for restoration of tempera and other works at Stenhouse Mansion, Edinburgh. This project, originally undertaken by the Trust in association with the Environment Department, is now entirely run by the Department.

Of the three painted ceilings at Crathes one carries a miscellaneous assembly of figures; but the others each have an ambitious theme, vigorously executed. One shows the Nine Nobles—the stock pagan, Old Testament and Christian heroes of the troubadours' repertoire—each with a eulogistic rhyme. The other is the Chamber of the Nine Muses, where in addition to the figures of the four muses the painter has added figures for five virtues to make up his set of nine.

The gardens were given their formal plan at the beginning of the eighteenth century. Lime avenues were planted leading to the river, and yew hedges, now grown to twelve feet, were established to mark the division of the garden into rectangular sections. The various divisions of the garden have now been planted with a very great variety of shrubs and plants, some native and others from North and South America, Africa, India and New Zealand.

KIRKCUDBRIGHTSHIRE

BRUCE'S STONE *6 miles west of New Galloway* A granite boulder on Moss Raploch where Bruce defeated the English in 1307.

$$\iff$$

ROCKCLIFFE *about 7 miles south of Dalbeattie* There are several properties here, including a house and some cottages in the village (not open). The Mote of Mark is the site of a hill fort; Rough Island is a bird sanctuary; there are nine acres of coastline near the Merse; another fifty acres of rough coastline between Rockliffe and Kippford.

$$\iff$$

Threave

2 miles from Castle Douglas

The gardens of Threave House, which are open to the public, are the Trust's School of Practical Gardening. This provides a two year course for sixteen to twenty year olds with a diploma that is recognized by education authorities.

The house, which is not open, was given by the late Major A. F. Gordon of Threave with the 1300-acre estate.

Threave Wildfowl Refuge, on the estate, and on and near the Dee, is a roosting and feeding place for many species. There is restricted access.

LANARKSHIRE

BLACKHILL: STONEBYRES *3 miles west of Lanark* A view-point commanding the Clyde valley.

$$\iff$$

Provan Hall

in Auchinlea Road, Glasgow E4

Built in the fifteenth century, Provan Hall is probably the most perfectly preserved pre-Reformation mansion house in Scotland. It was given to the Trust in 1935 by a group of people who also had the building restored.

Provan Hall, near Stepps, Glasgow, Lanarkshire

MIDLOTHIAN

INVERESK LODGE GARDEN *at Musselburgh* The seventeenth-century house is not open but the garden displays a range of plants suitable for the small garden.

━◦ ◦━

NAIRNSHIRE

BOATH DOOCOT: AULDEARN *2 miles east of Nairn* A seventeenth-century dovecote on the site of an ancient castle. Montrose flew the standard of Charles I here at battle on 9th May 1645 when he defeated the Covenanters. Battle plan on display.

━◦ ◦━

PERTHSHIRE

Ben Lawers

26 miles west of Aberfeldy

On the southern slopes of Ben Lawers (below), and the nearby Ben Ghlas and Coire Odhar the Trust now has an eight-thousand-acre property. Ben Lawers rises to 3,984 ft—the highest mountain in Perthshire—and many rare alpine plants grow there. From the summit there are views of both the Atlantic and the North Sea. Coire Odhar is popular for winter sports. The property was bought in 1950 from the Trust's Mountainous Country Fund—a fund formed by Mr P. J. H. Unna.

The Trust has published an extremely interesting and informative book on Ben Lawers containing expert accounts of its history, plant and animal life and the skiing areas in the range. In his notes on its plant ecology Dr Duncan Poore of the Nature Conservancy describes Ben Lawers as far famed for the richness of its alpine flora and rightly called 'the botanists' Mecca'. To this the Trust's introduction to the book adds a rider that one of the main objects in acquiring Ben Lawers was to ensure the preservation of the rare alpine flora and urging visitors not to uproot and 'collect' these flowers as speciments. In 1972 a Visitor Centre was opened here. This gives

Ben Lawers, Perthshire: seen from a point west of Killin, looking north-east

Killin, Perthshire: the bridge over the River Dochart, Ben Lawers in the background

information about alpine flora and other features of the area and provides a base for guided walks and activities arranged by ranger-naturalists.

Mr Unna, who died in a climbing accident near Dalmally in 1950, was a president of the Scottish Mountaineering Club in the 1930s. His generosity and his active interest have enabled the Trust to acquire or to accept Glencoe and Dalness, Kintail, Ben Lawers and Torridon.

Dunkeld

15 miles north of Perth

The Trust has achieved an excellent work of preservation and restoration at Dunkeld (below). In the early 1950s almost all the charming little houses between Atholl Street and the cathedral, dating from the rebuilding of the town after the battle of Dunkeld (1689), were half derelict and being considered for demolition. Between 1954 and 1966 the Trust restored twenty of these houses and the Perth County Council another twenty. The charm of the exteriors has been retained while the interiors have been improved to modern standards. The Trust was enabled to carry out this work by receiving

Dunkeld, Perthshire: little houses

most of the property as a gift from the Atholl Estates and by the response to a public appeal for funds to pay for its restoration. (See also the Little Houses, Fife, page 410.) Stanley Hill, an artificial mound of 1730, given to the Trust in 1958, provides a wooded background to the Little Houses.

The Hermitage

2 miles west of Dunkeld

The Hermitage (below), also once called Ossian's Hall, was the centre-piece of an eighteenth-century garden and sited to command a dramatic view of the waterfall below. It was built by the third Duke of Atholl in 1758 and decorated inside in 1783 with paintings of Hospitality, supported by Justice, and Fortitude and Harmony, attended by Temperance and Prudence. It suffered damage from vandalism during the nineteenth century but was restored, in simplified form, by the Trust in 1952 as the centre-piece of a delightful walk through the woods along the River Braan. Together with fifty acres of the woodland it was given to the Trust in 1943 by the eighth Duke's widow in accordance with his wishes.

The Hermitage, near Dunkeld, Perthshire

Pass of Killiecrankie, Perthshire: the railway viaduct over the River Garry

Pass of Killiecrankie

2½ miles north of Pitlochry

The Pass of Killiecrankie (page 429) ranks for preservation as well for its beauty as for its historical association. The view-point towards the head of the Pass has long been admired by visitors, among them Queen Victoria, who came here in 1844.

The site of the battle of 27th July 1689 was the hillside above the main road a mile north of the Pass. But it was through the Pass that King William's men advanced to engage the Jacobite army led by 'Bonnie Dundee', and through it that many of them later fled in retreat.

The Trust property of fifty acres here was given in 1947 by Mrs Edith Foster.

Perth: Branklyn Garden

Dundee Road

A small garden (two acres) with an outstanding collection of plants, particularly alpines. Bequeathed in 1967, with an endowment, by Mr John G. Renton who had made it with his wife—starting in 1922 with a derelict orchard. The City of Perth is giving practical support for its maintenance.

Pitlochry

The Trust has two small properties close to Pitlochry. At Craigower, though only thirteen hundred feet up, there is a viewpoint commanding wide views over country typical of the Perthshire Highlands. A mile and a half further along the A9 are fifty acres of the banks of the Tummel and the Garry. This Linn of Tummel property (which includes a nature trail) adjoins Trust property in the Pass of Killiecrankie.

RENFREWSHIRE

PARKLEA FARM *near Port Glasgow*   A strip of land on the south bank of the Clyde leased to the Town Council as a recreation ground.

———

WEAVERS COTTAGE *in Kilbarchen village, 10 miles south-west of Glasgow* An eighteenth-century weaver's cottage which now houses a collection of weaving equipment and domestic utensils.

———

ROSS AND CROMARTY

CORRIESHALLOCH GORGE *12 miles south-east of Ullapool*   A spectacular mile-long gorge and the 150-ft Falls of Measach. A suspension bridge provides a good view-point. Given in 1945 by Mr John J. Calder of Ardargie.

———

Hugh Miller's Cottage

in Cromarty

The seventeenth-century thatched cottage (below) in which Hugh Miller was born is one of the buildings which are preserved by the Trust rather for their association with some famous Scotsman than for their architectural interest. (Carlyle's birthplace and Barrie's also come into this category, as does the Bachelors' Club at Tarbolton.)

Hugh Miller's Cottage, Ross and Cromarty: birthplace of the geologist

Miller, who was born in the cottage in October 1802, was a man of great versatility. He was a stonemason by trade, and was for a time accountant in the Commercial Bank of Cromarty. As a man of letters, he contributed to Mackay Wilson's *Tales of the Borders*. He also gained wide recognition as a geologist. The cottage now houses a small museum.

The cottage was given to the Trust by the Cromarty Town Council in 1938.

> ———⊃ ⊂———

Inverewe

85 miles west of Inverness

The garden of Inverewe in Wester Ross was begun just over a hundred years ago, not on the site of an earlier garden, nor in an area where exotic plants already flourished. Quite to the contrary: Mrs Mairi T. Sawyer wrote of the place her father, Osgood Mackenzie, chose that it was almost devoid of vegetation; that the only soil was acid black peat and that the exposed position caught nearly every gale that blows. But in conclusion she wrote: 'To counter the more vicious of the elements there is the benevolent warm flow of air emanating from the Gulf Stream.'

So, supported by the Gulf Stream and an annual rainfall of sixty inches, and armed with both a love of trees and flowers and a knowledge of the coast (his father and grandfather had been Lairds of Gairloch), Osgood Mackenzie began in 1862 to make the garden which today delights visitors from all over the world with its profusion of exotic plants.

Frost is not entirely unknown at Inverewe—indeed the Fahrenheit thermometers showed twenty-five degrees below freezing-point in early 1947 and during the winter of 1954–5—but it is unusual, and Mrs Sawyer was able to claim that her father could grow 'as many and as good plants at Inverewe in the open air as is possible at Kew under glass'.

Establishing them called for windbreaks, the physical importation of soil, and time. Mackenzie planted Corsican pine and Scots fir as his windbreak with a variety of other trees in support. His daughter has recorded that: 'To Corsican pine he awarded first prize for rapidity of growth on bad soil and exposed sites and confessed that among the trees, many of the foreigners were far and away hardier than most Scottish natives.'

After about fifteen years Mackenzie felt he was making real progress and introduced eucalyptus and Monterey pine. Some of these trees have now grown to a great size, and twining on them are creepers introduced from many parts of the world. The general layout of the garden is informal,

Inverewe, Ross and Cromarty: view of Ben Airrdh Char from the walled garden

winding paths leading from section to section. The names of some of the sections are self-explanatory, thus: 'Grove of Big Trees' and 'Azaleas', but others, like 'Peace Plot' and 'Bambooselem', need explanation. 'Peace Plot' is a post-1914–18 war planting of the more tender rhododendrons. 'Bambooselem' covers not only bamboos but also massed hydrangeas and a twenty-eight-foot-high *Magnolia stellata*.

The Trust's guide to Inverewe, edited by D. J. Macqueen Cowan, former assistant keeper of the Royal Botanic Garden in Edinburgh, includes a list of what he describes as 'the more noteworthy plants and flowers to be found in the garden'. This list totals no less than 320 items.

Mrs Sawyer, who for many years helped her father at Inverewe and after his death in 1922 continued the work which he had set in hand, gave the garden to the Trust, with endowment for upkeep, in 1952. This endowment was added to by the Pilgrim Trust and an anonymous donor.

433

STAGE HOUSE: INVEREWE   An abandoned army camp, between Inverewe Gardens and Poolewe village, has been made by the Trust and Shell-BP Ltd into a caravan and camping site.

Kintail, Balmacara, The Falls of Glomach

The Trust has three large properties in Wester Ross, Kintail (below) of nearly thirteen thousand acres, Balmacara of eight thousand and the Falls of Glomach of two thousand. They preserve a magnificent stretch of West Highland scenery embracing the Five Sisters of Kintail, which rise abruptly from the lochside to three thousand feet, most of the Kyle-Plockton peninsula, and the 370-ft Falls of Glomach.

Kintail is a perfect countryside for climbers and for hill walkers, and the Trust's property is freely open to them at all times of the year. The walker here is rewarded not only by magnificent views but in early summer also by a wealth of bird life—from meadow pipits to the golden eagle. The Falls of Glomach, the highest in Britain, are remote and difficult of approach and

The Peaks of Kintail, Ross and Cromarty: Loch Duich in the foreground

live up to their name—Glomach being in Gaelic 'forbidding'. The water sweeps down a high wild glen before making its abrupt drop, to be splintered on a rock projection three hundred feet below and fall again to the bottom pool. Balmacara is a well wooded property and shows some exceptionally fine Douglas firs.

The Kintail estate was given to the Trust in 1944 by the late Mr P. J. H. Unna; the Balmacara estate was bequeathed in 1946 by the late Lady Hamilton; the Falls of Glomach were given in 1941 by Mrs B. C. M. Douglas of Killilan and Captain the Hon. Gerald Portman of Inverinate.

SHIELDAIG ISLAND   A thirty-acre island, almost entirely covered in Scots pines in Loch Torridon, off Shieldaig. It was acquired with the aid of the Trust's Coastline and Islands Fund.

STROME CASTLE *beside Loch Carron*   Ruins of the ancient castle, which was destroyed in 1602.

Torridon, Ross and Cromarty: looking across Upper Loch Torridon to the Torridon mountains

Torridon

The fourteen-thousand-acre Torridon estate includes some of the finest mountain scenery in Scotland. The north-western boundary of the estate runs along the summit ridge of Beinn Eighe (3,309 ft); to the south is the great mass of Liathach (3,546 ft), its seven tops linked by narrow ridges nearly five miles long; and to the west the mountain of Beinn Alligin (3,232 ft). In addition to their scenic beauty the mountains hold great interest for geologists.

There is a diversity of wild life on the estate, including red deer, pine marten, wild cat, golden eagle, peregrine falcon and seals.

The estate, less the mansion-house and adjacent woods, was given to the Trust in 1967 by the Treasury, who had accepted it in payment of death duty following the death of the fourth Earl of Lovelace. During his last few years the earl had been in consultation with the Trust and others with a view to arranging for public access to the Torridon Mountains.

The Trust now also owns Alligin Shuas, two thousand acres which adjoin the western extremity of the Torridon estate and were formerly part

Plockton Village, Loch Carron and the hills of Applecross, Ross and Cromarty

of it. This was given, by their three sons in Montreal, in memory of Sir Charles and Lady Edith Gordon. Sir Charles was owner of the whole Torridon estate from 1927 to 1947.

ROXBURGHSHIRE
Turret House, Kelso

Turret House (below), though altered and enlarged during the eighteenth and nineteenth centuries, was probably built in the seventeenth to contain two or perhaps three sets of apartments.

It was restored by the Trust in 1965 with the co-operation of St Andrew's Episcopal Church, Kelso, to whom it is now leased as a church hall.

Turret House, Kelso, Roxburghshire

STIRLINGSHIRE

Bannockburn Monument

2 miles south of Stirling

The battle area has for the most part been built on. But about sixty acres around the Borestone were bought for preservation in 1930 and later given to the Trust. The purchase in 1930 was made from a public subscription which was raised by a national committee led by the Earl of Elgin, head of the Bruce family. According to tradition the Borestone site was Bruce's command post before the battle, and takes its name from a large stone block with a socket in which it is said that he placed his standard. Only fragments remain.

On the 24th June 1964, the 650th anniversary of the battle, Her Majesty the Queen unveiled the statue of King Robert the Bruce which now stands on the site.

The statue (below), a bronze by C. d'O. Pilkington Jackson, was presented to the Trust by the King Robert the Bruce Memorial Fund Committee which had commissioned it.

The visitor centre provides an audio-visual presentation of the Wars of Independence and the battle entitled 'The Forging of a Nation'.

Bannockburn, Stirlingshire: statue of the Bruce

WEST LOTHIAN
The House of the Binns

3½ miles east of Linlithgow

The site has been inhabited, traditionally, since Pictish times, but the house of the Binns (below) is now substantially early seventeenth-century, with some additional rooms acquired in the middle of the eighteenth century, and battlements early in the nineteenth century. The battlements were substituted for crow-stepping and pointed turrets. Four of the main rooms have very fine ornate plaster ceilings that date from 1612 to 1630. It has not been established whether this beautiful work was carried out by Italians or by Italian-trained Scots, though there is good evidence that the latter were concerned in it.

In 1944, when Eleanor Dalyell of the Binns gave it to the Trust, the house had been the home of the Dalyells for more than three hundred years. Included in the contents of the building, which formed part of her gift, are a number of interesting family portraits. Among those portrayed is the builder of the house, Thomas Dalyell. He had accompanied James VI to London in 1603 and there made such a fortune that on his return to Scotland, nine years later, he was able to buy the Binns and enlarge and transform the house. Also, there is his son, the famous General Tam Dalyell of the

The Binns, West Lothian

A moulded plaster ceiling in the Binns

Binns. It was in 1681, while he was commander-in-chief of the forces in Scotland, that the regiment which became known as the Royal Scots Greys was formed and held its first musters at the Binns. Succeeding generations of the family have given loyal and gallant service in the armed forces of the Crown, and Sir John Graham Dalyell, author of works on a variety of subjects, was knighted in 1836 for his services to literature and science.

LINLITHGOW: NOS. 44 AND 48 HIGH STREET Sixteenth- to early seventeenth-century houses (not open).

SOUTH QUEENSFERRY: PLEWLANDS HOUSE This was built in 1643 (not open).

440

ZETLAND

Fair Isle

The most isolated inhabited island in Britain was acquired by the Trust in 1954 with the help of a grant from the Dulverton Trust. Housing and other improvements have been made with a view to retaining the existing population and encouraging new families to settle.

A bird observatory was founded here in 1948 by Mr George Waterston. About three hundred species have been noted and there are breeding colonies of great and arctic skuas. Access, twice weekly, in summer by boat from Shetland; also charter flights from Shetland. There is a hostel for bird watchers (apply to Warden).

The Little Houses Scheme

Some of the work done with the help of the Little Houses Restoration Fund is the subject of illustrations and notes on pages 414–15 and 427.

In the Trust's 1973 Year Book it was reported that the value of the work undertaken up to that time was over £200,000—exclusive of two major undertakings in which the Trust was agent of the Crown Estates Commissioners who provided the capital. The report goes on to say 'but impressive

St Monance

though these statistics may be, the value of the work in terms of amenity is even more important'. Places where, at the time of this report, work had been completed or was in progress are Anstruther, Arncroach, Cellardyke, Crail, Cromarty, Culross, Dunlop, Dysart, Falkland, Kelso, North Berwick, Perth, Pittenweem and St Monance (page 441).

The Trust has published a booklet, *The Trust and Little Houses*, which like other Trust publications is obtainable from 5 Charlotte Square, Edinburgh.

National Trust Properties
of Special Interest

The lists below will help those who wish to know at which of the Trust's properties they will find the things in which they have a special interest. I cannot suggest that they are comprehensive lists because one is always learning something new about the Trusts; but they cover a lot of the ground.

Barns

ASHLEWORTH	Gloucestershire
BREDON	Hereford and Worcester
BUCKLAND ABBEY	Devon
COTEHELE	Cornwall
EAST RIDDLESDEN	West Yorkshire
GREAT COXWELL	Oxfordshire
LACOCK	Wiltshire
WEST PENNARD, GLASTONBURY	Somerset

Castles

BODIAM	East Sussex
BRAMBER	West Sussex
BRODICK	Isle of Arran
CILGERRAN	Dyfed
CLOUGH	County Down
COMPTON	Devon
CRAIGIEVAR	Aberdeenshire
CRATHES	Kincardineshire
CROFT	Hereford and Worcester
DUNSTANBURGH	Northumberland
LINDISFARNE	Northumberland
LUNDY	Devon
PALACE OF FALKLAND	Fife
POWIS	Powys
SIZERGH	Cumbria
SKENFRITH	Gwent
TATTERSHALL	Lincolnshire

Churches and Chapels

BRADLEY MANOR	Devon
BROWNSEA ISLAND	Dorset
CLEVEDON COURT	Avon
CLUMBER	Nottinghamshire
COMPTON CASTLE	Devon
COTEHELE	Cornwall
FALKLAND PALACE	Fife
FARNE ISLANDS	Northumberland
GIBSIDE CHAPEL	Tyne and Wear
HAM HOUSE	Surrey
KELD	Cumbria
KILLERTON	Devon
LITTLE MORETON HALL	Cheshire
LOUGHWOOD MEETING HOUSE	Devon
LUNDY	Devon
MOSELEY OLD HALL	West Midlands
PETWORTH	West Sussex
ST MICHAEL'S MOUNT	Cornwall
SANDHAM MEMORIAL CHAPEL	Hampshire
SIZERGH	Cumbria
STAUNTON HAROLD	Leicestershire
THE VYNE	Hampshire

Country Parks

BOX HILL	Surrey
CLUMBER PARK	Nottinghamshire
CULZEAN CASTLE	Ayrshire
FELL FOOT	Cumbria
FRENSHAM COMMON	Surrey
HARDWICK HALL	Derbyshire
HATFIELD FOREST	Essex
LYME PARK	Greater Manchester

Dovecotes

BOATH DOOCOT	Nairn
BRUTON	Somerset
COTEHELE	Cornwall
GUNBY HALL	Lincolnshire
HAWFORD	Hereford and Worcester
KINWARTON	Warwickshire

NYMANS	West Sussex
PHANTASSIE DOOCOT	East Lothian
STOKE-SUB-HAMDON PRIORY	Somerset
WICHENFORD	Worcestershire
WILLINGTON	Bedfordshire

Gardens

ACORN BANK	Cumbria
ASCOTT	Buckinghamshire
BLICKLING	Norfolk
BODNANT	Gwynedd
BRANKLYN GARDEN	Perthshire
BRODICK CASTLE	Isle of Arran
CASTLE WARD	County Down
CLIVEDEN	Buckinghamshire
COTEHELE	Cornwall
CRATHES CASTLE	Kincardineshire
EMMETTS	Kent
GIGHA PLANT COLLECTION	Isle of Gigha
GLENDURGAN	Cornwall
GUNBY HALL	Lincolnshire
HARDWICK HALL	Derbyshire
HIDCOTE MANOR	Gloucestershire
THE COURTS, HOLT	Wiltshire
ICKWORTH	Suffolk
INVERESK LODGE, MUSSELBURGH	Midlothian
INVEREWE	Ross and Cromarty
KILLERTON	Devon
KNIGHTSHAYES	Devon
LANHYDROCK	Cornwall
LEITH HALL	Aberdeenshire
LYTES CARY	Somerset
MALLENY	Edinburgh
MONTACUTE	Somerset
MOUNT STEWART	County Down
NYMANS	West Sussex
OXBURGH HALL	Norfolk
PACKWOOD	Warwickshire
PECKOVER HOUSE	Cambridgeshire
PITMEDDEN GARDENS	Aberdeenshire
PLAS-YN-RHIW	Gwynedd

445

POLESDEN LACEY	Surrey
POWIS CASTLE	Powys
ROWALLANE	County Down
ST JOHN'S JERUSALEM	Kent
SALTRAM	Devon
SCOTNEY CASTLE	Kent
SHARPITOR	Devon
SHEFFIELD PARK	East Sussex
SISSINGHURST CASTLE	Kent
SPRINGHILL	County Londonderry
STOURHEAD	Wiltshire
TATTON PARK	Cheshire
THREAVE GARDENS	Kirkcudbrightshire
TINTINHULL	Somerset
TRELISSICK	Cornwall
TRENGWAINTON	Cornwall
UPTON	Warwickshire
WAKEHURST PLACE	West Sussex
WALLINGTON	Northumberland
WASHINGTON	Tyne and Wear
THE WEIR	Hereford and Worcester
WESTBURY COURT	Gloucestershire
WEST GREEN HOUSE	Hampshire
WESTWOOD MANOR	Wiltshire
WINKWORTH ARBORETUM	Surrey

HOUSES AND THEIR CONTENTS

This is a list of houses containing interesting decorations (D), furniture (F), pictures (P), china (C) and silver (S).

ANGLESEY ABBEY	P	Cambridgeshire
ANTONY HOUSE	F	Cornwall
ARDRESS HOUSE	D	County Armagh
ARLINGTON COURT	F	Devon
ASCOTT	FPC	Buckinghamshire
ATTINGHAM PARK	DFP	Shropshire
BENINGBROUGH HALL	D	North Yorkshire
BERRINGTON HALL	D	Hereford and Worcester
BLICKLING HALL	D	Norfolk
BRODICK CASTLE	FPCS	Isle of Arran
BUSCOT PARK	DFPCS	Oxfordshire

CASTLE COOLE	DF	County Fermanagh
CHARLECOTE PARK	P	Warwickshire
CLANDON PARK	DFC	Surrey
CLAYDON HOUSE	D	Buckinghamshire
CLEVEDON COURT	D	Avon
COTEHELE HOUSE	DF	Cornwall
COUGHTON COURT	D	Warwickshire
CRAIGIEVAR CASTLE	D	Aberdeenshire
CRATHES CASTLE	DF	Kincardineshire
CROFT CASTLE	D	Hereford and Worcester
CULZEAN CASTLE	D	Ayrshire
DYRHAM PARK	DFP	Avon
EAST RIDDLESDEN HALL	DF	West Yorkshire
FARNBOROUGH HALL	D	Warwickshire
FELBRIGG HALL	DFP	Norfolk
FENTON HOUSE	C	London
FLORENCE COURT	D	County Fermanagh
GREYS COURT	D	Oxfordshire
HAM HOUSE	DFPS	Surrey
HANBURY HALL	D	Hereford and Worcester
HARDWICK HALL	DFP	Derbyshire
HATCHLANDS	D	Surrey
HILL OF TARVIT	FPC	Fife
ICKWORTH	FPS	Suffolk
KELLIE CASTLE	D	Fife
KNOLE	DFPS	Kent
LANHYDROCK	DFP	Cornwall
LITTLE MORETON HALL	D	Cheshire
LYME PARK	DF	Greater Manchester
MELFORD HALL	FP	Suffolk
MOMPESSON HOUSE	D	Wiltshire
MONTACUTE	D	Somerset
MOTTISFONT ABBEY	D	Hampshire
NOSTELL PRIORY	DFP	West Yorkshire
ORMESBY HALL	D	Cleveland
OSTERLEY PARK	DF	London
OWLETTS	D	Kent
PACKWOOD	F	Warwickshire
PAYCOCKE'S	DF	Essex
PECKOVER HOUSE	D	Cambridgeshire
PENRHYN CASTLE	DP	Gwynedd
PETWORTH HOUSE	DFP	West Sussex
PHILIPPS HOUSE	DF	Wiltshire

POLESDEN LACEY	DFPCS	Surrey
POWIS CASTLE	DF	Powys
RAINHAM HALL	D	London
RUFFORD OLD HALL	D	Lancashire
SALTRAM HOUSE	DFP	Devon
SHUGBOROUGH	DFP	Staffordshire
SIZERGH CASTLE	DFC	Cumbria
SPEKE HALL	D	Merseyside
STOURHEAD	FP	Wiltshire
SUDBURY HALL	D	Derbyshire
TATTON PARK	FPS	Cheshire
TEMPLE OF THE WINDS, MOUNT STEWART	D	County Down
TOWNEND	D	Cumbria
TREASURER'S HOUSE, YORK	DFP	North Yorkshire
TRERICE	D	Cornwall
UPPARK	DF	West Sussex
UPTON HOUSE	PC	Warwickshire
THE VYNE	DF	Hampshire
WADDESDON MANOR	FPC	Buckinghamshire
WALLINGTON	D	Northumberland
WEST WYCOMBE PARK	DF	Buckinghamshire
WESTWOOD MANOR	DF	Wiltshire
WIGHTWICK MANOR	DP	West Midlands
YARMOUTH, NO. 4 SOUTH QUAY	D	Norfolk

HOUSES ASSOCIATED WITH FAMOUS PEOPLE

ALLAN BANK, GRASMERE	Cumbria	*Wordsworth*
THE ARCHED HOUSE, ECCLEFECHAN	Dumfriesshire	*Carlyle's birthplace*
BACHELORS' CLUB, TARBOLTON	Ayrshire	*Burns*
BATEMAN'S	Sussex	*Kipling*
9 BRECHIN ROAD, KIRRIEMUIR	Angus	*Barrie's birthplace*
BUCKLAND ABBEY	Devon	*Grenville and Drake*
CHARLECOTE	Warwickshire	*Shakespeare*
CHARTWELL	Kent	*Churchill*
NO. 24 CHEYNE ROW	London	*Carlyle*
CLAYDON	Buckinghamshire	*Florence Nightingale*
CLOUDS HILL	Dorset	*T. E. Lawrence*

448

COLERIDGE COTTAGE, NETHER STOWEY	Somerset	*Coleridge*
COMPTON CASTLE	Devon	*Humphrey Gilbert*
FLINT COTTAGE	Surrey	*Meredith*
HARDY'S COTTAGE, HIGHER BOCKHAMPTON	Dorset	*Hardy's birthplace*
HILL TOP, NEAR SAWREY	Cumbria	*Beatrix Potter*
HUGHENDEN MANOR	Buckinghamshire	*Disraeli*
JUNIPER HALL	Surrey	*Talleyrand*
LACOCK ABBEY	Wiltshire	*Fox Talbot*
LAMB HOUSE, RYE	East Sussex	*Henry James*
HUGH MILLER'S COTTAGE, CROMARTY	Ross & Cromarty	*Hugh Miller's birthplace*
MOSELEY OLD HALL	West Midlands	*Charles II*
QUEBEC HOUSE, WESTERHAM	Kent	*General Wolfe*
SHAW'S CORNER, AYOT ST LAWRENCE	Hertfordshire	*G. B. Shaw*
SMALLHYTHE PLACE	Kent	*Ellen Terry*
GEORGE STEPHENSON'S COTTAGE, WYLAM	Northumberland	*Stephenson's birthplace*
TY MAWR	Gwynedd	*Bishop Morgan*
WOOLSTHORPE MANOR	Lincolnshire	*Newton's birthplace*
WORDSWORTH HOUSE, COCKERMOUTH	Cumbria	*Wordsworth's birthplace*

INDUSTRIAL MONUMENTS

BEADNELL LIME KILNS	Northumberland
CONWY SUSPENSION BRIDGE	Conwy
CORNISH BEAM ENGINES	Cornwall
STRATFORD-UPON-AVON CANAL	Warwickshire
STYAL MILL	Cheshire
WEY AND GODALMING NAVIGATIONS	Surrey

MILLS

BEMBRIDGE	Isle of Wight
BOURNE MILL, COLCHESTER	Essex
BURNHAM OVERY	Norfolk
CASTLE WARD	County Down

449

FLATFORD	Suffolk
HIGH HAM, SEDGEMOOR	Somerset
HORSEY	Norfolk
HOUGHTON	Cambridgeshire
IVINGHOE	Buckinghamshire
MORDEN HILL, COTEHELE	Cornwall
NETHER ALDERLEY	Cheshire
PRESTON	East Lothian
SHALFORD	Surrey
WELLBROOK BEETLING MILL	County Tyrone
WICKEN FEN WINDPUMP	Cambridgeshire
WINCHESTER	Hampshire

NATURE RESERVES

This is a list of properties administered—in whole or in part—as Nature Reserves. Here the Trusts are given much help from the Nature Conservancy, the Field Studies Council, and a number of county naturalists trusts and other bodies. The term 'Nature Reserve' is not used by the National Trust for Scotland, but a number of its properties are for convenience included here; they have animal and plant life of very great interest and are administered with special regard for its preservation.

ARLINGTON COURT	Devon
BALMACARA	Ross and Cromarty
BEN LAWERS	Perthshire
BLAKENEY POINT	Norfolk
BROWNSEA ISLAND	Dorset
BROWNSHAMS, CLOVELLY	Devon
CHEDDAR CLIFFS	Somerset
COEDYDD MAENTWROG (FFESTINIOG WOODLANDS)	Gwynedd
FAIR ISLE	Zetland
FARNE ISLANDS	Northumberland
GLENCOE AND DALNESS	Argyll
GOATFELL	Isle of Arran
GOLDEN CAP ESTATE	Dorset
GOWER PENINSULA	West Glamorgan
GREY MARE'S TAIL	Dumfriesshire
HAWKSHEAD	Cumbria
HORSEY	Norfolk
KINTAIL	Ross and Cromarty

LEIGH WOODS, BRISTOL	Avon
LINN OF TUMMEL	Perthshire
MALHAM TARN	North Yorkshire
MURLOUGH, DUNDRUM	County Down
NAP WOOD	East Sussex
NEWTON POOL	Northumberland
RUSKIN RESERVE	Oxfordshire
ST KILDA	Inverness-shire
SALTHOUSE BROAD	Norfolk
SCOLT HEAD	Norfolk
STRANGFORD LOUGH	County Down
THREAVE WILDFOWL REFUGE	Kirkcudbrightshire
TORRIDON	Ross and Cromarty
ULVERSCROFT, CHARNWOOD FOREST	Leicestershire
WICKEN FEN	Cambridgeshire
WOOLTON HILL	Hampshire

PREHISTORIC SITES

About eighty properties have features of interest to those whose special study
is prehistory. Notes on them have been included in Trust publications—
Prehistoric Properties of the National Trust, by Phyllis Ireland; *Properties of the
National Trust*; *The National Trust for Scotland Year Book*; and in *The National
Trust Guide* published by Jonathan Cape. The list below is of properties
where, I think, the prehistoric features will interest the non-specialists.

AVEBURY	Wiltshire
CASTLERIGG CIRCLE	Cumbria
CISSBURY RING	West Sussex
COLDRUM	Kent
CROFT AMBREY	Hereford and Worcester
FIGSBURY RING	Wiltshire
HENTOR	Devon
HIGHDOWN HILL	Sussex
LANYON QUOIT	Cornwall
LITTLE SOLSBURY	Avon
LONG MYND	Shropshire
MIDSUMMER HILL	Hereford and Worcester
STONEHENGE DOWN	Wiltshire
STONES OF CLAVA	Inverness-shire
TRENCROM HILL	Cornwall

ROMAN ANTIQUITIES

AMBLESIDE—A FORT	Cumbria
ANTONINE WALL—	
THREE LENGTHS OF THE WALL	Stirlingshire
CHEDWORTH VILLA	Gloucestershire
HADRIAN'S WALL—	
A LENGTH OF THE WALL	Northumberland
HOUSESTEADS FORT	Northumberland
LETOCETUM—	
POSTING STATION	Staffordshire
RIBCHESTER—GRANARIES	Lancashire
SEGONTIUM—A FORT	Gwynedd

KEYS TO MAPS

Key to Maps

SOUTHERN COUNTIES

Figures in italics indicate page numbers

LONDON AREA

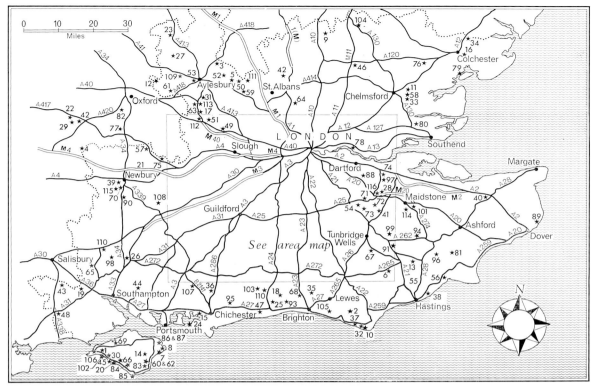

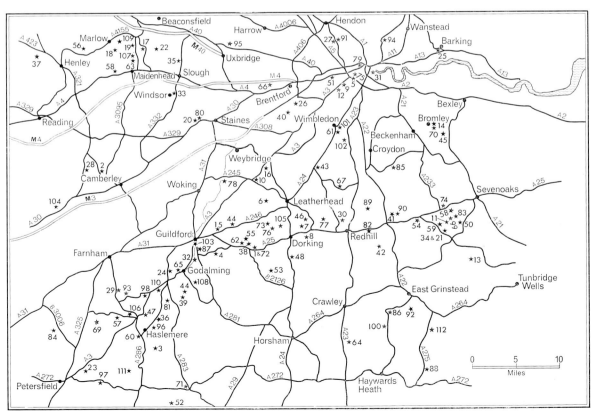

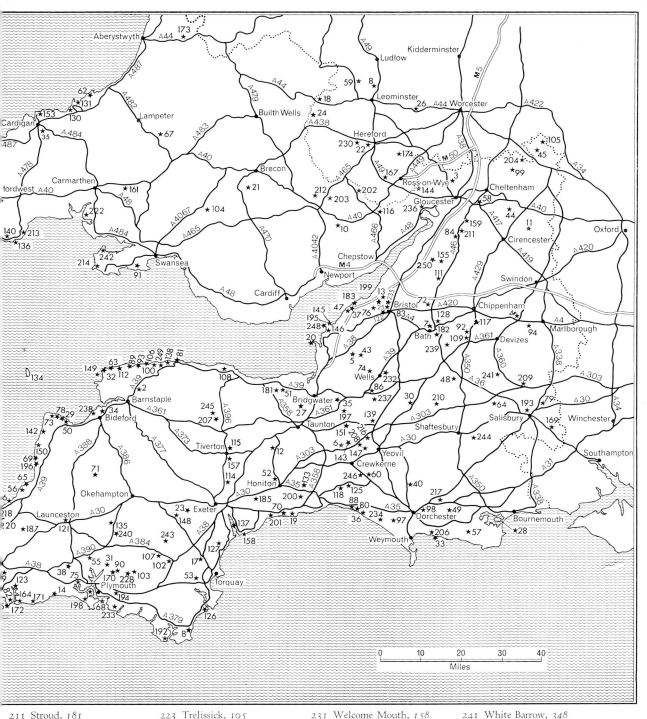

Key to Map
MIDLAND COUNTIES AND EAST ANGLIA

Figures in italics indicate page numbers

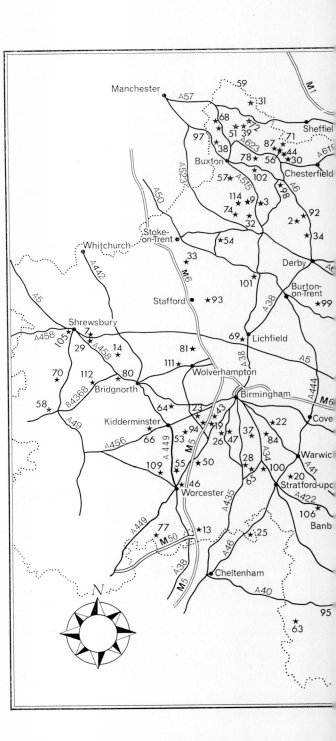

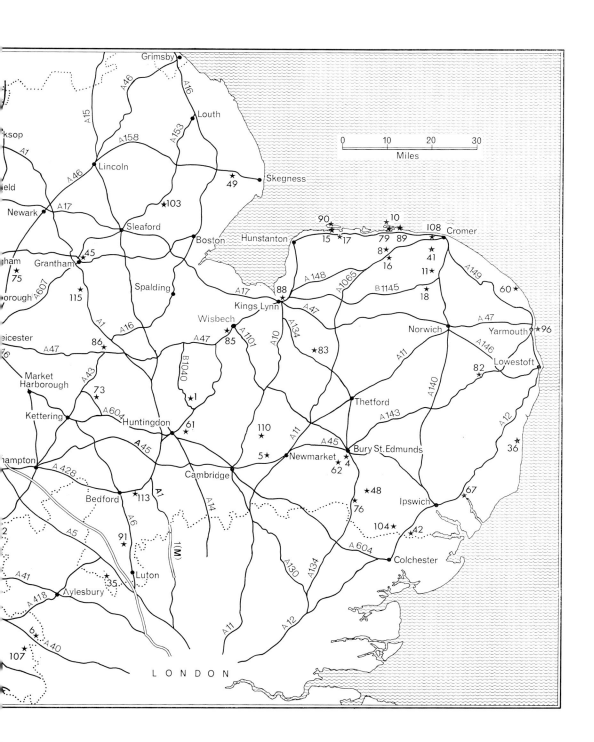

Grimsby

Louth

ksop

Skegness

Lincoln

Newark

A17

Sleaford

Boston

Hunstanton

Grantham

Spalding

Kings Lynn

Wisbech

Norwich

Yarmouth

Lowestoft

Market
Harborough

Kettering

Huntingdon

Thetford

Cambridge

Bury St. Edmunds

Bedford

Newmarket

Ipswich

Luton

Aylesbury

Colchester

L O N D O N

0   10   20   30
Miles

★49
★103
★45
★75
★115
★86
★73
★113
★91
★35
★6
★107
★1
★61
★110
★5
★85
★83
★88
★90
★15 ★17
★10
★79 ★89
★8
★16
★11
★41
★108 Cromer
★60
★18
★82
★48
★76
★104 ★42
★62 ★4
★36
★67
★96

Key to Maps

NORTHERN COUNTIES, NORTH WALES, ISLE OF MAN

Figures in italics indicate page numbers

LAKE DISTRICT

NORTHERN IRELAND

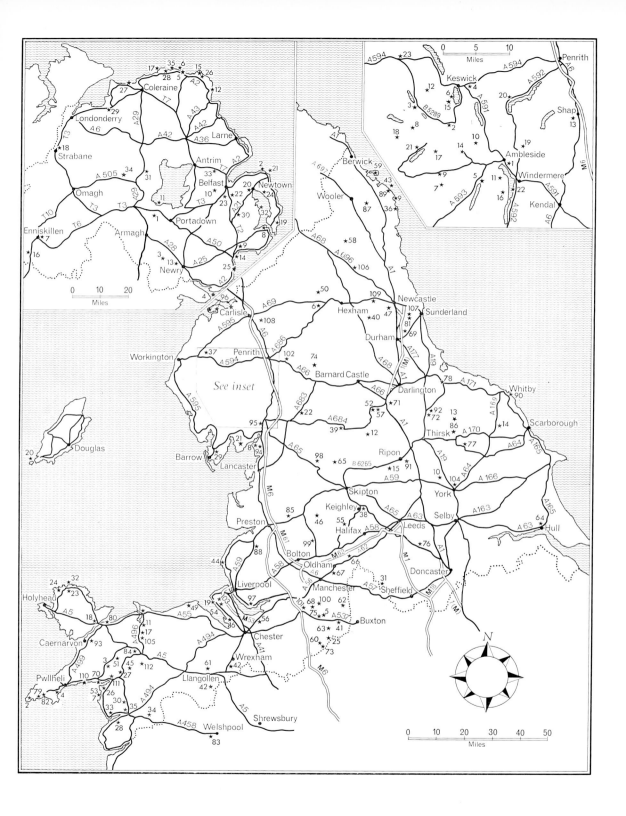

Key to Map
SCOTLAND

Figures in italics indicate page numbers

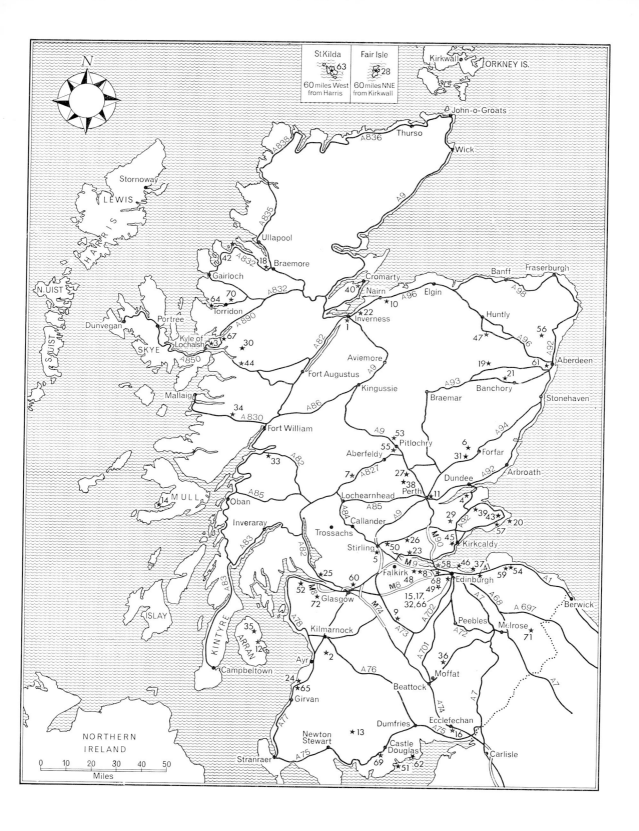

St Kilda ★63 60 miles West from Harris
Fair Isle ★28 60 miles NNE from Kirkwall

Kirkwall · ORKNEY IS.

John-o-Groats
Thurso
A836
Wick
A838
Stornoway
LEWIS
A9
Ullapool
A835
42 A832 18 Braemore
Gairloch A832
Cromarty
Banff Fraserburgh
40 Nairn
★10 A96 Elgin
A98
64 70 Inverness 22 Huntly
Torridon 1 47★ 56
Dunvegan A890 19★
Portree 67 30 Aviemore 21 A96 A92 61 Aberdeen
Kyle of Lochalsh ★3 ★44 A9 Braemar Banchory Stonehaven
SKYE A850 Fort Augustus A93
Kingussie
Mallaig A86
34 Fort William A830 A9 53 Pitlochry 6 Forfar
A82 Aberfeldy 55 31★
33 7★ A827 27★ Dundee Arброath
MULL 14 Oban A85 Lochearnhead 38 Perth 11 4★ A92
A85 29 39 43
Inveraray A84 Callander A9 45 57 20
Trossachs 26 M90 Kirkcaldy
★25 50 23 58 46 37 41
Stirling 5 M9 48 8 68 Edinburgh 59 54
52 60 Falkirk M8 49 A1
72 Glasgow 15,17 32,66 Berwick
M74 Peebles Melrose
ISLAY Kilmarnock A73 A702 A72 71
35 A78 36
ARRAN 12 2★ A76 Moffat
Campbeltown Ayr Beattock
24 65 A74
Girvan A7
A77 13 Dumfries Ecclefechan
NORTHERN Newton A75 16
IRELAND Stewart Castle Carlisle
Stranraer A75 Douglas
69 51 62

N

0 10 20 30 40 50
Miles

KINTYRE
A83
A82
N.UIST
S.UIST
HARRIS
A9
A92
A697
A68
A7
A701
A74

Index

Chichester family 142–3
Chichester Harbour 323
Chichester, Miss Rosalie
143, 151
Chichester, Sir Francis 143
Chick, The 92
Chiddingstone 207
Child, Francis 235
Chiltern Hills 50, 52, 53,
60, 197, 266, 269
Chilworth 296, 308
Chinese garden house 288
Chinese porcelain 306
Chipman Strand 92
Chippendale furniture 53,
157, 306, 336, 346
Chippendale, Thomas 336
Chippendale the younger,
Thomas 346
Chippenham 341, 342
Chipping Campden 176,
178
Chipping Sodbury 49
Chislehurst 229
Chun ware 53
Church Cobham 297
Church Cove 94
Church Hill, West
Wycombe 65, 66
Church House, Widecombe
150
Church Stile 119
Churchill, Sir Winston
206–7, 277
Churnet, River 284
Chute, Chaloner 188
Chute family 188
Cilgerran Castle 352
Cir Mhor 402
Cissbury ring 331
Cistercian buildings 177,
267, 410
City Mill, Winchester 188
Civil War 52, 98, 103, 107,
168, 215, 255, 262, 273,
315, 372, 399
Clachaig 394
Claife Woodland 130
Clamerkin Lake 204
Clandon Park 299
Clans, graves of the 415
Clappers, The 50
Claremont 299
Claude (Lorrain) 68
Claverton Manor 45
Claydon House 54–6

Clematon Hill 158
Clent Hills 191, 192
Clevedon 46, 47, 49
Clevedon Court 47
Cleveland Hills 261
Cley 250
Cley Hill 339
Clifden, Viscount 98
Clifton Suspension Bridge
45
Clive of India 368
Cliveden 56–8
Clock House 232
Close Farm 217
Cloud, The 76
Clouds Hill 161
Clough Castle 375
Cloutsham 278
Clovelly 146
Clumber Park 263–4
Clump Farm 193
Clutton, Henry 56
Clyde, River 431
Clyde Valley, the 423
Coaley Peak 177
Coastline and Islands Fund
435
Cobham, Kent 207, 217
Cock Hill 282
Cockermouth 111
Cockley Beck 118
Cockshott Point 130
Cockshott Wood 114
Codger Fort 259
Coe, River 394
Coed Llechwedd 360
Coedydd Maentwrog 358
Cofton Hackett 191
Coggeshall 171
Coire Odhar 425
Colchester 172
Coldharbour Hill 329
Coldrum Long Barrow 207
Cole, Sir William 382
Coleraine 383
Coleridge Cottage 277, 282
Coleridge, Samuel Taylor
277
Coleshill 266
Colliers Wood 236
Collin Glen 370
Colsterworth 226
Colston Bassett 264
Combe Martin 150, 151,
154, 155
Combe Raleigh 151

Combe Wood 151
Combegate Beach 151
Commanderies of the
Knights Hospitallers 211
Common Farm 130
Common Marsh 184
Commons, Footpaths and
Open Spaces Preserva-
tion Society xxxix, 183
communion plate, silver-gilt
222
Companies Act of 1895
xxxix
Compass Point 150
Compton Castle 146–7
Compton Down and Farm
205
Coney Island 373
Coneygree, The 176
Coneysburrow Cove 95
Conford Moor 183
Congleton 76
Coniston 112–13, 120–1
Constable, John 68, 289
Conwy 358–9
Conwy, Llyn 364
Conwy, River 356
Conwy Suspension Bridge
359
Conwy Valley, The 356
Conyngham, William Lenox
384
Cook, Mr E. E. 266, 267,
281
Cook, Thomas 63
Cookham and Maidenhead,
Manor of 51
Cookham Dean Common
51
Cookstown 384
Coombe 92
Coombe Allotment 115
Coombe End Farm 266
Coombe Hill 60
Coombe Road 182
Cooper's Hill slopes 309
Copeland Islands 376
Copenhagen, Battle of 295
copper mine workings 74,
356
Cordell, William 294
Corfe Castle 161
Cornish Engines 89
Cornish Rebellion 103
Cornwall Naturalists' Trust
99

472

474

Sèvres china 61, 63
Shaftesbury 348
Shakespeare, William 236, 313
Shalfleet Quay 202
Shalford Mill 300
Shallow, Mr Justice 313
Shap 125
Sharington, Sir William 342
Sharow 261
Sharpenhoe, the Clappers 50
Sharpitor 158
Sharrow Point 107
Shaw, G. B. 199
Shaw's Bridge 376
Shaw's Corner 199
Shee, Lanty 112
Sheffield 137, 284
Sheffield, Lord 170
Sheffield Park Garden 169–170
shell collection 143
Shell–BP Ltd 434
Sherborne St John 184
Shere 300, 305
Sheridan, Richard Brinsley 307
Sherriff, R. C. 163
Shervage Wood 282
Sherwood Forest 263
Shetland 441
Shiel, Loch 417
Shieldaig Island 435
Shining Cliff Wood 138
Shinto temple 83
Shipload Bay 146
Shippards Chine 205
Shipton 259
Shirehampton Park 46
Shirley, Sir Robert 220
Shoreham Gap 332
Shorestone Dunes 257
Shottermill Ponds 324
Shrewsbury 269, 274
Shrewsbury, Earl of 137
Shugborough 286–8, 378
Shute Barton 158
Sid Meadows 158
Side Farm 129
Side House Farm 122
Sidmouth 158
Sillery Sands 154
silver 80, 126, 290
Silverdale 125
silver-lead mine 100

Simons Wood 52
Simpson, Dr Douglas 385
Sissinghurst Castle 215
Sitwell, Sacheverell 136
Six Brothers Field 308
Sizergh Castle 125–7
Skegness 224
Skelwith Bridge 123
Skelwith Force 109
Skene, Loch 405
Skenfrith Castle 353
Skirrid Fawr 353
Skokholm Island 350
Skomer Island 350
Slieve Donard 378
Slindon Estate 328–9
Sling Pool 192
Slurring Rock Nature Trail 334
Smallhythe Place 216–17
Smallman family 274
Smythson, Robert 137
Snowdonia 356, 357, 361, 363
Snowshill Manor 179
snuffbox collection 143
Soames, Arthur G. 170
Soane Museum 301
soay sheep 154
Society for Protection of Ancient Buildings xxxix, 264, 281
Sole Street 217
Solent, the 202
Solva 300
Solway Commons 127
Somerset, Duke of 328
Somerset, Protector 262
Somerset Trust for Nature Conservation 277
Somerton 279
Souter Johnnie's House 395, 399
South Crofty Mine 89
South Downs 206, 323, 329, 332
South Harting 329
South Hawke 309
South Hill, Dulverton 279
South Leigh 269
South Quay, No. 4, Great Yarmouth 247
South Queensferry 440
South Ridge Farm 137
Southdown Farm 162
Southwark 236

Southwell family 72
Spanish Chestnut Avenue, Croft 193, 194
Spanish sheep 314
Sparrowlee 134
Sparsholt 184
Speke Hall 218, 238–9
Spence, Sir Basil 408
Spencer, Stanley 184
Spiers 210
Springhill 383–4
Sprivers 217
Squire's Mount 233
Stable Hills 114
Stafford 286
Staffordshire County Council 286, 288
Staffordshire figures 222
Stage House, Inverewe 434
stained glass, Kempe 264, 322
stained glass, Renaissance 184
Stainforth Bridge 262
Stalky and Co. 143
Stamford 250
Standen 329
Standish Wood 181
Stanford University of California 58
Stanley Hill 428
Stanton Moor Edge 138
Staple Island 254
Stapleford Park 222
Stapleton, Michael 372
Start Point 158
Station Wood 93
Staunton Harold Church 220–2
Steeple Point 92
Stenhouse Mansion 409, 422
Stephenson, George 259
Stephenson's railway bridge 357
Steps Bridge 148
Sterne, Lawrence 262
Steuart, George 269
Stevens, Mr Harry W. 309
Steventon 265
Steyning 323
Stiffkey 248
Stirling 438
'Stitchmeal' system 88
Stoatley Green 303
Stock Ghyll, the 108
Stockbridge Down 184

Wastwater 125, 129–30
watch tower 274
Watendlath 117
Waterend Moor 199
waterfalls 359, 368, 376, 405, 428
Watermeads 236
Waterslack Wood 125
Watersmeet 154
Waterston, Mr George 441
Watledge Hill 181
Watling Street 285
Watlington Hill 269
Watlington Park 269
Watt, Miss Adelaide 239
Watt, Richard 239
Watteau, Antoine 400
Watts-Dunton, Theodore 323
Waveney, River 288
Weald, the 217, 218, 325
Wear, River 165
Weavers Cottage, Kilbarchen 431
Webb, John 188
Webb, Philip 329
Wedgwood china 157
Weir, The 197
Weir House 300
Weir, Mr William 226
Welcombe Mouth 158
Well of the Dead, Culloden 417
Wellbrook Beetling Mill 384
Wellington 277
Wellington, Duke of 277, 330
Wellington Monument 277
Wells 277, 284
Wells Cathedral, Treasurer of 280
Wells, H. G. 331
Welshpool 368
Welton Hill 134
Welwyn 199
Wembury Bay 158
Wenlock Edge 274
Wensleydale 263
Went Hill 168
Wessenden Moor 336–7
West Bexington 163
West Clandon 299
West Cliff 164
West Drayton 172
West Green House 188

West Heath 304
West Hoathly Parish Council 328
West Humble Chapel 297
West Kirby 239
West Mersea 174
West Pennard Court Barn 279
West Pentire Farm 92
West Runton 250
West Sussex County Council 323
West Wight 204, 205
West Wittering 323
West Wycombe Park 63–5
West Wycombe Village 65, 66
Westbury College 46
Westbury Court Garden 181
Wester Ross 432
Westerham 206, 210, 217–218
Western Hill 94
Westhay Farm 164
Westleton 288
Westminster 236
Westminster Abbey 389
Weston, Richard 308
Weston-super-Mare 49
Westridge Woods 182
Westward Ho! 93, 143
Westwood 152
Westwood Manor 347
Wetheral Woods 130
Wey, River 183, 300, 308, 309
Wey Navigation, River 308–9
Weybridge 308
Weymouth 162
Weymouth Bay 163
Wha House Bridge 119
Wha House Farm 119
Wharfedale 261
Wheal Betsy 150
Wheal Prosper Mine 101
Whipsnade 50
Whistler, Rex 183
Whitby 260, 261
White Barrow 348
White, Gilbert 184
White Lady waterfall 149
White Moss Common 120, 123
White Moss Intake 120

White Park Bay 370, 371
White Sheet Castle and Downs 347
Whiteleaf Fields 60
Whitenothe Cliff 163
Whitesand Bay 107
Whitford Burrows 367
Whitgreave, Thomas 285
Whitmore Bottom 303
Whitmore Vale 303
Whitney-on-Wye 193
Wichenford Dovecote 197
Wicken Fen 72
Widbrook Common 51
Widecombe-in-the-Moor 150
Wigford Down 148
Wiggin, Mr W. 286
Wightwick Manor 322–3
Wilderhope Manor 69, 274–5
Wilderness, The, Burgh 394
Wilkite Riots 189
Willapark Headland 87
Willement, Thomas 361
Willett, William 229
William III 329, 430
William the Conqueror 262
Williams-Ellis, Mr Clough 360
Willings Walls Warrens 149
Willington Dovecote 51
Willoughby Cleeve 282
Willy Lott's Cottage 289
Wilmot, Lord 285
Wilmslow 80
Wilson, Dr E. H. 356
Wilson, Mackay 432
Wimbledon Common xxxix
Win Green Hill 348
Winchcombe 177
Winchelsea 168
Winchester 69, 184, 188, 347
Winchester City Mill 69, 188
Wind Hill 154
Winde, William 56
Windermere 108, 109, 123, 130–1
Windham, William 244–5
Windmill Hill, Avebury 338
Windmill Hill, Rhiw 363
Windsor 52, 339
Winkworth Arboretum 300